IN SEARCH OF FLORENTINE

CIVIC HUMANISM

In Search of Florentine Civic Humanism

ESSAYS ON
THE TRANSITION FROM
MEDIEVAL TO
MODERN THOUGHT

HANS BARON

VOLUME I

PRINCETON UNIVERSITY PRESS
PRINCETON, NEW JERSEY

LIBRARY OF CONGRESS CATALOGING-IN-PUBLICATION DATA
Baron, Hans, 1900–
In search of Florentine civic humanism.
Includes indexes.
1. Humanism—Italy—Florence—History.
2. Florence (Italy)—Politics and government—To 1421.
3. Florence (Italy)—Politics and government—1421–1737.
4. Renaissance—Italy—Florence. 5. City states.
6. Political participation—Italy—Florence.
I. Title.
DG737.55.B35 1988   945'.51   88–2328
ISBN 0–691–05512–2 (alk. paper: v. 1)
ISBN 0–691–05513–0 (alk. paper: v. 2)

Publication of this book has been aided by a grant
from The Andrew W. Mellon Foundation

This book has been composed in Linotron Bembo

Clothbound editions of Princeton University Press books
are printed on acid-free paper, and binding materials
are chosen for strength and durability. Paperbacks,
although satisfactory for personal collections, are not
usually suitable for library rebinding

Printed in the United States of America by
Princeton University Press,
Princeton, New Jersey

To Renate and Marcel Franciscono,
my indispensable helpers

PREFACE

FOR MANY YEARS I have devoted part of my time to preparing a book on Florentine civic Humanism which would differ in aim from *The Crisis of the Early Italian Renaissance* of 1955 and 1966. The *Crisis* was an attempt to understand the Florentine spirit during the first decades of the fifteenth century by examining the reactions of the citizens of the republic to its gravest crisis: the threat it faced from the long, victorious expansion through the Italian peninsula of the Duchy of Milan and the Kingdom of Naples. To fully grasp the moral, social, and politico-historical ideas that motivated Florentine humanists, one must use another approach as well. The originality and intellectual power of the pioneering period after 1400 become more visible when we investigate a larger portion of the Florentine development, confronting early Quattrocento thought with that of the Trecento, Petrarch's age, on the one hand and of the Cinquecento, Machiavelli's age, on the other. Up to a point, of course, scholars have always done this; the *Crisis* often raises the question how a specific idea or value accepted in the early Quattrocento appeared to citizens or writers a century before or would appear a century later. What I have in mind is something more systematic, however: an examination of selected Florentine conceptions and attitudes, followed up in essays tracing either their vicissitudes from the age of Petrarch to that of Machiavelli or their impact on later times. This approach has the benefit of putting the concept of the early Florentine Renaissance presented here on a broader and, therefore, more secure foundation, and also, incidentally, of sharpening our perspective of the ages of Petrarch and Machiavelli.

These are the goals I set myself in composing the present collection of published and unpublished essays on Florentine thought. A disadvantage of this method is that it necessitates repeated returns to the Trecento, or even earlier periods, after we have pursued other problems down the road to the Quattrocento and Machiavelli's time. It can be highly instructive, however, to revisit an already familiar terrain with related yet different questions in mind. I have, accordingly, sometimes used the same quotations in more than one essay. In such cases, I have done my best to demonstrate that the cited sources reveal new meanings when the perspective changes. To alert the reader to these recurrences, I have, whenever feasible, referred to parallel discussions elsewhere in the book.

The eighteen essays stem from widely diverse periods of my life, but most of the early ones were reworked and expanded later. Except for the first two, which have been left essentially as they were in order to show the point from which I started out, those from the 1930s were revised, rewritten, and augmented in the 1960s and early 1970s, after the *Crisis* was completed and I was at leisure to work on my second Florentine project. Each essay is preceded by a note on the time or times of its composition, and, where appropriate, its translation from German or Italian.

A special word of explanation is needed about the first essay, which serves as an introduction to my analyses of Florentine Humanism. Unlike most of the following essays, it does not trace a gradual development or sudden mutation of motifs and concepts, but rather presents a synthetic sketch of Florentine life and thought in the early Quattrocento, such as I had in mind when I embarked upon the more detailed inquiries. However incomplete or slanted parts of that youthful survey may appear today, its inclusion, after some bibliographical updating in the notes, seems to me justified because it affords an overview of many of the themes and materials at my disposal in the 1930s. The reader had best be familiar with them at the start.

I have added a few historiographical and autobiographical commentaries at the end that should provide helpful background for the approach to civic Humanism used here and in the *Crisis*. The most important of these is an essay on Burckhardt, which is intended not only to comment on my close ties to him but also to present an incipient critique of the Burckhardtian picture.

Cambridge, Massachusetts   H. B.
May 1986

CONTENTS

VOLUME I

I. AN ANATOMY OF FLORENTINE
CIVIC HUMANISM

One The Background of the Early Florentine
Renaissance   3

Two New Historical and Psychological Ways of
Thinking: From Petrarch to Bruni and
Machiavelli   24

Three The Changed Perspective of the Past in Bruni's
Histories of the Florentine People   43

Four Bruni's *Histories* as an Expression of Modern
Thought   68

Five The Memory of Cicero's Roman Civic
Spirit in the Medieval Centuries and in the
Florentine Renaissance   94

Six The Florentine Revival of the Philosophy of the
Active Political Life   134

Seven Franciscan Poverty and Civic Wealth in the
Shaping of Trecento Humanistic Thought:
The Role of Petrarch   158

Eight Franciscan Poverty and Civic Wealth in the
Shaping of Trecento Humanistic Thought:
The Role of Florence   191

Nine Civic Wealth and the New Values of the
Renaissance: The Spirit of the Quattrocento   226

Ten Leon Battista Alberti as an Heir and Critic of
Florentine Civic Humanism   258

Index of Names   289

xi

CONTENTS

VOLUME II

II. THE HISTORICAL SETTING AND INFLUENCE OF FLORENTINE HUMANISM

Eleven Fifteenth-Century Civilization North of the Alps and the Italian Quattrocento: Contrast and Confluence 3

Twelve A Sociological Interpretation of the Early Florentine Renaissance 40

Thirteen The Humanistic Revaluation of the *Vita Activa* in Italy and North of the Alps 55

Fourteen The *Querelle* of the Ancients and the Moderns as a Problem for Present Renaissance Scholarship 72

Fifteen Machiavelli the Republican Citizen and Author of *The Prince* 101

III. HISTORIOGRAPHICAL AND AUTOBIOGRAPHICAL COMMENTARIES

Sixteen The Limits of the Notion of "Renaissance Individualism": Burckhardt After a Century (1960) 155

Seventeen The Course of My Studies in Florentine Humanism (1965) 182

Eighteen A Defense of the View of the Quattrocento First Offered in *The Crisis of the Early Italian Renaissance* (1970) 194

Index of Names 213

PART I

An Anatomy of Florentine Civic Humanism

ONE

The Background of the Early
Florentine Renaissance*

I

OUR VIEWS of the Italian Renaissance are changing. The old conception of the fifteenth century was that of an age of unparalleled aristocratic patronage to which Renaissance Humanism and the new art owed their existence. Indeed, the early Renaissance was called the age of the Medici, after the Florentine family which contributed most to the encouragement of art and letters.

The truth is that Humanism and Renaissance art had flourished in Florence before the patronage of the Medici began; they were creations of pre-Medici Florence. Not only did they owe much more to the Middle Ages than scholars realized half a century ago but they bore the impress of a time when Florence had not yet become a Renaissance principality but was still a free city-state. What the Medici did for literature and art from the second half of the fifteenth century onward will never be forgotten. But we cannot maintain that Humanism was the culture of an age in which the political life of the Italian city-states was already at such low ebb that only the strong individual (the tyrant, the great artist, or the famous scholar) was esteemed. Actually, this was characteristic of Humanism in an advanced stage. Whoever wishes to understand its history as a whole must also study it in its youth, when Florence was still a free republic whose citizens were eager to absorb

---

* For the nature and intent of this introductory essay, see the preface above, p. viii. The essay was published under the title "The Historical Background of the Florentine Renaissance," without most of the notes, in *History*, n.s., vol. 22 (1938). It also appeared in an Italian translation, with more notes, as "Lo Sfondo Storico del Rinascimento Fiorentino," in vol. 1 of *La Rinascita* (1938). The text reprinted here is that published in *History*, with numerous stylistic changes and additional notes.

classical ideas about the state, society, and morals because they found a model for their own lives in the civic life of ancient Athens and Rome.

The contrast between the first and second halves of the fifteenth century can easily be perceived from the history of Florentine art. Individualism, so characteristic of the art of the Renaissance, had triumphed ever since the beginning of the century. But in the days of Donatello and Brunelleschi, the new art, steeped in the spirit of individualism, was for the most part not yet in the service of private patrons. The most commanding palaces of the Florentine Renaissance, erected by wealthy families as imperishable monuments to their own greatness, were not built, as we know today, until a much later time, when a principate of the Medici was already established. The new Medici palace (now known as the Palazzo Riccardi) was not constructed until 1444, ten years after Cosimo had risen to power. The palaces of the Rucellai, Pitti, Pazzi (now Quaratesi), and Strozzi followed even later.[1]

At the beginning of the fifteenth century architects and sculptors had still been working mainly in the service of the commune and the great guilds. The entire center of the city, between the cathedral and the Piazza Signoria, acquired at that time the impressive appearance it has retained to the present. From 1376 onward, the Loggia dei Signori (later called the Loggia dei Lanzi) provided a dignified background for the government (the "Signori") on public occasions. A generation later the bare walls of the little church of Or San Michele were gradually covered with their famous statues of saints, each the gift of one of the fourteen great guilds. Among them is the youthful, warlike figure of Donatello's Saint George (1416), whose feet are planted firmly on this earth like a very symbol

[1] A. Warburg, "Der Baubeginn des Palazzo Medici," in vol. 1 of *Gesammelte Schriften* (Leipzig, 1932), 165f., 366. H. Busse, "Der Pitti-Palast. Seine Erbauung 1458–1466," in *Jahrbuch der Preussischen Kunstsammlungen* 51 (1930): 110ff. For the Palazzo Pazzi-Quaratesi, see H. Willich, "Die Baukunst der Renaissance in Italien bis zum Tode Michelangelos," in vol. 1 of *Handbuch der Kunstwissenschaft* (1914), 33f.

of the early Florentine Renaissance. After 1419 the republic, with the help of the guilds, erected the new Foundlings' Hospital, the Spedale degli Innocenti, a public endowment on so lavish a scale that it became no less influential as a social institution than as a landmark in the history of art, thanks to Brunelleschi's building plan and Luca della Robbia's decorations.[2] While the baptistry, some parts of the exterior of the cathedral, and the upper floors of the campanile were being adorned with the epoch-making sculpture that marked the great forward strides in the plastic arts, Brunelleschi rebuilt, in the west of the city, the Palazzo dei Capitani della Parte Guelfa,[3] the headquarters of a political body that, like the guilds, cooperated with and confronted the government of the republic.

All these buildings were financed and supervised by the commune itself or by the great guilds. Citizens, not clerics, saw to the details of the buildings, chose the leading artists, even for the completion of the cathedral, and passionately discussed the plans for Brunelleschi's dome. When the consuls of a wool merchants' guild (the Arte della Calimala) entrusted Ghiberti with the work on the east doors of the baptistry in 1424, leading statesmen, such as Niccolò da Uzzano, served on the committee. The selection of biblical scenes to be represented on the doors was made by Leonardo Bruni, the most famous Florentine humanist and the city's first great historian, who a few years later became chancellor.[4]

---

[2] The claim that it was Leonardo Bruni who gave the impulse for the erection of the hospital—a claim once frequently repeated, for instance in vol. 1 of M. Dvořák's *Geschichte der italienischen Kunst im Zeitalter der Renaissance* (Munich, 1927), 666—is a legend of the seventeenth century, as was already established by L. Passerini, *Storia degli stabilimenti di beneficenza di Firenze* (Florence, 1853), 686. Cf. also G. Bruscoli, *Lo spedale di S. Maria degl'Innocenti* (Florence, 1900), 28.

[3] Shown by C. von Fabriczy in "Brunelleschiana," *Jahrbuch der Preussischen Kunstsammlungen*, Beiheft to vol. 28 (1907): 58ff.; see also Willich, *Baukunst der Renaissance*, 26f.

[4] Cf. Bruni's letter to "Niccolò da Uzzano und andere *Deputati*," in my edition of *Leonardo Bruni Aretino, Humanistisch-philosophische Schriften* (Leipzig, 1928), 134.

A generation that believed the new development of art to be primarily the concern of the Florentine community and felt a communal duty to promote and encourage it, cannot have been so far removed from the public spirit of medieval times as people usually imagine when they think of the Florence of the early Quattrocento. We are too easily tempted to contemplate the life and constitution of the city in the last period of her liberty from the viewpoint of the rising principate of the Medici. With regard to the city's constitutional evolution, it is true that the oligarchical tendency that marked the last pre-Medicean decades undermined some of the traditional institutions and indirectly paved the way for the predominance of a single family. Nevertheless, it is not enough to strive for an historical appreciation of pre-Medicean Florence merely by way of a knowledge of its later vicissitudes. The spirit of the age itself, the political mentality of the citizens before the end of the republic, is the essential clue to such an appreciation.

The changes in republican life had by no means yet transformed the old civic ideals. In a true oligarchy like Venice, the ruling families formed a closed circle of privileged patricians and monopolized the chief civic offices. In Florence at the beginning of the fifteenth century, however, the cultured classes and humanistic circles boasted that in the city on the Arno an able man could work his way up and share in the political life as well as the wealth of the city. "The liberty and equality of citizens" (this, of course, means those who enjoy full citizenship), not the rule of the few, is the basis of our constitution—this was Leonardo Bruni's highest praise for the Florence of his time. "Wherever men are given the hope of attaining honor in the state, they take courage and raise themselves to a higher plane; if this hope is lost, they grow lazy and stagnate."[5] As an historian, Bruni had already found the key to history in this thought. In 1415, when he described the

[5] *Oratio in Funere Johannis Strozzae*, in Stephanus Baluzius, *Miscellanea*, ed. Mansi, vol. 4 (Lucca, 1764), 3f. For the Latin text see Essay Two, note 14, below.

suppression of the individual life of the Italian provinces and towns by the universal empire of ancient Rome in his epoch-making *Histories of the Florentine People*, his judgment was rendered in almost the same words: "It is nature's gift to mortals that when a path to greatness and honor is open, men raise themselves more easily to a higher plane; when this hope is lost, they grow lazy and stagnate."[6]

Two decades later, Matteo Palmieri, a member of the Arte dei Medici e Speziali (the guild of doctors and druggists), wrote his *Vita Civile*, adapting Bruni's humanism for the use of citizens ignorant of Latin. He, too, declared that it was "just" for the lowly born to depend on their personal *virtù* rather than defer to the power of wealth and noble descent. "He who seeks fame in the ability of past generations deprives himself of honor and merit. He who lives on the reputation of his ancestors is a pitiable creature. A man who deserves honor should offer himself, not his genealogy—though we ought always to prefer the nobility as long as their achievements are equally good."[7] Contemporary documents and letters show

---

[6] *Historiae Florentini Populi*, ed. Emilio Santini, in vol. 19, pt. 3, of *Rerum Italicarum Scriptores*, new ed. (Bologna, 1926), 13 (in Lib. I, written in 1415). For the Latin text see Essay Two, note 20, below.

Meanwhile, Antonio La Penna has shown in a thoughtful analysis ("Die Bedeutung Sallusts für die Geschichtsschreibung und die politischen Ideen Leonardo Brunis," *Arcadia: Zeitschrift für Vergleichende Literaturwissenschaft* I [1966]: 255–76, and again as "Il significato di Sallustio nella storiografia e nel pensiero politico di L. Bruni," in La Penna's *Sallustio e la rivoluzione romana* [Milan, 1968], 409–31) that one of the significant literary sources for Bruni's political psychology was Sallust. It is all the more important to emphasize that the heart of Bruni's observations—namely, that participation in high offices of state was a powerful stimulus to citizens—had not played a serious role in Sallust's work, neither in his two proems nor in *Catilina* VIIff. and *Yugurtha* LXXXVff. This facet of Bruni's thought was not derived from Sallust, who after all had been read throughout the Middle Ages, but from experiences in contemporary Florence. For participation in offices in Bruni's time, see note 11 below.

[7] "Chi per le virtù de' passati cerca gloria spoglia sé d'ogni merito d'honore, et misero è certo colui che consuma la fama de' padri antichi. Dia exemplo di sé et non de' suoi chi merita honore, preponendo sempre la nobilità, quando

that those who participated in government were not unaffected by such views. A modern English writer has said of Rinaldo degli Albizzi—who was a brilliant leader of the powerful oligarchic group for a short time—that he, too, sometimes "dreamed of a Florence in which all citizens were equal and offices were awarded according to merit alone." At any rate, he appealed to the feeling for liberty in the city. "Without freedom, Florence cannot survive," he once said, "and without Florence, freedom cannot survive, because many lands [in Italy] will be subservient to lords and tyrants in the future."[8]

Another feature of the decades between 1394 and 1434 is also incompatible with the traditional picture. The constitutional development of Florence after 1390 cannot be explained merely as the result of the class warfare that shook the city to its foundations during the fourteenth century. It is true that the political influence of the lower levels of the population (above all of the workers in the wool industry), which was violently expressed in the revolt of the "Ciompi" in 1378, soon evaporated after this event. Perhaps this occurred because their temporary victory proved too great, or because the continuous decline of Florentine wool production and the increasing presence of foreign (especially German) elements among the native working population had weakened the latter's solidarity and energy. But the Arti Maggiori, which reorganized the state after the events of 1378, included the whole of the upper middle classes and cultured circles and were guided in the 1380s by leaders who were known as opponents

---

sono pari virtù. E sapientissimi antichi che molto dilatorono gl'imperii, spesse volti, forestieri, lavoratori et infime conditioni d'huomini rilevorono a' primi governi, quando in loro conoscevano spectabili excellentie di virtù" (*Vita Civile*, Autograph Florence *Bibl. Naz. cod. II, IV, 81*, fol. 66b–67b; now edizione critica a cura di Gino Belloni [Florence, 1982], 136f.).

[8] The modern English writer is Cecilia M. Ady, in *The Cambridge Medieval History*, vol. 8 (Cambridge, 1936), 204. Rinaldo degli Albizzi's appeal, "Quod sine libertate, Florentia durare non potest ac libertas sine Florentia, cum multe patrie servabunt dominis et tirannis," is quoted—from the minutes of the "Consulte e Pratiche" (1413) in the Florentine archives—by Gene Brucker in his *The Civic World of Early Renaissance Florence* (Princeton, 1977), 368.

both of oligarchic and of democratic extremes. For a long time afterwards, the middle sections of the population remained calm observers of the increasing restriction of the highest authority to a small circle, which retained remnants of the old nobility. Certainly the middle sections neither showed resentment nor refused to give the government both moral and financial support against the external dangers threatening Florence about 1400. Opposition did not arise till the very end of the period, when the leading group plunged the city into the unjust and fateful war against its sister city Lucca. It was only in the 1420s that the government began to fear the *homines novi* in the middle and lesser guilds, and not before the Lucca enterprise that a change took place in the attitude of the intellectual circles. Bruni, up to that time an adherent of the aristocratic regime, now joined the Medicean circle.[9] Pal-

---

[9] For Bruni's initially aristocratic view, cf. *Historiae*, Lib. II, on the recall of the exiled noble families to Florence in 1266: "Nobilitas . . . , maximum profecto civitatis ornamentum" (written between 1418 and 1419). See also his later praise of the constitution of Florence in an analysis περὶ τῆς πολιτείας τῶν φλωρεντίνων, where he says that it was a happy medium between aristocracy and democracy but was slanted more toward aristocrats and wealthy citizens (ἀποκλίνει μᾶλλον πρὸς τοὺς ἀρίστους τε καὶ πλουσιωτέρους); C. F. Neumann, ed. (1822), 68ff. On the eve of the war against Lucca, Bruni was present when the majority of the voters, led by Rinaldo degli Albizzi, decided in favor of hostilities, and the advisers of peace were not even able to make themselves heard; cf. *Commissioni di Rinaldo degli Albizzi*, ed. C. Guasti, vol. 3 (Florence, 1873), 191, and C. Pellegrini, *Sulla repubblica Fiorentina al tempo di Cosimo il Vecchio* (Pisa, 1880), 23, 28, 31.

Bruni's ability to remain chancellor in 1434, when the aristocratic faction led by the Albizzi was expelled by the Medici party, has often provoked the suspicion of opportunism in the eyes of modern historians. But such suspicions are mitigated by the circumstances which had prevailed in 1427 when Bruni was elected. At that time his predecessor, Ser Paolo Fortini, was removed as a bitter adversary of the Medici party, which, however, was not strong enough to have a Medicean nominee approved. The result was clearly a compromise: the selection of a neutral, prestigious intellectual. Bruni was chosen with the votes of both groups and therefore enjoyed, to a degree, a position that transcended the rivalry between the parties. See Dale Kent, *The Rise of the Medici: Faction in Florence, 1426–34* (Oxford, 1978), 225–27, esp. 227 n. 50; and Riccardo Fubini, "Osservazioni sugli *Historiarum Florentini Po-*

mieri, in his *Vita Civile*, declared resignedly that small groups of experienced citizens ought to be the best rulers of the state, but that in point of fact their rule was sometimes inferior to a democracy in which all interests are represented, because the self-interest of small cliques—human nature being what it is— easily leads to abuse of power.[10] If all citizens shared in government (this was the hope that was born when Cosimo de' Medici came to power, allegedly as the protector of a more democratic regime), their opposing interests would be adjusted and harmonized.[11]

---

puli libri XII di Leonardo Bruni," in vol. 1 of *Studi di Storia Medievale e Moderna per Ernesto Sestan* (Florence, 1980), 432f. n. 89.

[10] "Per questo adviene che la moltitudine civile, tracto però di quella sempre l'ultima plebe della città, rendono il iudicio migliore che non fanno i piccoli numeri degl'intendenti, non perché, essendo buoni cittadini, e pochi non fussino sufficienti a ogni governo, ma perché i cittadini coi quali in nel mondo le più volti si vive, spesso rivolti alla utilità propria, abandonono de' principali membri della città et forse alle volti tutta l'università publica quando sono pessimi. La multitudine comprende ogni membro et qualunche civile particularità; et non obstante che ciascuno sia disposto a l'utile proprio et secondo quello iudichi, ne segue di necessità che della magiore parte delle singularità si fa uno universale che è utile commune di tutto il corpo della republica; la quale commodità non può procedere delle specialità de' numeri piccoli. Questa è la nascosa ragione donde per sperientia si vede che i governi degli ignoranti popoli a tempo paiano buoni come quegli de' prudenti cittadini, ma di rado lungheza di tempo gli prospera" (*Vita Civile*, Autogr. fol. 95a–95b; edizione critica, by G. Belloni, 191).

[11] The puzzle—which this essay was unable to solve in 1938—is how Bruni and others could claim, in the same decades that saw the rise of an oligarchic trend, that it was possible for all full Florentine citizens to attain to leading offices of the republic. More recently, an answer was given which harmonizes with the assumptions of the present essay. First, several archival explorations (especially by Anthony Molho, Ronald Witt, and Lauro Martines) established beyond any doubt that from the 1380s onward substantially more Florentine citizens were admitted to office than at any time before. Eventually, John M. Najemy (in his *Corporatism and Consensus in Florentine Electoral Politics, 1280–1400* [Chapel Hill, N.C., 1982], 263–65, 276f., 292–300, 305–17) offered evidence that both tendencies existed in the political life of the early Florentine Renaissance: a broader opening of the government to many citizens and the rise of a strong oligarchic leadership. There are many relevant observations in Najemy's demonstration of how the formation of a new aristocratic power

II

It was thus not civil strife or any fresh conflict between classes that occasioned the strengthening of oligarchic trends within the Arti Maggiori from the 1390s onward. Rather, changes in the Florentine constitution were brought about by the stress of foreign politics.

From the end of the 1380s until well into the first half of Cosimo de' Medici's principate, the Florentines lived in extreme peril. The Visconti of Milan had established a powerful monarchy in Lombardy, which had already put an end to the independence of most of the northern and many of the central Italian cities. This new Renaissance tyranny made alluring propaganda for itself by promising to unite a large part of Italy under the Duke of Milan. Florence was in the utmost danger of becoming a dependent town in Viscontean territory, like Pisa and Siena, Perugia and Bologna, and of forfeiting with

---

center was constitutionally achieved under the relatively democratic conditions that existed for all full citizens. But he does not include the explanation given below: that the Florentine republic was increasingly threatened by the contemporary wars of the Italian states and may have needed to concentrate its power in a period of emergency. This is one of the themes which my *Crisis of the Early Italian Renaissance: Civic Humanism and Republican Liberty in an Age of Classicism and Tyranny* was to deal with nearly two decades after the present essay was written. (The two volumes of the first edition of the *Crisis* [Princeton, 1955] will hereafter be referred to as *Crisis*, vol. 1, vol. 2; the second, revised, one-volume edition [Princeton, 1966], as *Crisis*, 2d ed.)

Gene Brucker's interpretation of the Florentine regime during the 1410s and 1420s—in his *The Civic World of Early Renaissance Florence*, especially 252ff., 300ff., and 500ff., and also in the lucid pages of his *Renaissance Florence* (New York, 1969), in particular the chapters "The Patriciate" and "Politics"—leads to a perspective that is essentially compatible with the features elaborated by the other cited scholars, even though Brucker's estimate of the number of officeholders is somewhat lower (p. 253).

Much of what has gradually become known regarding the Florentine ideals of liberty and equality during the first decades after 1400 and as an undergrowth of Florentine life in the early Medicean period, is surveyed in Nicolai Rubinstein's "Florentine Constitutionalism and Medici Ascendancy in the Fifteenth Century," in *Florentine Studies: Politics and Society in Renaissance Florence*, ed. N. Rubinstein (Evanston, Ill., 1968), 442–62.

the loss of its autonomy the free development of the moral and intellectual resources on which its cultural preeminence during the Renaissance was based. With the economic power derived from its great industries and flourishing trade, Florence was no negligible opponent of the Visconti monarchy. But with authority vested in a large number of citizens, it was at a disadvantage against a tyranny imbued with the warlike desire for expansion. In Leonardo Bruni's *Histories of the Florentine People*, it is Rinaldo dei Gianfigliazzi, one of the moderate leaders of the Arti Maggiori after 1382, who realizes the extent of this danger and advocates a modification of the constitution to ensure prompter political action on the part of the republic. He attributes the inferiority of Florence to the fact that by their participation in all government measures, the people, unable to foresee future dangers, render the immediate prevention of hostile encroachments impossible. The leading men of Florence, he says, do not take the necessary steps in time, for fear of being accused of desiring war. So the initiative is always with the tyrant of Milan, whose plans are not known to anyone until they have been carried out. To defend itself against such an enemy, Florence must modify its constitution if there is no other way of preserving liberty. Decisions must be the responsibility of a few people who are independent of public discussion. "Promptitude and secrecy," says Bruni, are what the day demands, and "decisions made by the many are their deadly enemy." Such demands, he continues, did not fail in their effect.[12] The records of the time confirm this interpreta-

---

[12] Bruni, *Historiae*, Lib. XI, 276ff. He attributes the speech to the year 1399, when Giangaleazzo was at the peak of his power and aggression. The reliability of Bruni's characterization of Rinaldo dei Gianfigliazzi is supported by documentary evidence from a much later time. In 1424, on the eve of the wars against Filippo Maria Visconti, Rinaldo was again in favor of establishing a small governing board in time of war, "finaliter cum sententia ligargi [i.e., Lycurgi] concludens, ut per paucos ordinetur quod per multos deliberetur [that the few should carry out what the many have advised]: eligendo ex collegiis, officiis principalibus et civibus electissimis qui super premissis [i.e., the preparations for vigorous war against Milan] habeant examinare" (vol. 2 of *Commissioni di Rinaldo degli Albizzi*, 145).

tion by a contemporary historian. As early as 1384 the spokesmen of the oligarchic group had demanded the formation of a
small committee that could take quick advantage of the political situation. After 1393 executive power was in fact often
vested in a board of ten, elected for a short, fixed period, specifically as a central authority capable of acting quickly against
the Viscontean tyranny.[13]

If the Florentine constitution veered toward oligarchy during the time of the great wars with Milan, this did not necessarily mean that political and patriotic willpower among the
middle classes had weakened. Rather, it revealed the citizens'
determination to defend the liberty of the republic against the
concentrated power of the Milanese tyranny by every means
at their disposal. Along with the transformation of the constitution, a change took place in the intellectual sphere. In the
stormy years when Florence was defending its heritage of liberty, its intellectual life, too, took a new direction. A conception of education arose, whose object was not only to train
learned men but to produce good citizens; an education that
inspired men to take part in daily life and in the public affairs
of the community. At this point the citizens' ideas merged
with the humanistic mode of thought. The classical conviction that the personality of the individual grows toward maturity—both intellectually and morally—through participation in the life of the *polis* and *respublica* could be found in the
works of Aristotle and Cicero. The Humanism of the fourteenth century, which had retained the characteristics of medieval aloofness from the world, was now transformed into a
civic Humanism. The reawakening of the ancient civic spirit
became a parallel in the intellectual sphere to Donatello's and
Brunelleschi's rediscovery of Antiquity in the domain of art.

Whether the spirit of self-sacrifice and submission to the
often unjust and cruel will of the community was greater in

[13] Cf. the examination of Florentine politics in the early Albizzi period by
A. Rado, *Dalla Repubblica Fiorentina alla Signoria Medicea. Maso degli Albizzi e
il partito oligarchico in Firenze 1382–1393* (Florence, 1926).

Florence during this period than at other times cannot be ascertained, of course. In any case, during the first decades of
the Quattrocento, the civic virtues acquired new splendor
from the example set by the lives of the great Roman and
Athenian citizens as described by the classical authors. Florentines publicly embraced the civic ideal of Antiquity; and
even when they were not in the public eye, they were inspired
to conscious emulation. Like the chancellor Bruni, Cosimo
de' Medici, who was merely a powerful private citizen at the
beginning of the 1430s, was an opponent of the military enterprise against Lucca. But in a letter not meant to be read by
a third party, he admonished one of his relatives to do his utmost to ensure a successful outcome of the war in spite of the
disapproval in Medicean circles, "now that events have
reached a stage in which the honor of the commune is at
stake."[14] An equally strong public spirit persisted within the
ruling circle of the Albizzi. They were among the first to place
large sums of private capital at the disposal of the government
for the armaments that were needed on the eve of war with
Milan.[15] When the financial burden of the long years of war
lay heavily upon the Florentine state, the ruling aristocracy
levied a capital tax upon itself, the famous *catasto* of 1427,
which placed an obstacle in the way of the hitherto customary
protection of large fortunes in Florence.[16]

A few decades later, when Vespasiano da Bisticci wrote his
well-informed book on the *Lives of Illustrious Men of the Fifteenth Century*, one of the outstanding characteristics of the Albizzi period seemed to him to have been the devotion of Florentine citizens to their city, most impressive where party
dissensions in the city-state destroyed the lives of innocent
men. All the types of civic loyalty known to us from Roman

[14] Printed in vol. 2 of *Commissioni di Rinaldo degli Albizzi*, 350.

[15] Rado, *Dalla Repubblica Fiorentina alla Signoria Medicea*, 110, 174f.

[16] It is now considered certain that this was so and that the *catasto* was not a
measure inspired by the Medici to ingratiate themselves with the people (as
was long thought to be the case); cf. R. Caggese, vol. 2 of *Firenze dalla deca-
denza di Roma al risorgimento d'Italia* (Florence, 1913), 344ff.

authors reappear in Vespasiano's descriptions, in Florentine flesh and blood: Domenico Buoninsegni, who rather than complain of an arbitrary taxation far in excess of his resources, sold his precious manuscript of the Ptolemaic geography, the text and illustrations of which, with infinite patience and care, he had been among the first to copy; Giannozzo Manetti, who preferred financial ruin to sanctioning decisions of the Medicean group that went against his conscience and who continued his self-sacrificing labors in the service of the state, even though confiscatory taxation foreshadowed a time when he would be compelled to seek a livelihood far from home. Then the exiles: Manetti in Naples and Palla degli Strozzi (once the wealthiest citizen of Florence) in Padua. Both used their influence in favor of their ungrateful native city; neither ever spoke of Florence without reverence or—unlike Coriolanus, says Vespasiano admiringly—waited to be importuned before rendering assistance to their fellow citizens.[17] That these were not mere flattering legends is attested by Leon Battista Alberti, himself born and bred in exile. In his *Libri della Famiglia* the aged Piero Alberti recounts how Duke Filippo Maria Visconti had tried to make him abuse his native city when he sought, as an exile, to obtain a position at the court of Milan. He had quietly replied that a good citizen should not speak ill of his native land because its rulers have acted unwisely or unjustly, and by that very answer he won the tyrant's heart.[18] The same loyalty inspired Filippo degli Strozzi, whose family, after the triumph of Cosimo de' Medici, was banished to Naples. There he led such a life, his son contended, "that nobody who did not know the truth would have believed him to be an exile."

This was the world in which the classical conception of the unity of the individual with his *polis* or *civitas* was revived. In a humanistic dialogue of the time that describes a fictitious

[17] Vespasiano da Bisticci, *Vite di uomini illustri del secolo XV*, ed. L. Frati, vol. 3 (1893), 12; vol. 2 (1893), 192, 272; 3: 233; 2: 75f., 178, 181; 3: 273.

[18] L. B. Alberti, *I Libri della Famiglia*, ed. G. Mancini (Florence, 1908), 254f.; ed. C. Grayson, in *Scrittori d'Italia*, vol. 218 (Bari, 1960), 272f.

dispute between a patrician and a plebeian of ancient Rome, the victorious plebeian says that "the human spirit grows in excellence when it comes in contact with the life of the commonwealth."[19] Similar expressions recur in many writings by Florentine humanists. In 1427 Stefano Porcari, of Roman origin but twice Capitano del Popolo in Florence, referred to the classical praise of self-sacrifice for the *patria* in an official address before the authorities. Mutual protection in the community, he said, was the source of human culture; hence the unanimous teaching of the ancient philosophers that neither safety at birth nor family life, neither friendship nor honor among men, can exist outside the "common body" of the *patria*—"in it we live and thrive." In this address, delivered in the piazza of Florence, the Roman examples of self-sacrifice for the *respublica*, from Mucius Scaevola and Horatius Cocles to the Scipios, pass before the eyes of the Florentine citizens. "It was for their *patria* that the Romans took upon themselves such unheard of toil and danger, such wounds, and even the bitterness of death."[20]

The best proof that these convictions were in accordance with the sentiments of the Florentines is the unparalleled circulation of Porcari's orations in Florence and the insertion of his praise of a life led for the *patria* in Palmieri's *Civic Life*. This work, the finest blend of Humanism with Florentine civic spirit, begins with the statement that protracted historical studies had convinced the author that the perfect life is one which combines intellectual leisure with honorable activity in a rightly constituted *respublica*.[21]

---

[19] ". . . praeclariora tum fore mortalium ingenia, cum ad rem publicam accommodantur"; in Buonaccorso da Montemagno's "De Nobilitate Tractatus," in *Prose e Rime de' due Buonaccorsi de Montemagno* (Florence, 1718), 74f. For the correct text of this quotation see also Essay Six, note 14, below.

[20] Porcari, *Orazioni* (published in *Prose del giovane Buonaccorso da Montemagno* [Bologna, 1874], which wrongly ascribes them to Buonaccorso), *Oraz.* 2, pp. 14–23; see also *Oraz.* 5, 14, 15.

[21] ". . . et finalmente più che alcuna altra vita m'è paruta perfecta quella di coloro che in alcuna optima republica tale grado di virtù ritengono che ne' loro facti sanza errore o pericolo, et ociosi, riputati con degnità, possono vi-

III

In the fifteenth century, such ideas signified an intellectual and moral transformation. Although family, community, and state had constituted the milieu of the Italian citizen from earliest times, throughout the entire fourteenth century, mainly in consequence of the profound influence exercised by mendicant friars upon education and moral outlook, the intellectual training of citizens had contrasted sharply with the natural foundations of their existence. Even Petrarch and his first humanist adherents were deeply imbued with doubts about the value of a life devoted to the family and political community. However lightheartedly Boccaccio—Petrarch's closest friend in Florence—extolled the pleasures of love in his *Decameron*, he looked upon marriage as the greatest danger to a man of learning. In his biography of Dante—acknowledged to be the standard biography of the poet until the beginning of the fifteenth century—Boccaccio blamed Dante's unhappy fate on his having forgotten in the civic atmosphere of Florence

---

vere" (proem to *Vita Civile*). For Porcari's influence on Palmieri, compare Porcari, *Orazioni*, 14–23, with Palmieri, *Vita Civile*, Autogr. fol. 60a–61a (edizione critica [1982], 124–27). The classical examples are identical in both and for the most part described in the same words. One should compare the following sentences from the ends of these paragraphs: "Piene sone le greche, latine et barbare historie di memorabili exempli che dimonstrano quanto virilmente i nobili cittadini sprezavano ogni particolare commodo per salute della republica, per le quali opere sono nobilitati con somma gloria, et per eterna fama nel mondo immortali" (Palmieri, fol. 60b [p. 126]); "Passeremo . . . queste e molte altre Grecche, barbare e Latine storie, che tutte sono piene di opere gloriose de' cittadini verso le loro fortunate Repubbliche" (Porcari, p. 23); all the great Romans thought only of "la salute et acrescimento della republica, . . . per la quale multiplicate fatiche, affanni, disagi, pericoli, ferite, e crudelissime morti spessissime volti sofferivano" (Palmieri, fol. 60b [p. 127]); "Per la quale tanti affanni, tante fatiche, tanti pericoli, tante cicatrici, e crudelissime ferite, a morti ne' loro nobilissimi corpi acerbamente soffersero" (Porcari, p. 22). It is interesting to note Palmieri's dependence on Porcari, because it is a concrete example of the effect Porcari's orations had on the Florentine humanists. This is otherwise only deducible from the extraordinarily large number of manuscripts of speeches by Porcari circulating in Florence.

"what obstacles women are to studious life," thus forfeiting his intellectual peace through marriage and allowing himself to be drawn into the whirlpool of domestic and public cares that destroyed his life.[22]

Only a determined alliance with the classical ideas of citizenship could free the citizen from this medieval past. When Coluccio Salutati, Bruni's predecessor as chancellor of Florence, married at an early age, his only justification to other humanists was that he would emerge in time and recapture his soul, despite the fact that he was now experiencing the truth of the warning that man cannot serve both woman and philosophy. In later years, when the new civic Humanism had gained strength, he openly defended marriage against his master, Petrarch. In like spirit, the fictitious dispute between a Roman patrician and a plebeian to which I have already referred, ends with a picture of happy married life, in which husband and wife share the supreme intellectual pleasure of studying together in their library.

True breeding now seemed to the civic humanist to be possible only in the midst of family and society. As Bruni wrote in his biography of Dante (1436), real studies do not lead to idle solitude. "Among the stay-at-homes, who are withdrawn from human society, I have never seen one who could count to three. A lofty and distinguished mind does not need such fetters. . . . Standing apart from the interchange of ideas with others is characteristic of those whose inferior minds are incapable of understanding anything." Bruni's conception of Dante now displaced Boccaccio's earlier picture of the philosopher caught in the toils of marriage and politics. Petrarch's

---

[22] A particularly strong expression of Boccaccio's antipathy to marriage, with a list of all the evils arising from the bad habits of women and from married life, is found in his *Labirinto d'amore*. In spite of considerable differences in wording, the two versions of Boccaccio's *Vita* of Dante as handed down to us (the so-called *Trattatello in laude di Dante*, and the *Compendio della origine, vita, costumi e studii di Dante*) agree in declaring Dante's life as a married man and citizen to have been the ruin of his career as a philosopher.

weakness, declares Bruni, was that he lived only for himself.
Unlike this father of scholarly Humanism, the youthful Dante
worked for the government of his native city and proved his
courage in the citizen army at Campaldino, the decisive battle
between Florence and the city of Arezzo. The fact that he was
not afraid of marriage casts no shadow upon him but shows
that even great minds need not despise civic duties. The greatest philosophers—Aristotle, Cicero, Cato, Seneca, and
Varro—were fathers of families and served their communities.
Boccaccio's judgment is thus as frivolous as it is erroneous.
"In the opinion of all the philosophers, man is an *animale civile*.
The first union, the multiplication of which forms the state, is
that of husband and wife; there can be no perfection where
this primary condition does not exist."[23]

[23] L. Bruni, *Le Vite di Dante e di Petrarca*, in Bruni, *Humanistisch-philosophische Schriften*, 53ff., 68. Bruni's reconstruction of Dante's political career
and his discovery that Dante had fought in the battle of Campaldino were
repeatedly doubted by critics, because the Dante letters which Bruni claims
to have used cannot be found. Today, however, the correctness of Bruni's
statements is no longer doubted. Cf. I. del Lungo, *Dante ne' tempi di Dante*
(Bologna, 1888), 156ff.; E. Santini, in *Giornale Storico della Letteratura Italiana*
60 (1912): 321f., 329f.; N. Zingarelli, vol. 1 of *La vita, i tempi e le opere di
Dante* (Milan, 1931), 258f. One can understand why Bruni's discovery of the
youthful Dante living as a citizen among citizens seemed to give back to Florence the personality of her great poet. Regarding Bruni's defense of Dante as
the representative of Florence's historical traditions and Bruni's opposition to
the humanistic extremists who revered nothing but Antiquity, cf. V. Rossi,
"Dante nel Trecento e nel Quattrocento," in vol. 1 of *Scritti di critica letteraria*
(Florence, 1930), 293ff.

The intellectual situation, from which Bruni's *Vita di Dante* originated, is
illustrated through an oration composed by Francesco Filelfo, a few years before Bruni wrote his work. From 1429 to 1434, Filelfo was a teacher in the
service of the commune of Florence; in 1432 his oration on Dante was publicly
recited in the cathedral by one of his pupils. The most versatile of the migrant
humanists of the age, and accustomed to pleasing his alternating protectors,
Filelfo knew well what the Florentines wished him to say. He praised Dante
as the "liberatore" of his great "repubblica," who did for Florence in her dis-
tress what the Scipiones, Decii, and Metelli, as "cittadini romani," had once
done for Rome. "Molte furono le persecuzioni, molte le insidiazioni, molti i

This rehabilitation of Dante the Florentine citizen was but an echo of the humanistic rediscovery of Cicero the Roman citizen and statesman. In the Middle Ages Cicero had usually been conceived as an advocate of aloofness from the world. For a thousand years there had been no room for his civic doctrine that man is made to play an active part in his community and state and not merely to pursue solitary contemplation. Thanks to his new knowledge of Antiquity, Petrarch was the first to recognize the historical Cicero. But he was horrified by his discovery and bitterly accused the Roman statesman of failing in his duty as a true philosopher—just as Boccaccio accused Dante the citizen a short time afterwards. Petrarch could not forgive Cicero for deserting the calm of his studious life in order to defend the freedom of the state after Caesar's death. Salutati replied that Cicero had only obeyed the law attributed to Solon: in a time of civic strife the citizen who sides with neither party and desires to continue his private life is unfaithful and must be expelled from his city. Pier Paolo Vergerio, a pupil of Salutati's, added that Cicero had always

tradimenti, da che lui questa inclita città di Firenze più volte liberò. Quante guerre la città vostra . . . rimosse et al tutto estinse! . . . Tu finalmente in esilio fosti mandato per difensione della patria." But even in exile, "Dante sempre la patria lodava, sempre la magnificava, sempre la difendeva" (ed. Benaducci, in *Atti e Memorie della R. Deputaz. di storia patr. per le Marche* 5 [1901], 26f.). This was of course more fiction and high-flown rhetoric than truth. The exiled Dante attacked Florence rather than defending it. And when in his youth did he ever have an opportunity "di estinguere guerre" which threatened his city? It was, however, the very inconsistency between the patriotic praise accorded to the great Florentine and the real knowledge of his life that caused Bruni's documented discovery of Dante's civic career to be so cordially welcomed and very soon to become a characteristic feature of Florentine thought. The fourth book of Bruni's *Historiae Florentini Populi*, written in 1421, had already contained the first description of Dante at the battle of Campaldino and of his political activities during his priorate. But it was Bruni's *Vita di Dante*, written in the vernacular in 1436, which brought about the decisive change in the Florentine conception of Dante. The *Vita Dantis* by Francesco Filelfo's son, Giovan Maria Filelfo, is nothing but a highly rhetorical Latin adaptation of Bruni's work, which helped to make Bruni's views known during the fifteenth century.

professed in his writings that the existence of a man "who burdens himself with work for the state and the labor required by the *salus omnium* is superior to any other."[24]

Stimulated by such thoughts, Leonardo Bruni created the Florentine Cicero of the fifteenth century. In a biography written about 1415, at about the time Donatello carved his Saint George, Bruni made Cicero the symbol of the Renaissance conviction that a man's personality can only attain perfection through an active political life. The Roman author and statesman, who was not content with philosophical speculation—the Florentine biographer declared with reverence—made greater contributions to literature amidst the business of the vastest state on earth than did idle philosophers in their solitude, and at the same time gained added strength for his political work from his studies. "It was from the same sacred font of philosophy that he drew his actions in guiding the Roman Republic and the precepts of his books."[25]

Like Bruni, Palmieri joined the new conception of Cicero to the discovery that in his youth Dante had been a Florentine citizen in thought and deed. His book *Civic Life* transfers Scipio the Younger's vision (as described in Cicero's *Somnium Scipionis*)—in which citizens who have spent or sacrificed their lives in the service of their state are specially rewarded in the hereafter—from Roman to Florentine soil, that is, to the days when the youthful Dante bravely performed his duty with the Florentine army at Campaldino. After the victory (according to Palmieri's myth), Dante sees a fallen comrade-in-arms return to life for one short hour. The Florentine warrior, one of those whose sacrifice Palmieri equates with the heroic Roman deeds of Horatius Cocles and Curius Dentatus, describes to Dante the celestial gathering his soul has witnessed. "I saw there the souls of all the citizens who had ruled their states justly . . . and for the sake of their country had forgotten

---

[24] For Salutati, see Essay Five, 119f. For Vergerio, see his *Epistolario*, ed. L. Smith, in Fonti per la Storia d'Italia, vol. 74 (Rome, 1934), 440.

[25] Bruni, *Cicero Novus*, in Bruni, *Humanistisch-philosophische Schriften*, 114f.

themselves and their possessions." His final comment is that "no human work is more valuable than care for the welfare of the *patria*, the maintenance of the *città*, and the preservation of unity and harmony in a rightly ordered community." Thus the messenger from the beyond exhorts the youthful poet in the famous words of Cicero.[26] Palmieri assures us that he has heard this story "several times"; and the uncanny details of the raising of the dead on the battlefield and certain other incidents definitely point to a popular origin of the legend. There must have been a tendency among Florentine citizens to support the revival of classical civic ideals.

The view of Dante as the great exemplar of this way of life persisted into the sixteenth century. The first to follow Bruni's direction was Giannozzo Manetti, who two decades later described the lives of Dante, Petrarch, and Boccaccio in more detail. Of the three great *corone* (crowns) of Florence in the Trecento, said Manetti, the one who carried out the duties of a "free man" in addition to pursuing his studies was Dante, who did not remain aloof from public life but served his native city in high political office and in the citizen army. With even greater certainty than Bruni, Manetti declared that Dante, who had combined action and contemplation, was superior to Petrarch and Boccaccio, who had led the egoistic lives of humanistic literati. Henceforth almost every writer in Florence took this point of view until the end of the Renaissance.

In the second half of the Quattrocento, when the old traditions of Florence were overshadowed by the princely culture of the Medici, and when Platonism transformed the figure of Dante into that of a Platonic philosopher, the poet nevertheless remained the representative of civic life which he had become in the pre-Medicean epoch. In 1481 Cristoforo Landino published his commentary, which described the *Divina Commedia* as pervaded by Platonic ideas; but in an introduction dealing with Dante's life, even Landino emphasized, quoting

[26] *Vita Civile*, Autogr. fol. 100a to the end of the book (edizione critica [1982], 200–208).

Manetti as his source, that the great poet who had made the Florentine idiom preeminent in Italy had also done his duty in the service of the state and even on the battlefield. After the period of Platonism, the most widely read commentary on Dante's poem in the sixteenth century—that of Alessandro Vellutello of Lucca—carried on the conceptions of the early Quattrocento. It removed the Platonic veil from the figure of Dante as well as many of the characteristics that the Platonists had adopted from Boccaccio, and built in turn on Bruni's simple and powerful picture of Dante the Florentine citizen.

Thus, both the Florentine Cicero and the Florentine Dante remained in evidence throughout the Italian Renaissance. They are perhaps the most impressive testimony that patriotism and civic spirit were vital forces in Florence in the days when Renaissance Humanism and the art of the Renaissance were born.

New Historical and Psychological Ways of Thinking: From Petrarch to Bruni and Machiavelli★

I

H IGH on the list of priorities in the study of the Florentine Renaissance is the problem of the intellectual antecedents of Machiavelli's causal approach to historical change. Since the time when the ground-breaking works of Wilhelm Dilthey and Friedrich Meinecke were published, it has become common knowledge that one of the strongest roots of Machiavelli's image of the politico-historical world was a conception of *virtù*—the energy and resilience of man—that sprang from the Renaissance attitude toward life.[1] It is also known that this conception of *virtù* was stimulated by the reading of the classical authors and that it came to Machiavelli through the humanistic tradition which had taken form since Petrarch. But whether, or to what extent, the humanistic "conception and analysis of man" ("Auffassung und

★ First published in German in *Historische Zeitschrift*, 147 (1932), under the title "Das Erwachen des historischen Denkens im Humanismus des Quattrocento." In the present essay the sometimes complicated formulations of the original have been simplified; otherwise it is a faithful translation of the earliest piece in this collection. The Machiavelli characterized toward its end is more contemptuous of the common people and more estranged from the civic tradition of early Quattrocento Florence than I now believe him to have been. Readers who are troubled by my early opinion or wish to understand the subsequent change should read my 1961 essay "Machiavelli the Republican Citizen and Author of *The Prince*" in its final version in Vol. II below.

[1] W. Dilthey, *Auffassung und Analyse des Menschen im 15. und 16. Jahrhundert* (Leipzig, 1891); Fr. Meinecke, *Die Idee der Staatsräson in der neueren Geschichte* (Munich, 1924). E. W. Mayer's study, *Machiavellis Staatsauffassung und sein Begriff virtù* (Munich, 1912), was inspired by Meinecke.

Analyse des Menschen," in Dilthey's words) was applied to history and politics prior to Machiavelli has not been explored in any detail

Even the earliest phase of Humanism, however, yields relevant information. Not only do we find Petrarch using the concept and word *virtù* (or the Latin, *virtus*) in a sense similar to Machiavelli's, but like him Petrarch had already combined it with the idea of psychological *necessità*: coercion exerted by the state or by the relations between states can engender greater *virtù* in a nation. Petrarch, in fact, had already asked himself the question Machiavelli later posed in a more mature form: Does not a people cease to flourish when the removal of external danger minimizes its political and military *virtù*? Does not a people that no longer has enemies and has become self-satisfied face moral ruin?

When, in Petrarch's view, Genoa became excessively bellicose in 1352, after a Genoese victory over a Venetian fleet in the Bosporus, he pointed warningly in a letter to the example of the ancient *Respublica Romana*, which had tried to secure an untroubled existence for itself by destroying its historic adversary, Carthage, and thereby sapped its own strength. For a healthy military balance, Petrarch insisted, is necessary among powerful states. "Like corpulent bodies that look deceptively healthy, great and peaceful cities may be riddled with hidden disease. . . . Wars are often salutary for great nations, just as is exercise for obese bodies; and just as the body is made heavy and sick by excessive indolence, so is a city that lives too tranquilly. Such a life allows fluids to accumulate in the body, and in a nation it produces rivalries, discordant spirits, and clashing emotions. Moderate activity is the friend of good health; pleasant idleness prepares the way for disease. The *virtus Romana* would never have been destroyed if Carthage had been left standing. Once that burden of fear was lifted from the shoulders of the Romans, the way lay open for foreign vices and civil wars. The end of one great affliction was thus the beginning of an even greater one."[2]

[2] "Solet equidem ut exterior magnorum corporum sanitas, sic pax magna-

In another letter (*Epistola Fam.* XXII 14), probably written about eight years later under the influence of Sallust's remark that fortune changes along with mores and that domination passes from the less to the more suited, Petrarch depicted the perpetual shifting of political *virtus* from one people to another. Is it surprising, he asked, that *ingenia, virtus,* and *nomina* changed their location; that Macedonia, Carthage, and Rome rose to power each in its turn and sank again? When a people is satiated with prosperity it begins to fall back on its reputation. Indolence, the good life, and the enjoyment of luxury, which conquer armies and unnerve citizens, become widespread. Then another people, inured to danger and hardship, disdainful of pleasure, energetic and persevering, rises to the top. History has shown the only way to escape such change and degeneration. The greatness of Rome was upheld for many generations by the virile martial spirit—the *prisca illa Romana militia masculorum militum*—alive in the days of Scipio and of Metellus, by simplicity, discipline, and the contempt for soft living. Those times gave Petrarch a standard for denouncing both the misery produced by the mercenary system and the general degeneration of modern Italy—the same de-

---

rum urbium morbis abundare latentibus. . . . Sepe ut gravibus corporibus exercitia, sic magnis populis medicinalia bella sunt, et sicut quies immodica corpus gravat atque inficit, sic urbem immoderata tranquillitas; hec et in corpore varios humores et in populo simultates varias ac discordes animos gignit affectusque contrarios; agitatio temperata sanitatis amica est, leta quies male valitudini causas prebet. Nunquam romana virtus periisset si incolumis Carthago mansisset; ille terror cervicibus amotus, peregrinis vitiis et bellis civilibus viam fecit, magnique laboris finis maioris initium fuit" (Petrarch, *Epistolae Familiares*, ed. Rossi, vol. 3, pp. 121f., *Ep. Fam.* XIV 5 [17–19]). According to *Ep. Fam.* XII 2 (7), the inspiration for the Carthage statement came from Florus' description of Scipio's opposition to Cato's demand that Carthage should be completely destroyed; "ne, metu ablato emulae urbis, luxuriari felicitas nostre urbis inciperet," is the argument given by Florus' Scipio. There is also a reference in Petrarch's *De Otio Religioso* to the *securitas* that Rome expected from the elimination of Carthage and to the debility (*segnities*) of the Romans that actually resulted (*Opera* [Basel, 1581], 301; now in Rotondi's edition [Vatican City, 1958], 20).

nunciation that was to pervade Machiavelli's writings several generations later.

The question whether coercion or "necessity" could create military strength, another of Machiavelli's central themes, was taken up by Petrarch's school, which after his death included Florentine citizens who dreamed, long before Machiavelli, of replacing their foreign mercenaries with a native citizen army. In Matteo Palmieri's *Vita Civile*,[3] the idea that *necessità* produces military *virtù* is presented entirely in the Machiavellian sense. Palmieri's Greek literary model, Aristotle, had regarded the daring in battle which is owed to passion, coercion, or blindness to danger, as a flawed virtue. According to Aristotle, a brave man "ought to be brave not because he is coerced but because bravery is beautiful."[4] In contrast, the Quattrocento Florentine Palmieri was keenly aware that coercion could be a spur to brave deeds that otherwise would not be undertaken, a "great help to those imperfect people with whom one commonly lives." "For fear of dishonor, risks are taken in battle by a man who will not hold his ground because it is the right thing to do. Because he sees cowards scorned and brave men rewarded and honored, he stands firm so as not to be considered cowardly and base." Besides this psychological incentive, Palmieri says, there is the brutal *necessità* of battle, which leaves only the choice of dying or fighting bravely. With evident satisfaction he translated into the Florentine vernacular the words in which, according to Sallust, Catilina had once told his comrades *per tale necessità*—in a desperate situation on the battlefield—that for them there was only victory or death. Machiavelli was later to react with similar delight when he read in Livy the cry of a leader of the Volsci to his men, who had been surrounded by the enemy: Follow me, *necessitas* will make you victors![5]

---

[3] For the date of the *Vita Civile*—the 1430s—see Essay Six, note 13.

[4] Δεῖ δ'οὐ δι'ἀνάγκην ἀνδρεῖον εἶναι, ἀλλ' ὅτι καλόν (Aristoteles, *Eth. ad Nic.* III.8; Bekker, ch. 11, p. 1116). Palmieri's difference from Aristotle will be discussed in more detail in Essay Six, 155ff.

[5] Matteo Palmieri, *Vita Civile* (autograph), Firenze Bibl. Naz. cod. II, IV,

How could anyone tracing the rise and fall of *virtù* to natural causes and believing that culture and political power follow a psychologically conditioned cycle also retain the medieval belief in the eternal Roman Empire, which would endure forever according to divine plan and, in the role of judge, finally end the clash of nations? Yet Petrarch still held these conflicting notions. It is true that unlike Dante he understood the reluctance of other nations to submit to the Roman Empire and expressly stated that he no longer condemned it as a foolish and sinful rebellion against God's will;[6] and at least in his *Africa*, the epic of his youth, he showed himself to be undeceived by the medieval assumption that the German Holy Roman Empire was the same political institution that the Roman people had founded in the age of the Scipios. Nonetheless, Petrarch did not doubt that the ancient Roman world, whose literature and art seemed to be reviving after centuries of oblivion, could be brought back to political life as well. Like all the humanists of the Trecento, he was a political as well as a cultural classicist, whose dream of a Roman revival included the revival of its empire. What began to change with Petrarch was the medieval Christian idea of eternal holy Rome, which was giving way to the idea of *Roma Aeterna* found in the classical authors. In the final analysis, he was scarcely closer than writers of the preceding ages to gaining the historical insight that nothing of the past simply returns and that every state and people is bound to reflect its own time. In fact, between Petrarch's belief in the resurgence of Rome's everlasting empire and Machiavelli's historical conception, which ignores everything but the naturally conditioned rise and fall of peoples and states, there stretches almost the entire distance dividing the medieval trust in the permanence or renovatio of Rome from historical thinking in the modern sense.

---

81 fol. 32vf.; now edizione critica by Gino Belloni (Florence, 1982), 74ff. On Machiavelli, *Discorsi* III 12, cf. Meinecke, *Idee der Staatsräson*, 47.

6 Petrarch, *Epistolae Sine Nomine*, ed. Piur, *Ep.* IV, p. 174, to be compared with Dante, *Monarchia* II 1.

II

A decisive break with medieval thinking did not occur until the generation that saw the art of Donatello, Brunelleschi, and Masaccio. Now, a fresh, less dualistic view of man was elaborated by humanists, and it became the basis for a new psychology, which was eventually to leave its mark on historiography and historical imagination. Writers and educators began to acknowledge that ideas and ideals are unalterably rooted in natural drives, emotions, and passions. Humanists took pleasure in discovering a bond between lofty virtues and earthbound *humanitas* and rejected any ethical theory that might oblige them to suppress passion for the sake of spiritual isolation. Strong emotional impulses and a thirst for fame and power were discovered to be among the indispensable motivations of great achievement in politics and culture.

After a long stay in Florence, Pier Paolo Vergerio, in his *De Ingenuis Moribus et Liberalibus Studiis Adulescentiae* of 1402,[7] made the first attempt to formulate a psychology of adolescence that would allow room in pedagogy and moral teachings for youthful desires and that excess of "heat and blood" which makes the adolescent break all barriers and which is the source of his achievements and mistakes, of his élan and idealism as well as his arrogance and lack of moderation. Without ambition and the desire for fame—the emotions that urge the mind on to greatness—no education, Vergerio insisted, would have the power to fire the youthful mind and raise it beyond sensual desire and a materialistic outlook on life.

A frank defense of anger, that strong emotion which the Stoic orientation of Trecento humanists had unreservedly condemned as an impediment to reason, is common in humanistic discussions after 1400. How could devotion and bravery be possible in the active life without the welling up of justifiable wrath, asked Leonardo Bruni during the 1420s in an argument against the doctrinaire rationalism he claimed to be at the core not only of Trecento philosophy but of all Stoic

---

[7] For the date, see *Crisis*, 2d ed., 494.

and ascetic teaching. Woe to him, Bruni exclaimed, who "neither feels pain nor starts up in anger when his homeland, parents, or children . . . are humiliated." In defiance of the Stoic glorification of the rational, he insisted that "excitement and violent emotion are sometimes useful and certainly appropriate."[8] Many of the Florentine citizen-humanists agreed. Matteo Palmieri observed that a good part of a fighter's courage comes from violent anger, and as late as the 1480s Cristoforo Landino wrote that nature puts the emotion of anger into the soul of brave men not in order to shut out the light of reason but to serve the growth of bravery, just as the grindstone serves the blade in need of honing.[9]

A provocative and widely shared discovery of the first Quattrocento decades was that no moral strength or human greatness can develop without the help of passion. A humanistic chancery official at the Curia, Francesco da Fiano, who lived in Rome at the beginning of the century, is of interest to us in this connection because he had the benefit of friendly contacts with many humanists of the rising younger generation, among them the Florentine Bruni.[10] In his few surviving works, Francesco da Fiano shows that he knew how to make good use of the new psychology in defending or criticizing the poets and writers of the past. This curial humanist dared to suggest that although the Church Fathers had thought differently and Augustine in his *City of God* had condemned man's desire for worldly glory as a vice and sin, "we are all dragged toward the desire for glory by hooks, so to speak, firmly embedded in our humanity" (*quia omnes in cupiditatem*

---

[8] "Iuvant enim interdum et certe decent stimuli quidem et motus animi vehementiores . . ." (H. Baron, ed., *Leonardo Bruni Aretino, Humanistisch-philosophische Schriften*, 34).

[9] Palmieri, *Vita Civile* (autograph), fol. 33; edizione critica, 75f. Cristoforo Landino, *De Vera Nobilitate*, dedicatory copy, Bibl. Corsiniana (Rome) cod. 433, fol. 78; now ed. Maria Teresa Liaci (Florence, 1970), 108. For the comparison to a grindstone, see Cicero *Acad. Prior.* II.135.

[10] See *Interrogatio, ad Franciscum de Fiano, per Leon. Aretinum transmissa, videlicet quo tempore fuerit Ovidius* . . . ; in Bruni, *Humanistisch-philosophische Schriften*, 179.

glorie quodam, ut sic dixerim, humanitatis unco pertrahimur); God and nature have themselves given us our passions and "whatever else is human." Even the Church Fathers would not have written their great works "if they had not been fired by ardent longing for praise and glory among men" and "if passionate love for a writer's fame had not cajoled them into it." No Pompey or Marius would have rushed victoriously through vast lands, no Hannibal would have scaled the steep Alps, scarcely accessible even to the bird's flight, if these labors had "not been sweet to their glory-seeking hearts."[11]

III

At this point in the evolution of Renaissance thought, the city-state of Florence assumed a unique role. Florentine citizens, who were accustomed to seeing an intimate connection between the literary and artistic rise of their city on the one hand and its political and economic growth on the other, began to speculate about the psychological forces propelling the historical development of the Florentine people and about the dependence of Florentine culture on the changing vitality of the body politic. In 1436 Leonardo Bruni, in his widely read biographies of Dante and Petrarch, pointed out for the first time, and with remarkable persuasiveness, the correlation existing between political and cultural conditions in the various stages of Rome's development. Both the *Respublica Romana* and Roman literature, Bruni argued, were at their height in the time of Cicero, and it was true later as well that "literature and the study of the Latin language developed in parallel with the vicissitudes of the Roman state." For "when the Roman

[11] Francesco da Fiano, *Contra oblocutores et detractores poetarum*, Cod. Vat. Ottobon. lat. 1438, fol. 144f; now ed. by Igino Taù, "con appendice di documenti biografici" (Rome, Edizioni di Storia e Letteratura, 1964), 76f. Written before October 1404, because the recipient of the dedication, called Cardinalis Bononiensis, is the later Innocent VII, elected 17 October, consecrated 11 November 1404. Novati's notation in vol. 4 of *Epistolario di Coluccio Salutati*, 171, which would suggest 1405–1406, is thus deceptive.

31

people lost their freedom under the rule of the emperors, . . . their talent for scholarship and literary creativity came to an end, together with the flowering of the Roman state." So long as the state was in decline no true culture could flourish in Italy. Only after political freedom was regained by the expulsion of the Lombards did the Italian communes begin "to rise again politically and bring back life to studies," until a new age of maturity was once again reached with the appearance of Dante, Petrarch, and Boccaccio.[12]

Before long, the sociopolitical causation of cultural growth was extended to the fine arts as well. Their flowering came to be ascribed widely to the creative force of republican liberty. With its incorporation in some of the most important writings on Florentine Renaissance artists—Antonio Manetti's *Life of Brunelleschi*, the writings of Leon Battista Alberti, and later Gelli's collection of biographies of artists[13]—this assumption was even disseminated beyond humanistic circles. Together with the theory that republican life and a thriving literature were intertwined, it became a permanent element of historical philosophy.

A conviction that human nature must not be repressed lay behind all these theories. In Florence it was easily transferred from the field of psychology and pedagogy to an explanation of historical growth. Why had Florence been able to advance so proudly beyond other Italian states? Because it was politically free, answered the citizens of the last great Italian commune which could boast that it had never fallen for any length of time under the rule of a tyrant or of a restricted aristocracy. There was an intimate connection, they argued, between freedom and creativity. When Bruni in his oration of 1428 (patterned after Thucydides' *Funeral Oration of Pericles*) glorified liberty as the root of Florence's political and cultural greatness, he claimed that the source of the city's vitality and suc-

[12] Bruni, *Humanistisch-philosophische Schriften*, 64f.

[13] See W. Rehm, *Der Untergang Roms im abendländischen Denken* (Leipzig, 1930), 68 and 71.

cess was the opportunity it offered citizens to rise to high positions in public life and to make full use of their talents. "For when men are given the hope of attaining honor in the state, they take courage and raise themselves to a higher plane; if this hope is lost, they grow lazy and stagnate. Since such hope and opportunity are held out in our commonwealth, we need not be surprised that talent and diligence excel here in the highest degree."[14]

Did not, then, the same explanation apply to Florence's primacy in the arts and humanistic studies? Whenever man breaks the chains of tradition, Palmieri explained; whenever he has the courage not to bind himself, as did men in most centuries and as do the artisans in the guilds, who follow the lead of previous generations; whenever he has the will to advance freely and steadily and make new discoveries, golden ages of culture arise. This happened in Antiquity and was beginning to happen again in Florence. Before the Florentine artist Giotto, painting was dead (*la pittura morta*), because men were satisfied with what their fathers had done and made no attempt to improve art. Art reached a highpoint after Giotto, and so did literature and the liberal arts (*lettere e liberali studi*). For eight hundred years, said Palmieri, they were sterile and almost forgotten, until "our Leonardo Bruni" reestablished humanistic studies. "He who has been given a talent should therefore thank God for having been born in this period, when the noble arts of the mind [*l'eccellenti arti d'ingegno*] are in greater flower than they have been for a thousand years."[15] Such is the Florentines' evaluation of their own age. The word

---

[14] "Atque haec honorum adipiscendorum facultas potestasque libero populo, haec assequendi proposita mirabile quantum valet ad ingenia civium excitanda. Ostensa enim honoris spe, erigunt sese homines atque attollunt; praeclusa vero inertes desidunt; ut in civitate nostra cum sit ea spes facultasque proposita, minime sit admirandum et ingenia et industriam plurimum eminere" (*Oratio in Funere Johannis Strozzae*, in Stephanus Baluzius, *Miscellanea*, ed. Mansi, vol. 4 [Lucca, 1764], 3f.). This political creed of Bruni's was already referred to in Essay One, note 5.

[15] Palmieri, *Vita Civile* (autograph), fol. 17–18; edizione critica (1982), 44f.

"Renaissance" (*rinascere l'arti perduti*) appears here for the first time with the historical meaning we still attach to it.

IV

This new conception of freedom and its effect on human vitality and creativity, which gave Florentines a clearer understanding of their own time, proved equally effective as a key to the past. Had not freedom and active citizenship been at the root of what was great in Antiquity, just as they were in the present? When he tried to explain Rome's triumph over other ancient states, Petrarch had eventually fallen back on the medieval belief that the imperial Roman monarchy was loftier than any mere product of human action. It had seemed to him that the transcendent, God-willed Roman Empire was subject to the general causality of history only in that it would not always be at its height. Like everything human it would reach a peak and then decline, for even Roman *virtus* depended on the laws governing human affairs. But at the same time Rome was different. Its universal empire could never entirely disappear. It would eventually have to rise again if the order imposed by God upon the events of history was to prevail. For Bruni in the early fifteenth century, the Roman conquest which had so long dazzled the eyes of posterity lost the aura of a suprahistorical phenomenon. For the first time Roman history was seen entirely as the work of an historical agent: the Roman people, with its rising and waning power to shape political and cultural conditions throughout the world.

This new historical perception is formulated in the introductory book of Bruni's *Histories of the Florentine People*: "Under consuls, dictators [appointed for a fixed time], and military tribunes, the officials of a free people," the Roman Empire "in fact and in name" came into being through the strength "of a single city-state." As a product of history, it had to decay when the energy of the people who had created it began to decline. History shows that its degeneration was rooted in the transformation of the *Respublica Romana* into the authoritarian imperial monarchy. Although the emperors extended the outer boundaries of the Empire, internally they destroyed the civic spirit that had created it. "The decline of the Roman Empire [the *declinatio Romani imperii*—this expression, which finally parts with the medieval belief that the Empire is eternal, occurs here for the first time] must, therefore, have occurred at the moment when Rome forfeited her liberty and became subservient to emperors." For with the rise of autocratic monarchy, the psychological climate necessarily changed; during the centuries when the courtier replaced the Catonian champion of freedom, the courageous honesty of the age of the Scipios disappeared. Both physically and psychologically, the less valuable elements of society were favored. Terrible proscriptions decimated the traditional champions of the *virtus Romana*. "Thus strength gradually ebbed away, and for want of citizens the sunken power of the state began to pass into the hands of foreigners."[16]

Later in his life, in his biographies of Dante and Petrarch, Bruni was to trace in detail this decline of Roman—and soon even Italic—elements and the advance of foreign blood to the imperial throne itself. "In the end there was almost no one left who could master Latin culture [the *lettere latine*] with any degree of refinement."[17] That, Bruni emphasizes, was the true end of Roman history. Afterwards, its bearer, the Roman people, no longer existed either in body or in spirit. The German empire of the Middle Ages, as well as the powerless, demoralized townspeople of postclassical Rome, represented something historically different, despite the fact that they continued to bear the old Roman name. When, after a thousand years, Italy finally rose to eminence again, it was not because

---

[16] "Itaque paulatim evanescere vires et prolapsa maiestas interire caepit, ac deficientibus civibus, ad externos deferri" (Bruni, *Historiae Florentini Populi*, Lib. I, ed. Santini, *Rer. Ital. SS. Ed. N.*, vol. 19, pt. 3 [Bologna, 1926], 15; see also pp. 14 and 22).

[17] Bruni, *Humanistisch-philosophische Schriften*, 65.

ancient Rome or her empire had revived but because of the free Italian communes, which, having been given room to expand by the expulsion of the Lombards, brought a new political and cultural vigor to the Italian peninsula.[18]

Such was the first attempt to formulate a history of Rome and Italy in which an historical entity—the ancient Roman people—replaced *Roma Aeterna*. Of course, before the medieval belief in the suprahistorical role of Rome could finally die, the rise of the Roman state had to be viewed as a natural historical phenomenon within the framework of the power balance of the ancient states; but even this final step was taken with Bruni's efforts to reconstruct the genesis of the Florentine republic in Roman times. To achieve world rule, Bruni reflected in his *Histories*, the *Respublica Romana* had to draw together the strength of Italy. This centralization by force, however, also represented an irreparable loss, because it obliterated all local and regional independence outside of Rome and thus destroyed the very forces the Florentines considered essential for political health and the flourishing of culture.

In the early days of Italian history—as Bruni described this process—the map of Italy was covered with city-states filled with vitality. This showed itself most impressively in the cultural and political flowering of Etruria, whose city-states had special significance for the Florentines because they were the first great historical creation of the Tuscan race. The rise of Rome brought with it the merciless annihilation of this multiplicity. "Just as tall trees stand in the way of young plants that spring up near them and prevent them from growing, Rome dominated its surroundings and no longer permitted the ascent of other cities in Italy. Even cities that had formerly been great lost their strength and declined under the repressive dominance of Rome. For how could any city still grow in power? Without sovereignty they could no longer enlarge their territories, or even wage war. Their officials no longer had adequate jurisdiction, for their authority was sharply re-

---

[18] Ibid., and Bruni, *Historiae*, 7 and 23f.

stricted and even within its narrow limits was subordinate to that of the Roman authorities." In the same way, Rome's economic development led to the concentration of growth in one place. "And so, by attracting every outstanding man born in Italy, Rome drained the other Italian cities of their strength."[19] With these conclusions a new way of thinking historically, of understanding history in causal, organic terms, has undermined, if not yet formally attacked, the medieval idea of *Roma Aeterna* as an instrument of God.

An indispensable prerequisite of this new, secular approach was the optimistic psychology of the early Quattrocento. As we have seen, humanists had come to recognize that a nagging ambition for distinction and a yearning for the free development of naturally given capabilities were the forces at work in creative minds. In Bruni's conception of Roman history, this psychological discovery was applied to the struggle of the city-states for independence. According to Bruni, without a place in the sun, without freedom to develop their energies, without opportunity for the ambitious to enter upon significant careers, peoples as well as individuals languish and wither, like plants striving vainly toward the sun. "It is nature's gift to mortals," said Bruni in his *Histories*, "that when a path to greatness and honor is open, men raise themselves more easily to a higher plane; when they are deprived of this hope, they grow lazy and stagnate. Thus, when rule [in Italy] passed to the Romans, and people [outside Rome] could no longer attain to public honors or occupy themselves with matters of great import, the Etruscan *virtus* languished, overcome much more by leisure and inaction than by the sword of the enemy."[20]

---

[19] "Ita [Roma] quidquid egregium per Italiam nascebatur ad se trahens, alias civitates exhauriebat" (Bruni, *Historiae*, 7).

[20] "Est enim hoc mortalibus natura insitum, ut via ad amplitudinem honoresque exposita, facilius se attollant: praeclusa vero, inertes desideant. Tunc igitur imperio ad Romanos traducto, cum neque honores capessere, neque maioribus in rebus versari liceret, etrusca virtus omnino consenuit longe plus inerti otio quam hostili ferro depressa" (ibid., 13).

V

Machiavelli inherited this causal and psychological approach. As we know today, Bruni's *Histories* served him at many points as a guide for his *Istorie Fiorentine*, and he shared (at least in its essentials) Bruni's conception of the abundant vitality of Italy in pre-Roman times and the repression of this vitality by the ascendancy of Rome. The picture of Rome's role in the struggle of the Italian city-states set forth by Bruni must have been in Machiavelli's mind[21] when he concluded that history is an unending process of growth and decay, and when he formulated the principle that "since all mortal things are in constant motion and cannot remain stable, they must either rise or fall."[22] Like the Florentine humanists of the early Quattrocento, Machiavelli held the antithesis of Dante's medieval belief that "the world needs a single monarch" and that "the evil lies in the multiplicity of states"; for like Bruni he reasoned that it is precisely the multiplicity of autonomous, competing states that creates historical vitality. "Where there are many states," he wrote, "many capable men are produced; where there are few states, few are produced" and there is correspondingly little *virtù*.[23]

Yet Machiavelli's view of man and history did not include the entire legacy of Bruni's age. Even before Machiavelli, the optimism of the first Quattrocento generations, with their unquestioning belief in the positive value of the unrestrained growth of man's full nature, with all its passions, had widely turned to disappointment. Just as Botticelli's spiritualized art followed upon the earthy style of Donatello, so in the days of

---

[21] As was suggested by P. Joachimsen, in vol. 1 of his *Geschichtsauffassung und Geschichtschreibung in Deutschland unter dem Einfluss des Humanismus*, 224, and E. Santini, in *L. Bruni Aretino e i suoi Hist. Flor. Populi Libri XII*, 118ff., both published in 1910.

[22] Machiavelli, *Discorsi*, 1 6 and 11 preface.

[23] "Est igitur monarchia necessaria mundo. . . . Malum autem pluralitas principatuum, unus ergo princeps" (Dante, *Monarchia*, 1 10). "Conviene pertanto che, dove è assai potestadi, vi surga assai valenti uomini; dove ne è poche, pochi" (Machiavelli, *Arte della Guerra*, toward the end of Book 11, in S. Bertelli's edition [Milan, 1961], 393).

Florentine Neoplatonism a more dualistic view of human nature succeeded the early Renaissance confidence in the beneficial effect of vigorous emotions. The classic witness of this reaction is Cristoforo Landino, whose dialogues, the *Camaldulensian Disputations*, arrive at the reluctant conclusion that although noble spirits come to maturity only when they are driven by strong passion, that passion contains a latent danger which especially threatens the best minds. "It is easy for the man who has allowed higher things to enter his soul to disdain sensual pleasures. Even wealth . . . is soon held in contempt by a noble soul. But the desire for political honor, public position, and power to rule ensnares even a lofty mind, because these goals appear to have within themselves something great and outstanding. . . . Without doubt nature has so made us that we constantly long to be first in all things. . . . Yet if this natural desire is not restrained by clear reason, it drags us toward ambition and unjust power, . . . until we lose even our humanity and are changed into passion-drunk monsters."[24]

To describe this eternally thorny road of the soul in psychological terms was one of the tasks of Landino's work. By explaining how passion and great aspiration drive men to great deeds, it continued the humanistic tradition; by pointing out how easily a noble impetus degenerates into selfishness, it began a trend that went beyond early Humanism. The moral

---

[24] "Facile est enim contemnere voluptates ei, qui iam maiora mente concepit: divitiae vero etsi speciem maximorum bonorum a principio nobis ostendant, postremo tamen ab excellenti animo negliguntur. At vero honores, magistratus et imperia, quoniam excellens quoddam et eminens in se continere videntur, specie decori atque magnifici animum etiam excelsum decipiunt. . . . Est enim natura nobis inditum, ut semper superiores in rebus omnibus evadere cupiamus, cedere autem aut succumbere turpissimum putemus. Quae quidem naturalis cupiditas, nisi recta ratione temperetur, in ambitionem ac postremo in tyrannidem nos rapit, in qua multa adversus humanitatem crudelia, taetra nefariaque committimus et, cum natura ipsa, nisi depravata fuerit, ad magnanimitatem erigat nos, ad superbiam et dominatum omnia rapimus. Hinc fraudes, hinc caedes, hinc reliqua inmania flagitia insurgunt. Quibus rebus ipsam humanitatem exuti in truculentissima monstra convertimur" (Cristoforo Landino, *Disputationes Camaldulenses Lib. Tertius* [Paris: Jean Petit, 1511], fol. Lᵛf.; Peter Lohe ed. [Florence, 1980], 155f.).

ambiguity inherent in the drive for power was fully exposed here for the first time. "What incited the Spartans and Athenians, of all the Greeks, to annex a large part of Asia to their domain?" Landino asked in the *Disputations*. "What persuaded Hannibal to extend his grasp toward Rome, the center of the world, after Spain and Gaul had been subdued? What drove our own [leaders in ancient Italy] Sulla, Marius, Caesar, Pompey, Octavian, and Anthony, to such fury that they filled the world with the blood of citizens? What else but mad greed for glory? . . . Only one who is himself evil can call these people good. Yet is it not true that even the best members of human society, those who were most willing to give their lives for their state, went to their deaths with open eyes, driven not only by love of their homeland but also by a thirst for glory that made them accept death more willingly? Could anyone be naïve enough to believe that the Athenian Themistocles, during the sea battle at Salamis; Epaminondas, in his triumph over the Lacedaemonians; or the Spartan Leonidas, in the heroic battle at Thermopylae, never thought of their reputation? I, at any rate, am convinced that neither Brutus . . . nor Scaevola . . . nor the Decii . . . nor the innumerable others who put the freedom of their homeland before their own lives considered the reputation they would leave to posterity to be unimportant."[25] These wise but rather sad observations recall

[25] "Quid apud Graecos, Spartanos aut Athenienses excitavit, ut magnam Asiae partem suo imperio adiungerent? quid Hannibali suasit, ut Hispaniis Galliisqae subactis Romam orbis caput peteret? quid apud nostros L. Syllam prius ac C. Marium, deinde Iulium Caesarem Cn.que Pompeium ac postremo Octavium et M. Antonium eo furore accendit, ut civili sanguine cuncta replerentur? nisi insana quaedam famae cupiditas. . . . At nemo, modo ipse malus non sit, huiuscemodi viros bonos dixerit. Sed quid, si optimi quoque in hominum societate viri ac pro re publica emori promptissimi praeter id, quod patriae caritate in manifestissimam mortem ruebant, gloriae quoque cupiditate extremum casum aequiore animo ferebant? Quis enim sibi persuadeat aut Themistoclem Atheniensem in navali proelio apud Salamina gesto aut Epaminondam in ea victoria, qua de Lacedaemoniis potitus est, aut Spartanum Leonidam in Thermopylis viriliter pugnantem nihil de gloria cogitasse? Ego enim neque Brutum singulari certamine adversus regis exulis filium concurrentem neque Scaevolam tanta animi constantia dexteram exurentem neque Decios illos in confertissimos hostes irruentes neque innu-

Francesco da Fiano's audacious faith in glory at the beginning of the century. From the early Quattrocento delight in the discovery that strong emotions can be a spur to moral conduct, the road had led to an understanding of how egotistic tendencies are bound to dilute the ethical purity of political aims.

This was already understood when Machiavelli began to formulate his views of history and historical change. Responding to the political conditions of his time, he, too, concluded that the psychological optimism of the early Quattrocento was due to the naïveté of writers who had failed to perceive the evil in man's psyche. This was the reason for his critical assessment of Bruni. He himself believed in an active, productive *virtù* only for those few great founders and rulers of states whose natural vices of greed, self-interest, and desire for power are excused because they are linked to a political mission. In Machiavelli's eyes, the large majority of men belong to the indolent masses and are filled with petty instincts and capable of achieving *virtù* only under the coercion exerted by the state and the law.[26] In the *Discorsi* the assumption that people do what is right only if they are driven to it by necessity is frequently repeated. In the period about 1500, it was held that great individuals alone, not ordinary men, have creative power. As Machiavelli sees it, the architect of a state is like the artist who shapes the stone; it is he who gives form to the people, the defective raw material that often resists the efforts of the leader.

The focus of Machiavelli's writings, in consequence, alternates between discussions of stratagems to be applied by the head of a state and explorations of patterns discernible in the psychological reaction and conduct of a people. There exists, accordingly, a twofold *necessità*: the coercion exerted by the activities of a prince or leader, and that exerted by the natural process of historical growth and decay. It is with this dichotomy in mind that Machiavelli approaches the historical past.

---

merabiles alios, qui patriae libertatem suae vitae praetulerunt, famam, quam de se posteritati relicturi essent, nihili unquam fecisse arbitror" (ibid. [Paris: Jean Petit, 1511], fol. cxxiiiif.; Peter Lohe ed., 228).

[26] Cf. E. W. Mayer, *Machiavellis Geschichtsauffassung*, 42f.

His interest no longer lies in the reconstruction of Italy's distinctive history of change from an age of city-state liberty to one of imperial centralization and finally, in the Middle Ages, back again to one of civic freedom and independent states. Although he adopted all these elements from early-Quattrocento Humanism, the focus of his study is different. For Machiavelli, history is a process determined by the rules inherent in the uniformity of human nature, but it nevertheless offers the statesman a raw material that can be modified, even though the natural trend of change from rise to decay will eventually reassert itself.

This outlook on history explains why only certain aspects of the original humanistic conception are carried on in Machiavelli's work: the emphasis on the bond between *virtù* and *necessità* and the basic view of relations between states—including Rome and its empire—as a struggle for survival which must be judged in terms of natural cause and effect. However, the other mark of early Quattrocento thought, the optimistic faith in the free and autonomous development of human energies—in individuals as well as in the body politic—has disappeared. Where Leonardo Bruni sees *virtù* emerging from the struggle for independence and from political liberty, Machiavelli's world is shaped by a few great individuals who alone are capable of slowing down the blind race of history through its predestined cycles. The earlier interpretation of human affairs in the light of a psychology of noble passion has been followed by a systematic, scientific observation of the laws of history in the service of rulers and their politics.[27]

[27] The "separation of [Machiavelli's] *virtù* into original and derivative"— i.e., into the "inborn and creative" virtue of the great founders of states on the one hand, and on the other that of the masses, which is based merely "on organization, not on a gift of nature"—was first postulated by Meinecke, *Idee der Staatsräson*, ch. 1, esp. 40f. According to what I wrote in this essay in 1932, this distinction is basic for our understanding of Machiavelli's relationship to the humanistic psychology of the early Quattrocento. I would now say that although this is not entirely wrong, much more of early Quattrocento civic Humanism remained alive in Machiavelli. See the introductory note to this essay regarding my changed understanding of him.

THREE

The Changed Perspective of the Past in Bruni's *Histories of the Florentine People**

I

THE ultimate evidence that a new way of historical thinking developed in Florence soon after 1400 is provided by Leonardo Bruni's *Historiarum Florentini Populi Libri XII*. This first humanistic history of an Italian city embodies the civic Humanism of early Quattrocento Florence like no other literary product of the time. The work was begun in 1415. The first nine books were officially presented to the Signoria in 1429 and 1439, and at Bruni's public funeral in 1444 the civic authorities paid the deceased author the highest honor by laying the work ceremoniously on his breast.[1]

This public recognition does not mean that the *Historiae* had

---

* Essays Three and Four, on Bruni's modernity as an historical thinker, were outlined during the 1930s and put into the form in which they now appear at the Center for Advanced Study in the Behavioral Sciences in Stanford, California, where I held a fellowship in 1967–1968. Both essays are intended to add detail and precision to the picture of Bruni adumbrated in Essay Two. Neither Three nor Four has previously appeared in print.

[1] It should be stated at this point that I am disregarding the question of how many of the ideas in the *Historiae Florentini Populi* of 1415–1444 which we are going to analyze were contained in a rudimentary form in Bruni's *Laudatio Florentinae Urbis* of 1403–1404. The *Laudatio* has been widely discussed in the last decades, ever since it was discovered that this pamphlet is far more than a mere product of rhetoric. There is no need to take up the problems connected with the *Laudatio* in the present book, since I have dealt with them in the *Crisis* and in the chapter "Imitation, Rhetoric, and Quattrocento Thought in Bruni's *Laudatio*" in my book *From Petrarch to Leonardo Bruni* (1968). An informative survey of many recent contributions to *Laudatio* scholarship is found in H. M. Goldbrunner's "Laudatio Urbis: Zu neueren Untersuchungen über das humanistische Städtelob," *Quellen und Forschungen aus italienischen Archiven und Bibliotheken* 63 (1983): 313–28.

been commissioned by the government. In contrast to the many histories of Italian cities and states later written in the pay of governments or princes, the *Histories of the Florentine People* was neither a work of propaganda nor a product shaped by any kind of censorship; it was the independent creation of a humanist and citizen who from his youth had dreamed of becoming the Livy of Florence. But from the moment the book appeared, its wholly original conception of history became the model for Florentine thinking in the Renaissance. After the completion of the first six books in 1429, no other historical work was so generally read, acknowledged, cited, and imitated in Renaissance Florence. Every Florentine who afterwards reflected on history was significantly indebted to it. It goes without saying that the great chroniclers of the previous century, especially the three Villani—Giovanni, Matteo, and Filippo—continued to be read. But although they remained an inexhaustible stimulus for the historical and epic imagination, the *Historiae Florentini Populi* was the model for historiographical writing well into the times of Machiavelli and Guicciardini.[2] It not only taught the humanistic form of historical presentation and initiated the criticism of medieval legends (in this respect, too, the influence of the *Historiae* was without parallel) but was the source of the outlook on universal history that distinguished Florence from the rest of Italy in the fifteenth century and allowed it to set the direction in Humanism. This is true especially of Bruni's ideas regarding the historical role of political freedom and power, and his new periodization and accentuation of the history of Rome, the Italian Middle Ages, and Florence itself.

The idea of treating the history of Florence as a modern counterpart to Rome took shape in Bruni's mind under the influence of earlier chronicle writing. The concept of an ana-

[2] As has been acknowledged by Eduard Fueter, *Geschichte der neueren Historiographie* (Munich, 1911), and Eric Cochrane, *Historians and Historiography in the Italian Renaissance* (Chicago, 1981), who both begin their works with Bruni and make his influence the core of the subsequent development of historiography.

logue to Rome had been of no basic importance for humanists of the fourteenth century. Before 1400, the humanistic attitude toward ancient Rome had been too closely bound with the belief, or hope, that the *Urbs Aeterna*—that is, the *Imperium Romanum*—had not yet played out its role and that sooner or later it would experience a revival together with the return of Latin letters. Petrarch's faith in a political rebirth of Rome was dimmed for only a short while, after Cola di Rienzo's attempt to restore some aspects of the hegemony of ancient Rome had failed. At the same time, Petrarch's direct involvement in the struggles of the north Italian states as an envoy and publicist (during the 1350s) led him to view some of the modern Italian city-states as counterparts to Rome; but his thinking followed this course only as long as he was actively in touch with the contemporary politics of the Italian states. With this short-lived exception, his prevailing sentiment was hope for a political survival of *Roma Aeterna*.

In other words, Bruni's work—the history of a city other than Rome—tended more in the direction of the Florentine chroniclers than of Petrarch's historical ideas; but it changed rather than continued that direction. In the introductory book of the *Historiae*, as a background to the subsequent history of the Florentine state, Bruni draws a brief but truly remarkable outline of the founding of Florence within the framework of the general development of Italy from the *Respublica Romana* to the *Imperium Romanum*. Criticism of the monarchical absolutism that replaced the Roman republic in Caesar's time is perhaps the most striking feature of this background sketch, but it is merely one aspect of the story Bruni tells. If republican value judgments serve him as a key to the history of Italy from Antiquity onwards, it is because for him the struggle between liberty and monarchical power not only expresses a political rivalry between republic and monarchy but involves all aspects of historical life. To Bruni's way of thinking, the internal tendencies of a government correspond to its external relations. In the history of Italy as a whole, he finds a crucial antagonism between the coercive power of states bent on building empires on the one hand and the creation of political *virtus* and the cultural energy characteristic of smaller states on the other (in particular, the many city-states that enabled citizens to participate in public affairs and thereby molded the conduct and outlook of city-state policies).

This new turn of historical interest was the result of experiences of the time around 1400, which saw the clash between surviving city-state liberty and the expanding despotism of the great monarchies of northern and southern Italy. In Bruni's judgment, as was already implied in his *Laudatio Florentinae Urbis* and was fully stated in the *Historiae Florentini Populi*, it was precisely the contest between rising great powers and smaller states, often republics, that afforded a new view of the rise and fall of ancient Rome. Of course, one has to become familiar not only with the striking prelude of the first book but with Bruni's entire history in order to place the significance of this change in perspective. Suddenly, fundamental phenomena of interstate life that had previously been subordinated to the historical theology of the "Sacrum Imperium" could be approached with sympathetic understanding and given a causal explanation. Existent assessments of Florentine historiography, it seems to me, have not yet paid enough attention to these forward-looking aspects of Bruni's work, although the recent intensive study of many of his technical achievements has led to growing appreciation of him as an historical scholar and writer.[3]

[3] I am thinking here of E. Santini, *Leonardo Bruni Aretino e i suoi "Historiarum Florentini Populi Libri XII"*, reprinted from *Annali della R. Scuola Normale Superiore di Pisa* 22 (1910); B. L. Ullman, "Leonardo Bruni and Humanistic Historiography," in his *Studies in the Italian Renaissance* (Rome, 1955); D. J. Wilcox, *The Development of Florentine Humanist Historiography in the Fifteenth Century* (Cambridge, Mass., 1969); E. Cochrane, *Historians and Historiography*; R. Fubini, "Osservazioni sugli *Historiarum Florentini Populi Libri XII* di Leonardo Bruni," in vol. 1 of *Studi di Storia Medievale e Moderna per Ernesto Sestan* (Florence, 1980), 403–48; and my *Crisis of the Early Italian Renaissance*, especially the sections entitled "Republicanism versus Dante's Glorification of Caesar," "A Vindication of the Roman Republic in Leonardo Bruni's Ear-

II

I have already said that ancient Rome, whose rise and fall seemed comparable to the vicissitudes of some of the medieval Italian cities, had often served in prehumanistic times as a model for citizens in central and northern Italy. In 1087, a poet had commemorated a Pisan naval expedition to northern Africa in a Latin song evoking the memory of Rome's triumph over Carthage:

> I am going to write the history
> of the famous Pisans,
> and revive the memory
> of the ancient Romans:
> For Pisa only carries on
> the admirable glory
> which Rome once achieved
> by vanquishing Carthage.[4]

Two centuries later, after the fall of the Hohenstaufen, when Florence began to excel in the eyes of contemporaries, an inscription on the new *palazzo del podestà*, the Bargello, referred to Florence as a "second Rome."

Some feeling of this sort probably prevailed in every aspiring Italian city, but in Florence the historical parallel had a broader sweep. There it went beyond mere political reminiscence: Florence seemed to be a modern counterpart to Rome even in the birth of its new literary culture. Fifty years after the Bargello inscription was composed, Florence possessed a *divinus poeta* who could bear comparison with the Roman Virgil. It was then, too, that several magnificent Florentine chronicles were begun whose narratives were not remotely

---

liest Works," and "The Thesis of the Foundation of Florence by Republican Rome" (2d ed., 48–64).

[4] "Inclytorum Pisanorum scripturus historiam, / antiquorum Romanorum renovo memoriam: / nam extendit modo Pisa laudem admirabilem, / quam olim recepit Roma vincendo Carthaginem." The entire song of triumph is found in Fedor Schneider's *Fünfundzwanzig lateinische weltliche Rhythmen . . . VI. bis XI. Jahrhundert* (Rome, 1925), 34–42.

47

matched by those of other Italian cities; they were the forerunners of Florence's later preeminence in humanistic historiography. Giovanni Villani conceived the idea of writing his chronicle of Florence during his pilgrimage to Rome in the year of jubilee, 1300, amidst the ruins of ancient Rome. Reflecting on how his own city might one day lie in ruins as ancient Rome did now, he resolved to immortalize its deeds while it was still on the rise, just as Livy and Sallust had written the history of Rome when it was at its peak. Several decades later, his nephew Filippo Villani initiated a kind of cultural history with his collection of biographies of famous Florentines. This work was initially conceived as a separate biography of the poet Dante. To his own surprise, Filippo became aware that Florence possessed not only one great poet but a whole group of living and dead *poetae*, including Petrarch, Boccaccio, Zanobi da Strada, and Claudianus, the last classical poet, who in the fourteenth century was considered to have been a Florentine. Rome, instead, had been able to claim only four famous *poetae* of Roman origin and few leading men in the *ars dicendi*. Filled with patriotic pride, Filippo Villani enlarged his biography of Dante, undertaking the hitherto unheard-of task of compiling a comprehensive presentation of the Florentine poets, to which he added characterizations of other famous Florentines as well.[5]

Bruni's humanistic history of Florence belongs to this line of late medieval historiography. His dual contribution was a deeper understanding of ancient Italy and a more acutely developed comparison between Rome and Florence. The result was a method of discussion that has occasionally reminded Bruni's readers of Machiavelli's *Discorsi sulla Prima Deca di Tito Livio*. The relationship of Bruni's work to earlier Florentine city-chronicle writing and its divergence from humanistic writings outside Florence is illustrated by the fact that as late as the fifteenth century, non-Florentine humanists still

---

[5] That is, Filippo Villani's *Liber de civitate Florentiae famosis civibus*, ed. G. C. Galletti (Florence, 1847).

carried on Petrarch's conception of Rome and rejected the Florentine claim that the city on the Arno was a counterpart and heir to the ancient city. No less a humanist than Lorenzo Valla protested vehemently against the Florentine interpretation, informing the Florentines that the Roman people were still alive and needed no heir. "The Roman people of whom *I* speak," Bruni responded, "have long been dead and buried. The motley multitude which now resides in Rome is not a sovereign people but a subservient crowd. We are indeed talking about the legacy of a dead, not a living [people]."[6]

The Florentine claim was eventually accepted by humanists elsewhere in Italy, even in Rome. In his *Historiarum ab inclinatione Romanorum imperii decades*—the first humanistic history of the Middle Ages—Flavio Biondo, who was born in the States of the Church and became a Roman in the course of his life, developed what had been intimated by Bruni in his *Historiae*. Rather than taking the survival, or even revival, of eternal Rome as his primary theme, he followed Bruni and wrote (as his title indicates) a history of the development of new centers of political life: the reappearance of numerous cities and states, especially in medieval Italy. Moreover, the idea of a rivalry with Rome, which had been steadily developing in Florentine chronicles since the time of Giovanni Villani, involved considerably more than a partisan point of view that the Florentines sought to elaborate at the expense of Rome. Behind

---

[6] For Valla'a attack, see L. Barozzi and R. Sabbadini, *Studi sul Panormita e sul Valla* (Florence, 1891), 75ff. Bruni's critique of modern Rome is found in his letter to F. Picolpassi, archbishop of Milan, *Leonardi Bruni Arretini Epistolarum Libri VIII*, ed. Lorenzo Mehus (Florence, 1741), vol. 2, *Ep.* VIII 4, which shows that Bruni's opponent had followed Valla's argument (cf. F. P. Luiso [a cura di L. Gualdo Rosa], *Studi su l'Epistolario di Leonardo Bruni* [Rome, 1980], 145, n. 27; first half of 1440, according to Luiso, p. 144). Bruni's letter to Picolpassi reads: "At reprehensor meus . . . negat Populum Romanum esse mortuum, meque delirare putat, qui hereditatem viventis ad alium pertinere scripserim. . . . Sed certe Populus ille Romanus, de quo ipse loquor, jampridem mortuus et sepultus est: haec autem, quae nunc Romae habitat, collectitia turba non dominatur, sed servit. Quare de mortui agitur, non de viventis hereditate" (Mehus, vol. 2, p. 113).

the Florentine claim lay a new and reflective historical way of thinking. By emphasizing the dependence of the Roman Empire on the destiny of the *populus Romanus*, Bruni showed the course of Roman history to have been inextricably linked with the natural rhythm of demographic forces. Rome was no longer viewed as an exceptional empire playing a suprahistorical role.

This new point of view became prominent in Bruni's generation. Had not Italy been a land of independent cities in pre-Roman times as it was in the present, and had not its early cultural and political flowering been due to its extensive political division? Did not Rome, which gave so much to Italy, also threaten to deprive Italy of its vigor by preventing its cities from developing the local strength which nurtured their efflorescence in pre-Roman times? Bruni's importance as an historical thinker rests not least on his having been the first to formulate these questions.

III

Throughout Bruni's history of Florence, Italy is presented as a world in which independence of states, peaceful exchange, and militant struggle between many local centers were the rule. In his *De Monarchia*, Dante had argued that any resistance to Rome's subjection of Italy and ultimately of the world was sinful rebellion against God's inscrutable decree. He had no understanding for the forces that had acted alongside and against Rome before it succeeded in subjugating the other peoples to its might. It is this opposition to the Imperium and Rome—an opposition no longer regarded as sinful—which is the most important mark of Bruni's view of history. He saw the historical process, from the days when Sulla founded Florence as a colony of Roman veterans in the territory of the Etruscan Faesulae, with realistic eyes. Since the land colonized by Sulla was not an empty space, one has to ask how it was possible, says Bruni, that free land was available for a new settlement in the midst of the ancient Etruscan domain. The answer is that Rome had enervated the old independent life in this region shortly before Sulla's time, during the wars between the Romans and their allies. "War was waged especially against the Piceni and Etruscans; indeed Asculum, the most thriving city of the Piceni, was destroyed by the Romans, as is the usual practice against enemies. . . . In addition to the losses and sacrifices of war, great injuries were inflicted upon the Aretines and Faesulani, due to which . . . the cities were practically emptied of their inhabitants."[7]

Bruni's readers are thus made aware, early in the *Historiae*, of the shadow cast by Rome over the rest of Italy. When he subsequently introduces the newly founded city on the Arno as it begins to play its role on the historic stage, he initiates the dialogue of the Moderns on ancient Rome by commenting on the inevitable decay and ultimate fall of the *Imperium Romanum*. What he seeks to explain is that as long as the Roman Empire endured, the young Roman colony, Florence, was forced to grow in a political ambiance that robbed it of the freedom it needed to flourish. Great buildings were soon erected on the Arno, to be sure, and the population of the city increased, but healthy evolution was "prevented by the proximity of the Roman might." We have already become familiar with Bruni's impressive simile of a huge tree preventing neighboring plants from receiving sunlight and maturing.[8] Growth through trade was no help, he adds, for even economic progress was most easily achieved in Rome. Rome had great masses of people, opportunities for conducting business, contacts with tax farmers and harbors, and buildings for rent. There, imposts could be established and favors granted and received. With all this available, no other city could compete. The most gifted people migrated to Rome, because at home they were confronted by far greater obstacles. "And so, by

[7] *Historiae Florentini Populi*, ed. Santini, in vol. 19 of *Rerum Italicarum Scriptores*, new ed., pt. 3, p. 5.
[8] See Essay Two, p. 36.

attracting all outstanding men born in Italy, Rome drained the other Italian cities of their strength."[9]

These ideas were shared by other historians of the Quattrocento. Bruni's comparison of Rome to a tall tree that robs weaker plants of light and life was taken over almost verbatim by Flavio Biondo in his *Decades* and was disseminated throughout Italy and Europe by this much-studied general history. It is no exaggeration to say that, for the history of historical thinking, something like a Copernican revolution was achieved through Bruni's work. Just as Copernicus later destroyed the conception that the stars revolve around a stationary Earth, thus making it one celestial body among many whose movements are all subject to the same natural laws, so here, a century before, a more modest but kindred revolution had begun in the area of historical thought: the world of human history ceased to revolve around Rome. No matter that Rome may have had a unique importance for mankind, it was no longer the fixed point in the movement of history but one natural phenomenon among many, all governed by the same causality and the same pattern of rise and fall.

Petrarch's humanistic ideas had pointed this way with his postulate that constant movement and struggle are a psychological necessity if political and cultural vigor are to survive.[10] Through Bruni, this psychological conception became linked with Florentine resistance to the idea of *Roma Aeterna*, thereby initiating a whole new idea of historical change. The most disastrous effect of Roman domination, we are told in the *Historiae*, was not the visible, external devastation of war and conquest, but the internal, creeping poison of "enervating inactivity" (*marcescente otio*), which demoralized the subjugated areas of Italy after the conquest, even though—like the ancient Etruscan cities—they were not outwardly suppressed and in fact were given the honorable name of "associates" (*so-*

[9] "Ita quidquid egregium per Italiam nascebatur ad se trahens, alias civitates exhauriebat: quod antecedentia simul et sequuta tempora manifestissime ostendunt" (*Historiae*, 7).
[10] See Essay Two, pp. 25–26.

cii). To repeat Bruni's crucial argument once more: "It is nature's gift to mortals that when a path to greatness and honor is open, men raise themselves more easily to a higher plane; when they are deprived of this hope, they grow lazy and stagnate. Thus, when rule [in Italy] passed to the Romans, and people [outside of Rome] could no longer attain to public honors or occupy themselves with matters of great import, the Etruscan *virtus* languished, overcome much more by leisure and inaction than by the sword of the enemy."[11]

The true significance of a new way of historical thinking is determined, however, by the fruitfulness of the perceptions which flow from it; for once our eyes have been opened, hitherto unnoticed facts and aspects enter our field of vision. How revolutionary the break in the partisanship for Rome really was can only be measured by turning our attention to the entire long-ignored province of the past revealed in Bruni's historical picture: the world of pre-Roman Etruria and the Etruscan roots of Florentine history.

IV

The fact that Florence had not only a Roman but an Etruscan past had never been totally forgotten in Tuscany. But the recognition of this fact remained unfruitful so long as Rome was believed to be the sole source of political and cultural greatness. In his invectives against his ungrateful native city, Dante had condemned, indeed reviled,[12] the contamination of the noble Roman founders of Florence by the inferior blood of the barbaric Etruscans of Faesulae as the source of Florentine vulgarity: "Let the Fiesolan beasts make fodder of themselves and not touch the plant (if any yet springs up upon their dungheap) in which survives the holy seed of those Romans who

---

[11] See Essay Two, note 20.

[12] In Dante's *Ep.* VI 6, the Florentines are called the "most wretched offshoot of Fiesole" and "barbarians" because of this partially non-Roman descent.

remained there when it became the nest of so much wicked-ness."[13]

Even when Dante alluded to Etruscan descent in a less po-lemical context, his conception of ancient Etruria was far too nebulous to influence his Rome-centered image of the past se-riously. This is true of his treatment of the founding of Virgil's native city, Mantua, to which a long passage is devoted in the *Inferno*. Virgil had reported in his *Aeneid* that Mantua was founded by Ocno, son of the prophetess Manto (a daughter of the Theban Tiresias, who originated the art of prophecy, *man-teia*) and of the "Tuscan stream," the Tiber; Virgil had con-cluded from this that the Mantuan populace sprang "Tusco de sanguine."[14] In Dante's re-creation of this founding myth, all memories of the Etruscan past and of pride in the Etruscan people have disappeared. He tells us only that Mantua was founded by the Greek Manto. He even expressly puts a warn-ing in the mouth of Virgil that only this version of the found-ing history of Mantua is valid; everything else is a "lie."[15]

In the Florence of Dante's day, only the usual medieval an-tidotes were circulated to counter the denigration of the city's Etruscan roots. The contrast between its Roman founders, of whom a Florentine could be proud, and the contaminating Etruscan strain, of which one was ashamed, was explained away in medieval fashion by tracing the origin of the inhabit-ants of Fiesole back to the same genealogical roots from which the Romans were fabled to have sprung: the Trojan nobility. In this way the Florentines of the Middle Ages tried to counter the reproach that bad, non-Roman blood flowed in their veins. Atalante, father of the ancestral hero Dardanus—so went their reply to Dante—was also the founder of Fiesole; hence Romans and Fiesolans, the two founding peoples of Florence, came from the same Trojan roots. This legend ap-

[13] Dante, *Divina Commedia*, "Inferno," xv, 73ff. (trans. Charles S. Single-ton).
[14] *Aeneid* x.198ff.
[15] Dante, "Inferno," xx, 55ff.

pears in Giovanni Villani's chronicle[16] as well as in a book by his nephew Filippo. Toward the end of the Trecento, the latter reproduced the entire legendary cycle, apparently without skepticism, this time depicting Atalus, Atalante's son, as the founder of Fiesole and as the father of Italus, Dardanus, and Sicanus, who colonized all the Greek and Roman coasts of the Mediterranean Sea.[17] The Florentines themselves contributed in this way to the obliteration of the memory of Tuscany's Etruscan past; or at any rate justified it by making the Etruscan world a part of the Trojan and, therewith, Roman tradition, outside of which there reigned nothing but darkness and oblivion.

Before the end of the Trecento, however, the credibility of this legend was slowly undermined, thanks to the growth of philological criticism among Petrarch's disciples. In his commentary on Dante, Boccaccio cast doubt on the legendary founding of Fiesole by Atalante, and did so despite everything he had read about it in Giovanni Villani's chronicle; none of it, he said, was verified by a reliable source.[18] The most determined rejection of all—"quae omnia reputo frivola"—is encountered in the work of another commentator on Dante, Benvenuto Rambaldi da Imola, a semi-humanist who treated the legends of King Atalante and Dardanus with irony and attributed their origin to the desire of their inventors to trace their descent to as pristine a source as possible. But Benvenuto's criticism was still exclusively destructive and resulted in mere skepticism. When he was asked to explain who really founded Fiesole, he could only reply "I do not know, nor at

---

[16] "Come il re Atalante primo edificò la città di Fiesole" (Giovanni Villani, *Cronaca*, I 7).

[17] Filippo Villani, *De origine civitatis Florentiae et eiusdem famosis civibus*, ed. G. C. Galletti (Florence, 1847), 4. Filippo's chapter titles read: "De aedificatione civitatis Fesularum facta per Atalum . . ."; "De Italo, Dardano et Sicano, Atali filiis, et quas orbis oras inabitaverint"; "Quibus ascendentibus, signo et planetis fundata sit Florentia."

[18] But he nonetheless called Atalante "edificatore della città di Fiesole." See Boccaccio, *Del Comento sopra la Commedia*, lezione 14.

what time; it often happens that the origins of even major cities remain unknown. Yet I am certain that if this city was really so noble [as a Trojan origin would make it], the ancient writers would surely have mentioned this in one way or another."[19]

It is the retrieval of the Etruscan past that made a positive solution of such uncertainties possible. But the discovery was not the consequence of any crucial find of unknown sources. Bruni used only classical authors who had long been read: Livy, Pliny the Younger, Virgil, his commentator Servius, and Horace. At most, a few insignificant references in Plutarch and Dionysius of Halicarnassus could qualify as newly disclosed information. And yet, from mostly well-known sources there now emerged a world turned upside down. Scarcely anything demonstrates better than this example that it is not always the discovery of new sources which provides the incentive for such an upheaval; often it is the posing of new questions which leads to the discovery of new information, because it draws attention to perspectives previously overlooked.

Bruni's reconstruction of the past assumes an abundance of independent cities existing side by side, not only in the Etruscan region but throughout pre-Roman Italy. Rome was initially one among many, and not even the most important. As the narrative in the first book of the *Historiae* stresses, it was not at all evident at the time that Rome would one day rule over the whole of Italy. Before the rise of the Roman Imperium, Bruni tells us, the Etruscans had been the most powerful people in Italy, both in war and in peace. He describes their twelve tribal divisions, which initially existed under a common king but later ruled over all central Italy as a mighty league of free Etruscan cities. Colonies were founded from Capua to Mantua, and names were given to two seas. Finally, about 600 years after the Trojan war, when Etruria was al-

[19] Benvenuto Rambaldi da Imola, vol. 1 of *Comentum super Dantis Aldigherij Comediam*, ed. William Warren Vernon (Florence, 1887), 510.

ready in full flower, and 170 years after Rome was founded, the Gauls invaded Italy, overpowering the Etruscan cities and robbing them of all their territories north of the Apennines.

These conditions on the peninsula formed the background for the rise of Rome to dominance. Northern Etruria was already weakened, Bruni emphasizes, when Rome began to gather strength in the south and occupy the southern Etruscan borders. Hemmed in between two powerful adversaries, Etruria was at a disadvantage from the start. Nevertheless, it continued to flourish for some time and to wage a battle in which Rome on more than one occasion nearly lost its prospects for a great future. To no other people did Rome ever have to give hostages; Porsenna of Clusium forced Rome to do so, in fact at a time when Etruria had already been impaired by the invasion of the Gauls ("quod post transitum Gallorum in Italiam fuisse admirabilius est"). Indeed, Porsenna presented a direct threat to Rome; otherwise Horatius Cocles, who had neither captured an enemy province nor conquered an Etruscan army, but merely made possible the timely destruction of the bridge over the Tiber, would not have been given such high honors. And later the citizen army of Veii even managed to advance to the Janiculum in Rome. "This single Etruscan city, sometimes entirely by its own strength, sometimes with the help of other cities, dragged out the war beyond Rome's 350th year." The eventual surrender of Veii in the war was due only to the disunity of the Etruscans, whose other cities gave Veii no support at the time. For all that, Veii was taken only after a ten-year siege, and then only by cunning. The Romans even thought momentarily of moving into the rich conquered city; Veii nearly became their home. After Veii, the cities of Etruria fell one by one. By the time the Etruscans finally realized that their disunity was causing them to lose everything, it was too late. Thus Rome, which was able to summon both its strength and that of its allies, eventually triumphed, "either because of the constant hostile vicinity of the Gauls, the dissension between Etruscan cities, or fate, which was already drawing everything to the Romans, or because all these together prevented the Etruscans from entering the war in league." Bruni's final verdict is "there is certainly no doubt that if the Etruscans had conducted the war according to a single plan, all Etruria could have been defended longer and more gloriously."

A second observation made possible by the rediscovery of the Etruscan past was that the cities of Etruria exerted a fertilizing influence on the culture of Rome. Although it became stagnant after it had been conquered, it was the Etruscan region of Italy that provided Rome and the better part of the peninsula with the important elements of a more highly developed cultural life; later, Greece was to exert a similar influence. Rome took over the names and forms of Etruria's civic institutions, its style of clothing, and its *literas disciplinasque*. Just as the Greek *literae* were taught in later centuries, so in early Rome young boys were instructed in the Etruscan *literae*. Religion and worship came to Rome from Etruria, as well as the art of prophecy, which in fact the Romans subsequently called the *etrusca disciplina*. Thus, Rome peacefully submitted to its most dangerous political opponent in cultural matters, the *Historiae* tells us. It took over from its neighbors "what no one accepts from those one hates and disdains." Romans remained in close contact with Etruscans, in contrast to the gulf that separated both of these peoples from the barbaric Gauls of the north. This is the rounded, balanced picture of Florence's Etruscan past found in the first book of Bruni's *Historiae*.[20]

It goes without saying that this revolutionary new interpretation had more than one motivation: in addition to the joy derived from an unanticipated expansion of the historical horizon, it swelled the local pride of the Florentines. The revaluation of the Etruscan past undoubtedly found so great a response among the Florentine citizenry because, like the contemporaneous hypothesis of the founding of Florence by Sulla's veterans (that is, by citizens-in-arms of the republican

[20] *Historiae*, 7–13.

period of Rome),[21] it flattered self-esteem. Whereas Florentines had found satisfaction throughout the Trecento in the thought that their Etruscan forebears could trace their genealogy to the Trojans and Romans, in the Quattrocento they considered it a great honor that they were not only descendants of Rome but also the heirs of the powerful free cities of ancient Etruria and of a culture to which even Rome had submitted. "Est enim civitas nostra Romanorum colonia, veteribus Tuscorum habitatoribus permixta," as Bruni put it in later years in his funeral oration for Nanni degli Strozzi; "but the Tuscan people were always the foremost of Italy, the leaders in reputation and authority. . . . From this one people, the cult of the immortal Gods and the *disciplinae et litterae* spread throughout Italy. From this one people, the other peoples of Italy took all their *ornamenta* for war and peace."[22]

Soon after his rediscovery of the Etruscan past in the *Historiae*, Bruni gave a similar argument to Francesco Gonzaga of Mantua, whom he wished to turn from his belief in Dante's founding fable and in whom he hoped to instill pride in the Etruscan origin of his city.[23] The Gonzaga princes did not have to be ashamed that their city was founded by Etruscans, Bruni wrote. Again he referred to the power of Etruria, which extended from the Alps as far as Sicily; to the victories of the Etruscans over Rome, which no other people could match; and to the cultural influence that the Etruscans had had over Rome, until the Greeks took their place—an influence on all the political and religious rituals, on cults and the art of prophecy, on official insignia (like the *sella curulis* and the *toga prae-*

---

[21] This second and complementary thesis of Bruni's regarding the origin of Florence—Florence as a colony and heir of republican Rome in the land of the Etruscan city-states—has been examined in detail in *Crisis*, 2d ed., pp. 61ff. There is no need to go into the history of this hypothesis—which became vital for the Florentine political outlook of the Quattrocento—within the context of the present essay.

[22] Stephanus Baluzius, *Miscellanea*, ed. Mansi, vol. 4 (Lucca, 1764), 3.

[23] Bruni, *Ep.* x 25, in Mehus, vol. 2, pp. 227–29.

texta) and on the institution of the twelve lictors.[24] At the same time, Bruni presented the Mantuan prince with proof of Mantua's founding as an Etruscan colony, demonstrating that the mythical history of its foundation that appears in Virgil could easily be reconciled with his argument if one accepted the descent of the city's founder, Ocno, from the "Tuscan stream" as evidence of the Etruscan roots of its original inhabitants. Bruni was indignant over Dante who, "although he was himself a Tuscan, . . . apparently never read or noticed what so many famous [ancient] authors had written about the might of the Tuscans."

V

Local Tuscan pride is not the most important aspect of the historical picture given in the *Historiae Florentini Populi*, important as it was for the powerful effect that the rediscovery of the Etruscan past had on Florence. In the *Historiae*, the introduction of ancient Etruria into the perspective of the past serves primarily as a means for realizing a history of Italy in which the idea of *Roma Aeterna* no longer plays the central role.

It was still true for Petrarch, as we have noted, that the meaningful historical development of Italy came to an end, as it were, with the fall of the Roman Empire. What followed during the Middle Ages, Petrarch felt, was not further historical growth but a time without history, an interval of waiting for a revival of the past that would continue until, as Petrarch so fervently wished, the Roman Empire regained life and strength. Only when pre-Roman Etruria was rediscovered did the picture of Italy become so rich that Italian history could no longer be thought synonymous with that of Rome. All those vital forces on the peninsula which had had to stagnate so that Rome might live and bring honor to Italy's name were able to revive after Rome's fall: this is Bruni's fundamen-

---

[24] Mehus, vol. 2, p. 229.

tal vision, one in which the decline of ancient Rome was not the end but rather the beginning of a new chapter, "because before the Romans took control—this is a well-established fact—there were many cities and peoples flourishing throughout Italy, which all lost their vitality under the *Imperium Romanum*. Conversely, in later times, as soon as Rome ceased to dominate, the other cities began to lift their heads and flourish, so that what the rise [of Rome] had taken from them, its decline gave them back."[25] Of course, the storms of the barbarian migrations, with all their consequences, had to end before this could occur. But the decisive hour arrived when the title and rule of the Imperium were transferred to Germany after the fall of the Carolingian Empire, and the foreign emperors could maintain only a few garrisons on Italian soil. "The Italian cities gradually began to recall their freedom, to give only formal recognition [*verbo magis quam facto*] to the Imperium, and to honor the name of Rome and Rome itself more out of respect for its former strength than out of present fear. At last all the cities in Italy that had survived the many barbarian inundations prospered anew, came to flower, and rose again to the height of their former power."[26]

Through its inclusion in Bruni's vernacular *Vite di Dante e di Petrarca*, this historical picture from the *Historiae* quickly became known everywhere in Florence, even outside humanistic circles. Moreover, in the *Vite*—intended for the general reader since it was written in the Volgare and concerned with the historical understanding of the emergence of Petrarch's humanism—Bruni expressed in even clearer terms than in his history of Florence the idea that the fall of Rome was followed not only by a political but also by a cultural renewal and a creative upsurge. When the *Imperium Romanum* was succeeded during the barbarian migrations by the rule of "foreign barbarian nations" like the Goths and Lombards, we read in the

---

[25] *Historiae*, 7.
[26] "Denique quotcumque ex variis barbarorum diluviis superfuerant urbes per Italiam, crescere atque florere et in pristinam auctoritatem sese attollere [coeperunt]" (ibid., 23).

Vite, a "gross and rude" (*grossa e rozza*) era began in the field of studies as well. But after this flood, when the *populi Italici* regained their liberty, "the cities in Tuscany and elsewhere began to recover their strength and to devote time and effort to studies," until in the days of Dante and Petrarch the level of classical times was regained.[27] Bruni retained this positive evaluation of the restructuring of Italy in the Middle Ages until his final years, when his interest in the overall history of the peninsula became even keener. In his *De Bello Italico Adversus Gothos Gesto* of 1441, he tried to create a kind of substitute history of the survival of Italy during the time of the Germanic migrations by reworking the account of Procopius. Although it was a sad period of decline and destruction, he explained in his introduction to this work, one would still not wish that the time of trial had never existed. Hercules would have achieved little fame if difficult situations had not given him the opportunity to earn it. By the end of the period of migrations, Italy had conquered all intruders, and it was then that its "citystates, distinguished through great deeds and power, once again showed vigor, and they have remained vigorous to the present day."[28]

With all of this, the historical conception of the role of Rome in Italian history took on an ambivalence which made it far richer and more realistic than the classicistic belief in a golden age of Antiquity followed by stagnation or decline. The reasons why fifteenth-century Humanism was able to go beyond literary classicism to achieve a more historical way of thinking are nowhere better illustrated than in Bruni's works. Briefly summarized, he depicted how in German hands the medieval *Imperium Romanum* was bound to become a largely passive factor in Italian history—an institution which, through its weakness after the fall of the Hohenstaufen, unwittingly promoted the flourishing of the free Italian com-

[27] *Crisis*, 2d ed., pp. 147f.

[28] "Civitates in ea [Italia] ornatissimae magnis opibus magnaque auctoritate viguerunt hactenus hodieque vigent" (*De bello Italico*, Prooemium; in *Bruni, Humanistisch-philosophische Schriften*, 148).

munes. Bruni's consistent framework in all of this was the medieval Guelph polemic against an empire that had unlawfully called in question the authority of the Church. There are comments in the *Historiae* that carry on the old medieval partisan position—papacy versus empire—with the most extreme partiality. The Empire was reestablished by Charlemagne to protect the papacy and Church, his final verdict runs, but it was then manipulated by Charles' German successors as if it had been instituted for the persecution and overthrow of the papacy. His strongest criticism is directed toward the Hohenstaufen—especially, of course, Frederic II—whose policy is seen as the destruction of the Church.[29] Moreover, the deeds of an emperor like Louis of Bavaria, who was in standing excommunication, are judged to be nothing but criminal madness.

It is true that Guelphism appears changed here, for its national Italian, anti-German components are far more intense than anything previous of the sort. The old definition of the Guelphs as friends of the pope and enemies of the emperor, and of the Ghibellines as friends of the emperor and enemies of the pope, was broadened in the *Historiae Florentini Populi*. Included now under the banner of the Guelphs were "those who clung to the freedom of the people [the *populi* of the city-state republics] and considered the rule of barbarians over Italians unworthy," in contrast to the Ghibellines, "who, in submission to the imperial name, unmindful of freedom and the honor of their forebears, preferred to obey foreigners than to be governed by their own compatriots." But in the final analysis, even this more nationalistic accentuation of Guelphism is of secondary importance for Bruni's new historical conception of the history of Italy; in a way, the Guelph-Ghibelline controversy had lost its relevance. Because belief in the historical right of the Italian communes to be free replaced faith in a predestined Roman dominance, Bruni was able to write an Italian history of the Middle Ages without engaging in a direct

[29] *Historiae*, 26.

63

polemic against the Dantesque World Empire of the Germans. Beyond all quarrels between Guelphs and Ghibellines, his two main changes in the perspective of the history of Italy—the inclusion of the *Imperium Romanum* in the cycle of historical rise and fall and the acknowledgment of the independence of the rich regional and city-state life on the peninsula—permanently undermined the idea of the superiority and unique mission of the Roman Empire.

VI

What replaced Rome and the Empire as the major theme of Bruni's historical analysis is in part the conception of a shifting balance of power not only among the states and regions of the peninsula but also—especially in the period in which the political range of Florence did not yet reach beyond the borders of Tuscany—among the various Tuscan city-states, the successors of the Etruscan cities. The end of the introductory book of the *Historiae* therefore includes a detailed statement on the local balance-of-power system that of necessity evolved in medieval Tuscany. As Bruni promises at the beginning of his description of the region, it will let us see "which cities in Tuscany began to flourish after Roman dominance came to an end, which of them again lifted their heads, and what power they all possessed."[30]

Thus, the task Bruni set for himself in an inherently modern fashion was twofold: it entailed an objective assessment of the relative strengths and interests that came to characterize the larger city-states of Tuscany and an attempt to understand the reasons why these strengths and interests resulted in a closely interwoven network of four Tuscan power centers. As he tries to show, an elaborate system began to develop in Tuscany—in place of the profusion of rival cities in Etruscan times—in the epoch that saw the gradual weakening of the imperial monarchy due to its transfer to Germany after the end of the

[30] Ibid., 7.

chaotic conditions resulting from the barbarian migrations. So Bruni returns time and again to a comparison of the Tuscan cities of his age with those of Etruscan times, because only by tracing the survival or decline of the ancient cities, he maintains, can one discover why Florence's allies and rivals, Pisa, Siena, Perugia—and Florence itself—eventually eclipsed the other Tuscan cities.

Pisa (the analysis begins), a city which was neither Etruscan nor Italian in origin but a Greek colony, became the foremost harbor of Tuscany, because all the strong coastal cities of ancient Etruria—Tarquinia, Luna, and Populonia—had perished. "This is why, I believe, this city [Pisa] had no power so long as Etruria flourished on land and at sea; but when our maritime cities were destroyed it gained the opportunity to increase its strength." Thus, Pisa began to flourish only in the period following Charlemagne. Since that time, its superior position has rested on its maritime foundations, in contrast to Florence, which has always been an industrial inland power.

The causes of Siena's dominance in southern Tuscany were different. It, too, was a city-state that only came to flower late in history. Its potential Etruscan rivals were weeded out of southern Etruria, owing to the disastrous effect of Rome's proximity—initially because Rome overshadowed them, and later because, as outlying Roman country towns, they were especially affected by Rome's decline. That Siena could not have existed in Roman times Bruni infers not only from the lack of Roman information concerning it but from the fact that in the Middle Ages Florentine and Aretine real estate reached close to its walls. In the centuries following the fall of Rome, Siena ultimately became the leading city in its region because a group of outstanding families (Bruni had the great Sienese banking families in mind) lived there and made possible an unusually luxurious urban life. Bruni's conclusion is similar to the one he reached about Pisa: "It was the fall of Rusellae and Populonia, its initial [Etruscan] neighbors, that provided Siena with the *potentiae materia*."

His analysis then proceeds to Perugia. Lying in the eastern

part of Tuscany, it was able to maintain a city-state of the first rank from Etruscan times, thanks to the great fertility of its region and to its central location. In pre-Roman times, it was one of the three leading cities of Etruria and never ceased to be at least of second or third rank. But why Perugia and not Arezzo, which lay in the same eastern region, had likewise survived since Etruscan times, had the similar advantage of a good location and fertile ground, and possessed, besides, an unusually large expanse of territory? Bruni's studied answer to this is that Arezzo's position between the territories of Florence and Perugia prevented it from rising to the level of the ranking powers. Hemmed in by two strong neighbors, it was unable to evolve to its potential might.

Among the weaker towns of Tuscany, some succeeded in maintaining their independence and finding a place within the provincial balance of power by taking sides in the struggle between the leading cities. With their inclusion, the balance-of-power system in Tuscany becomes complete. Since the early Middle Ages, Bruni points out, there existed among the Tuscan cities two groups tending toward alliance. One of them included Florence, which was able to maintain friendly relations with Perugia and Lucca "because, I am convinced, on one side the intervening territory of Pistoia and on the other the intervening territory of Arezzo separated their borders and their interests and kept them from becoming objects of dispute." The second natural, enduring alliance existed between Siena and Pisa; these cities were separated by the territory of Volterra and were thus insulated against territorial conflicts.

This was the basic scheme in Tuscany; but it continued to change according to the partisan emotions and special interests of the ruling factions at home and in the allied cities; "for the people always follow willingly without deliberation what each respectively finds most advantageous. And, indeed, I suppose that in the time immediately following the departure of the barbarians, harmony reigned among our cities. Before long, however, when they began to grow and to lose their fear of an external enemy, envy and rivalry set them against each other" in a struggle that soon became intertwined with that of the emperors and popes, and their Ghibelline and Guelph partisans.[31]

This describes the first attempt to explain in analytical terms the friendly and hostile relations growing within a political balance-of-power system. It was accomplished by distinguishing the permanent factors of political geography from the changing influences of ruling and contending groups. In short, the exploration of the small regional system of Tuscan states undertaken by the Florentine humanist Bruni not long after 1400 was a prologue to that great historical art of political analysis which came to fruition after the fifteenth century and had as its subject the entire Italian, and eventually European, system of states.

[31] Ibid., 25.

FOUR

Bruni's *Histories* as an Expression of Modern Thought*

I

THE brilliant outline of the history of Tuscany and Italy from pre-Roman times to the end of the Hohenstaufen period in the first book of Leonardo Bruni's *Historiae Florentini Populi* is centered on two lines of historical development: the rise and decay of the Roman Imperium on the one hand and the cycle of freedom, subjection, and restored freedom undergone by many Italian city-states on the other. In Book II, Bruni shifts his perspective to the gradual development of a single city, Florence, presenting it as a model of republican liberty and ultimately as a nascent major power whose links to other powers extend beyond the Alps as far away as Germany and France. In so doing, he turns his new historiography—focused on cause, growth, and continuity—toward a task wholly peculiar to him: interpreting the history of a city not only as the result of geographic necessity and diplomatic planning but also in the humanistic manner, *psychologically*, as the result of reactions by citizens to situations in which their public spirit is tested under the impact of dramatic political events.

We will search in vain in the earlier historiography of Florence and other Italian communes for a precedent to Bruni's method. The question of how the ascendancy of an individual city might be explained in natural terms had, to be sure, often been raised by medieval chroniclers. But however much could be learned about the general course of human history from the conception of *Roma Aeterna* and a divinely ordained universal monarchy, it was of little help in determining the forces that

---

* See the preliminary note to Essay Three.

shaped the history of cities other than Rome. In principle, it is true, civic historiography was at liberty to indulge in secular explanations, independent of the religious preordination of the general history of Christianity and mankind. Yet, when all is said, the medieval chronicles of individual cities and states did little to satisfy the interest in underlying causes beyond assuming the existence of unchangeable laws imposed by the power of the stars. This "astrology of history," which appeared beside the older "theology of history," began to penetrate Europe from the Islamic countries in the twelfth century. Occasionally, its practitioners dared to cast the horoscope of cities, states, and religions, indeed of Christianity itself, and to predict the time of their inevitable end. Although heresies were suppressed whenever possible, in the course of the Trecento astrological interpretations of history became widespread among Italian city-chronicle writers. This was true even of more religiously minded chroniclers, who feared the consequences of applying astrological causation to the whole of Christian history, but condoned the admission of this kind of interpretation into narratives of everyday life.

When we look among Florentine city chroniclers for the ascription of natural causes to the profusion of events depicted in their chronicles, we encounter as an explanation for political rise and fall almost nothing but the influence of the stars that dominated the heavens when a city was founded or grew old. No really historical interpretations, based on an understanding of specific Roman and Florentine conditions, were available for the two events that induced Giovanni Villani to compose his chronicle of Florence—the decline of Rome and the rise of Florence. Villani was conscious only of a cycle of rise and fall which, for all cities, was regulated by the stars. His confidence in the present and future of Florence was based on the constellations present at its founding, which promised centuries of ascent, in contrast to Rome, which had run the course predicted for it by the stars and was condemned to future decline.

After Giovanni Villani, this astrological key to the phenomenon of Florence's rise was passed from hand to hand well into humanistic times. In the next generation, Giovanni's nephew, Filippo, included in his book on the origin of Florence a chapter entitled "Quibus ascendentibus, signo et planetis fundata sit Florentia," together with a casting of the city's horoscope. In his biography of Petrarch, Filippo made Dante predict an imminent revival of poetry, based on Dante's interpretation of the conjunction of the stars: the revival was verified, Filippo stated, by Petrarch's appearance "according to the promise of the stars." Even Salutati had no qualms about crediting the geographer Ptolemy with foresight of the future greatness of Florence "through knowledge of the stars, of which Ptolemy was the most conscientious of investigators." Nor did Salutati have misgivings about explaining the rise of the Guelph and Ghibelline parties on the basis of astrology; for if the stars can do so much in the lives of individuals, they must certainly have an effect upon the decisions and deeds of a whole people, even if they do not completely take away free will. About 1400, in his *Invettiva contro a cierti caluniatori di Dante e di Petrarca*, the somewhat younger Cino Rinuccini, a member of the Florentine Wool Guild, defended astrological predictions of the fate of individuals and cities against the skepticism of some of the younger humanists. In a political pamphlet against Milan, he, too, ascribed the course of Florentine history to astrological causes, blaming the city's first calamity, its alleged destruction by Attila the Hun, on the baleful influence of Mars, under whose aspect the Romans had founded Florence. Charlemagne, he added, began to rebuild the city at precisely five in the afternoon of April 1, 801, "ascendente l'Ariete casa di Marte e principio del Zodiaco," in a year ruled by Jupiter, the bringer of good fortune. Thus arose a new and successful Florence, which "will continue to grow for eight hundred years," a prognosis the veracity of which the past six hundred years "have already borne out."[1] The city could thus

[1] "... per ottocento anni debbe continuo crescere, come si manifesta secento anni passati" (Cino Rinuccini, *Risponsiva alla Invettiva di Messer Antonio*

still look forward to two more centuries of advancement and prosperity with the scientific certainty only astrological calculations can bring.

It is essential for our understanding of the historical place of Bruni's work to recognize that when his predecessors searched for general causes for the rise or decay of Florence, they had nothing to fall back on but the abstract and arbitrary "laws" of astrological effects. Such computations do not appear in Bruni's history, even though some of his humanist successors were to show a less reserved attitude toward astrology. It is true that we have no general or theoretical statement by Bruni in this regard, but he clearly exhibits a new approach: in place of astral causes, he systematically applies the fundamentals of humanistic psychology to the political *virtus* of the Florentine people and at the same time carefully examines the effects of international relations. The very fact that Bruni calls his work a "history of the Florentine people" rather than simply a "history of Florence" shows that he had a program: just as he explains the *Imperium Romanum* as the creation of the *populus Romanus* and its *virtus*, he identifies the history of Florence with the growth of Florentine *virtus*, which made it possible for the *populus Florentinus* to build its state.[2]

Lusco, in appendix to *Invectiva Lini Colucii Salutati . . .* , ed. Dominicus Moreni [Florence, 1826], 206f., 224f.). Cf. Cino Rinuccini in his *Invettiva contro a cierti caluniatori di Dante*, in A. Wesselofsky's *Il Paradiso degli Alberti*, Scelta di curiosità letterarie (Bologna, 1867), vol. 1, pt. 2, pp. 308f.: Some younger people wrongly deride the astrology "per lo cui sapere molte città siano aventuratamente edificate, molte nazioni d'uomini calculate, molti mali pronosticati per comete ed eclissi, congiunzioni magiori fugiti."

[2] There is no easy answer to the question of whether astrological thinking was already abating when Bruni introduced his new approach. Louis Green, in his "Fourteenth-Century Florentine Chronicles" (*Journal of the History of Ideas* 28 [1967], 173), remarks about two of the most interesting Florentine chroniclers of the generation preceding Bruni—Marchionne di Coppo Stefani, who composed his chronicle between 1378 and 1385, and the so-called Anonymus of 1385 to 1409—that they "mention occasionally the position of the stars, but with growing indifference and even skepticism as to their possible bearing on events." That a skeptical attitude was not common as yet, at

II

A prelude to Bruni's view of the gradual rise of Florence is already encountered in his description of conditions in Italy during Roman times. It is a remarkable psychological reconstruction of the birth of Florentine public spirit and its impact on the early development of the city. To be sure, given the inaccuracy of the historical sources available for that time, the result is for the most part a product of Bruni's historical speculation. But for this very reason it allows us to see how dominant psychological issues were for him.

To begin with, part of the evidence that could be drawn upon for the early history of Florence consisted of the visible remains of the former Roman city, which since Giovanni Villani's time was believed to have been laid out along the lines of Rome, with its capitol, forum, and circus. Furthermore, there were several statements of Cicero and Sallust which, besides giving an account of the founding of Florence by Sulla's veterans[3]—"viri optimi et fortissimi," as Cicero called them—told how the original settlers (after rapidly accumulating wealth) squandered through wanton luxury the goods that luck had thrown their way and began to long for the return of dictatorship and proscriptions that would permit them to reap immediate rewards, as they had in Sulla's time. All of this, Bruni argues, explains why the Florentines befriended Catilina's rebels more quickly than did the citizens of other cities. Their attempt to re-create the impressive layout of Rome throws light not only on the Roman origins of Florence but also on the character of its settlers: their incentives must have been "a desire to better themselves" (*levandi desiderium*) and love for the ancient Roman *patria*. One observation in particular confirmed this interpretation for Bruni: architectural ruins proved that Roman Florence had built an aqueduct on

---

least as far as the total course of Florence's history was concerned, is proven by what we have observed regarding Filippo Villani and Cino Rinuccini.

[3] For the significance of the thesis that Florence was founded by Rome in the time of Sulla, see *Crisis*, 2d ed., 61–64.

the Roman model, stretching many Roman miles from Monte Morello, even though ample springs within the city made such procurement of water superfluous for Florence. The settlers' desire to emulate Rome serves as Bruni's psychological key here. It was their endeavor to develop their new home on a grand scale that drove them beyond their strength; "bellicose and accustomed to civil war" and to the rewards due the victor by the rights of war, "they had no understanding at all of how to live peacefully" (*quietos esse nullo pacto sciebant*). This is why some of them joined Catilina.

The bloody events of the Catilinian war waged before the eyes of the city, bringing a number of the new citizens to their ruin, must have taught this warlike and ambitious but unruly original population a decisive lesson. However great the immediate danger was for the survival of the young city, this experience eventually proved to be a blessing. The settlers saw at first hand what misery had been brought to the followers of Catilina by their desire for war and booty. The character of the people began to change. They learned to respect other people's property, to be satisfied with their own possessions, to live modestly and frugally, and to teach their children to do the same. After this "cleansing of habits," the settlers were able to coalesce into an integrated political body. New colonists arrived, lured by the advantages and pleasantness of the area; as a result the number of buildings increased and the population grew.

But now the well-known obstacles appeared which were to prevent the opening bud from coming to full flower for a long time: first, there was Rome's oppressive weight on the rest of Italy, followed by the pressure of the barbarian invaders during the period of migrations, and finally, centuries of dominance by the German emperors. Although the foreign masters were not strong enough to prevent the revival of liberty in the Italian cities for any length of time, the last of them, Frederic II, managed to slow the process by intensifying the struggle between Guelphs and Ghibellines in every city, and he especially concentrated on the total suppression of the Guelph

73

party in Tuscany. The death of Frederic II and the collapse of the rule of the Hohenstaufen in Italy in the middle of the thirteenth century was thus the real beginning of Florence's freedom. From this point on, reliable historical data were available for Bruni's psychological reconstruction, and his second book begins.

The time had now come for the *populus* to rise up against the arrogant Ghibelline nobles who had ruled under the Hohenstaufen; the citizens took the rule of the state into their own hands. And it is wonderful to see, says Bruni, "how powerful the people now became. For, to tell the truth, the same individuals who had formerly served the princes and their helpers rebelled with all their might as soon as they experienced the sweetness of freedom and the people became masters and guardians of their own honor. Thus it became increasingly possible to exercise good judgment and industry at home and military efficiency and valor in foreign affairs."[4]

These and other events (to follow Bruni's conception of Florence's development as closely as possible) made the Florentines strive eagerly for even greater things. Before long the people of Florence had successfully invaded Siena and Volterra, with an armament such as the city had never seen before. Although the Florentines had to fight under unfavorable tactical conditions, their awareness of the now tested Florentine *virtus* and their memories of the spoils of victory redoubled their strength.[5] In Florence the increasing power of the people resulted that same year in the laying of the cornerstone of the Bargello Palace, the seat of the *Podestà*; formerly, private houses had served for official meetings and churches for popular gatherings. In one surge of strength, all of Florence's social and political relationships, internal and external, were changed.[6]

---

[4] *Historiae Florentini Populi*, ed. Santini, in *Rerum Italicarum Scriptores*, new ed., vol. 19, pt. 3, p. 27.

[5] "Sed conscia virtutis mens, insignisque victoriarum memoria, adversissimis etiam locis superare in animum induxit" (*Historiae*, 30).

[6] "Ita et foris et domi eo anno populi maiestas exaltata est" (ibid.).

Florence's move toward independence, once the shackles of imperial rule were removed, proves that the powers of a people increase when history affords the latter the opportunity for free development. The experience of Florence attests that the internal and external policies of a state are mutually dependent. In the rise and fall of states, these policies are joined, because when *virtus* increases, the state is strong domestically and externally; when *virtus* decreases, the state is weakened in both respects. From here on, the interaction between the internal and external development of Florence is one of Bruni's principal subjects. By extending his narrative to the last third of the thirteenth century, that is, to the time when the nobility was finally tamed and the rule of the *populus* was established, he again demonstrates that all history in principle has "two parts or limbs, as it were," which must always be considered together; that "internal conditions," as he puts it, should be given the same weight as "external wars."[7]

This interaction throws light on the progressive transformation of Florentine society and institutions from the late thirteenth century on. This development began as a logical consequence of the social conditions of the time. The intense demands made by the *populus* for participation in civic affairs were a necessary counterblow to the earlier supremacy of the nobility. Because of the immense power of the local noble families, the struggle between nobility and *populus*, a phenomenon that occurred in many states,[8] was particularly bitter in Florence. "Only when it was master in the state, so that the nobility could not exceed its own despotic authority . . . for its own ends, could the *populus* feel safe." The various results of this struggle were the creation of the Priorate, which excluded the nobles unless they joined the guilds; the organization of the guilds for military service; and the commissioning of a *vexillifer iustitiae* for the discharge of judgments against the unruly powerful.

[7] *Historiae*, 78, lines 44ff.
[8] Ibid., 79, lines 1ff.

Because of its effect on the internal balance of power, foreign policy played a decisive role in the establishment of this system of government, which was created through the "Ordinamenti della giustizia" of 1293. Not long before, Florence had launched powerful attacks against Arezzo and Pisa. "After that the *populus* began to entertain a higher conception of itself and to turn its attention from wars against external enemies to its internal freedom." It was elation over their military successes that led the people to institute the Ordinamenti, after which it was the turn of the nobles to fear the *popolani* as much as these had previously feared the nobles.

III

After showing in Book II how the *libertas Florentina* became firmly established through the Guelph victory over the Hohenstaufen and the triumph of the *populus* in the government of the commune, Bruni turns in the following books to the defense of Florentine liberty at home and abroad. Not that he viewed the history of the republic during its last 100 or 150 years without serious misgivings. His praise for the Florentine laws ends at the point where, in 1323, the demand of fully enfranchised citizens for equal participation in public offices led to election by lot and thereby repeated the pattern followed by the Athenian government. This seemingly technical change, Bruni asserts, contained the seed of inevitable decline. Its immediate advantage, namely, that quarrels were reduced during elections, was far outweighed by the disadvantage that it was now the unworthy who were often picked; and what gave life to a free state, competition among individuals, was extinguished. "It discouraged striving for the rewards of excellence [the *studium virtutis*], for if men had had to compete in elections and publicly risk their reputations they would have been more cautious." We see here clearly how inseparable was Bruni's approval of the political development of Florence from his civic ideal, which taught him to accept free develop-

ment and the competition for power as moral and psychological necessities.

Once the limits to the benefits of equality afforded by the
Florentine constitution have been discussed, Bruni's other two
main themes come to the fore: the clash of republican liberty
with tyrannical usurpation, and the final growth of Florence
into an Italian power.

Bruni's account of this twofold development begins with
the rise and subsequent expulsion of Florence's only tyrant,
the Duke of Athens, in 1342–1343. Because his account leans
heavily upon, yet profoundly deviates from, that of Giovanni
Villani, who was an eyewitness to the events, few pages of the
Historiae point up so well the differences between Bruni's historiography and the chronicles of the Villani family.

The fact that Giovanni created a colorful and detailed picture of the time and that Bruni drew from it with great selec-
tivity and added to it sparingly has often led modern historians, who use Giovanni and Matteo Villani as rich sources of
information, to praise the medieval chroniclers and criticize
the humanistic historian. But the decisive point is that although Giovanni painted the episode of the "tyrant" in vivid
detail, he failed to grasp its significance for the course of Florentine history. Giovanni relates the story of the Duke of Athens as an epic tale. He tells us that some of the greatest Florentine mercantile companies were in financial difficulties, or
even bankrupt, and wished to be governed by a strong master
who could make new laws at will, especially in favor of the
ruined houses. Treacherously, in secret, they asked the duke
for help, and since at the time he was a prince without a state,
he agreed. He managed to become dictator, but he was cruel
and unjustly accused many citizens who got in his way. He
even had them put to death, among them some from the old
families of the *popolo*. He tried to divert all state income to his
coffers and promised everyone something, without keeping
his promises. Soon he had nothing but enemies in the city, and
three separate groups of conspirators, who knew nothing of
one another due to the general fear of the duke, discovered

when they finally decided to act that everyone in Florence was dissatisfied and part of a conspiracy. The duke was lucky to escape with his life. Giovanni's narrative, and his interest in the event, ends with the duke's flight.

Three aspects of this episode and its outcome, about which the chronicler had not given a thought, were of major interest to Bruni: Why, he asks, were the citizens, who had never before bowed to a tyrant, prepared to do so at that particular time? Why, cruel or not, did the duke fail after only a few months, when the Florentines had initially made his triumph so easy? And finally, did the episode, short as it was, really have no lasting consequences—as Giovanni Villani would have it—for the power and survival of the Florentine state? There is no need to elaborate the point that these are among the questions that must be posed in any modern history of Florence.

As to why despotism arose precisely when it did, it is easy to see why Bruni, unlike Giovanni Villani, did not give a decisive or even a primary role to the downfall in 1342 of the great banking and mercantile houses.[9] Major bankruptcies had occurred before; what had to be explained was the willingness of many, and perhaps even of the populace as a whole, to recognize a *dominus*. In other words, as is so often the case, Bruni was interested in a psychological phenomenon. In the decade preceding the catastrophe of 1342, he explains, the Florentine republic had been bled almost to death, financially and militarily, by the wars for the possession of Lucca, a city that had always served as a gateway to Tuscany for north Italian despotism. In the end, in 1342, it had to forsake all influence over Lucca. "In no other war had the name of the *populus Florentinus* been more dishonored," begins the account of the episode in the *Historiae*, "and before long the ignominy suffered in foreign affairs was followed by a major disgrace at home," a violent coup.[10] For, as is often the case after great

---

[9] He mentions it first for 1345.

[10] "Et traxit mox ignominia foris accepta aliud domi dedecus maius" (*Historiae*, 161).

disasters, everyone felt helpless and blamed someone else; the most painful defeat in Florence's history had weakened the city internally and made it vulnerable as never before. Giovanni Villani had given no consideration whatever to this change in the normal political climate of Florence. Neither had he offered any other series of causes that might have explained the catastrophe of 1342. If the years around 1340 had seen every possible misfortune, "floods, dearth, famine, high mortality, defeats, shameful political enterprises, loss of property and money, the bankruptcy of merchants, damaged credit, and eventually impaired liberty,"[11] these were for him "afflictions" (*flagelli*) visited by God upon the Florentines for their "sins," which should exhort the populace to mutual love and accord so that God would not have to pour out the full measure of his wrath. Nothing in this account could be called an "historical interpretation."

Second, nothing written prior to the *Historiae* could explain why, after a meteoric rise, the duke was not successful in his enterprise. For Bruni, human weakness and sin are merely contributing factors; the duke's exceptional cruelty led to his rapid downfall not simply because he was wicked but because he had worked against the spirit and traditions of the Florentine state. "Because he was a Frenchman used to the customs of France, where commoners are treated almost like serfs, he merely smiled at the terms 'guilds' and 'guildsmen' [*artes* and *artifices*]; it seemed ridiculous to him that a city should be ruled by the decision of the many." It was his policy to ally himself with the nobility and to offer his protection to the workers and humble people in the belief that they could be easily won over, for the duke asssumed that they lacked all sense of dignity and the desire for liberty. But this was not the decisive issue. "There was still the central group of the *populus*. This

---

[11] "diluvio, carestia, fame, mortalità, sconfitti, vergogne d'imprese, perdimento di sustanze e di moneta, fallimenti di mercantanti, e danni di credenza, e ultimamente di libertà" (Giovanni Villani, *Cronaca*, XII 3).

was his basic problem."[12] Because he lacked understanding, he "pursued a most perverse internal policy," even though his foreign policy was not incompetent; "in that respect he was careless and foolish."[13] With total disregard, he undermined the position of the officials and magistrates through which the *popolo* had so long ruled the republic: the Priorate, the old head of the republic, was reduced to a position with little prestige; the troops of the citizen militia (the *societates populi*) with their banner bearers were disbanded; the right to levy taxes and handle finances was taken from the citizens and put into the hands of non-Florentines; preparations were begun to transform public buildings belonging to the commune into strongholds for an autocratic ruler. As a result the *popolo* was provoked to the utmost, despite being intimidated by the duke's cruel and unjust death sentences, which fell even on those with whom he had been on friendly terms. A race between fear and hate ensued, and when hate overcame fear, this regime, which had been so destructive to Florentine traditions, came to an end.

A detached political analysis and a sharpened conception of the injury done to the historically established character of the Florentine body politic have here replaced the moral and religious invective characteristic of the medieval chroniclers. This is most striking in Bruni's discussion of the duke's dealings with those authorities who had held the sovereign power in the republic: the *Priori*. The Florentines would have found it easier to bear, Bruni argues, if the duke had done away with the office altogether. Instead, he did the worst thing possible psychologically and thereby helped to prepare his own overthrow: he robbed the priors of their authority, expelling them

---

[12] "Primo nobilitatem . . . suam fore totam arbitrabatur. . . . Tenues vero et opifices ac totam illam civitatis turbam nullum negotium putabat ad se traducere; nullam enim iis neque dignitatis neque libertatis curam intelligebat esse. Restabat medius populus. In eo difficultas omnis versabatur" (*Historiae*, 162).

[13] "Haec foris provisa non incaute: domi vero omnia perverse; quaedam etiam leviter et stulte" (ibid., 163).

from their customary seat so that he could take it over as his own residence, but allowed the institution of the *Priori* to remain—"a bitter and mournful spectacle for the eyes of the citizens."[14] This is the kind of psycho-political argument a Florentine historian of the sixteenth century could have made; Machiavelli would not have been ashamed to use it.

That Giovanni Villani had nothing to contribute to this phase of politico-historical thinking is equally evident when we turn to Bruni's third theme: the consequences of the Duke-of-Athens episode. Giovanni had been satisfied to note that when they were informed of Florence's rebellion against the duke, Arezzo, Pistoia, and Volterra, the cities within the Florentine territory, rebelled against their own ducal garrisons. That sealed the duke's fate, Giovanni said, and therewith he ended his account.

Bruni went more thoroughly into this aftermath of the episode because he saw it from a wider perspective: not merely as an aspect of the duke's destiny but as the beginning of a new *libertas* for the three major cities of the Florentine territorial state, which were united in their refusal to again submit unconditionally to Florence. Thus, though the duke's reign was short, its consequences for the position of Florence in Tuscany and for Florence's relationship to its neighboring city-states were enormous: the unity that in the course of history had developed within the Florentine territorial state was destroyed for the foreseeable future. "Outside the city everything that had been gained by the labor of many years and with the greatest exertion was lost and ruined."[15] What was historically significant in this outcome was not the duke's personal fall from glory, but the beginning of a new phase in Florence's relationship to the members of its territorial state and to the other states of Italy. As in his discussion of the causes of the

[14] "quasi spectaculum quoddam acerbum miserabileque in oculis civium dereliquit" (ibid., 164).

[15] "Foris igitur unum sub tempus cuncta perdita profligataque iam erant quae dudum multorum annorum labore plurimisque contentionibus fuerant acquisita" (ibid., 167).

81

duke's rise to power, Bruni shows himself to be keenly aware of the impact his fall had on both events at home and the republic's foreign relations. To Bruni, Florence's experience with the duke was closely bound up with developments elsewhere within the territory, especially in Arezzo after the troops of the duke were expelled and the Aretines declared their *libertas*. Florence was prepared formally to renounce its right over its former dependency. Bruni reports, on the basis of an Aretine source consulted by him, that a Florentine legation was sent to Arezzo to congratulate the Aretines on the recovery of their freedom and to convince them that the goals of Florentine policy had changed. An alliance was soon formed between four republics, in which Arezzo stood formally on an equal footing with Florence, Siena, and Perugia. Only at this point in the story was Bruni satisfied that the episode of the Duke of Athens had been fully told.

In addition to their role in the history of the *libertas Florentina*, the events of this period of Florentine history have thus been put to two historical uses: to illustrate the gradual rise and retardation of the Florentine state and to identify and explain the changing phases of Florence's foreign policy and interstate relations. Of these, it is the second, the successive changes in Florence's foreign policy, that increasingly predominates in Books VII-XII, the second half of the *Historiae Florentini Populi*.

IV

The menace hanging over the republic due to the steady expansion of the most powerful monarchic states of the peninsula—primarily Milan under the Visconti, but also Naples under King Ladislaus—shaped Bruni's political outlook well into his old age. But the closer his narrative draws to the present, the more his work becomes a history of those international entanglements on whose outcome depended the preservation and the future strength of the Florentine state. Moreover, the fact that the last six books of the *Historiae* were written between the late 1430s and 1444 is highly significant for their tone and outlook.[16] When Bruni composed them, the wars with Giangaleazzo Visconti and King Ladislaus lay in the past, and the Medici party under Cosimo's leadership had taken the reins in Florence. The Florentines no longer had reason to feel that the republic was in daily peril of war and that an imminent battle was being fought in Italy between civic liberty and monarchic despotism. In the second half of the *Historiae*, therefore, a more pragmatic point of view, oriented toward power politics, replaced the passionate emphasis—common to all of Bruni's works from 1400 until the early 1430s—on the unique role played by the *libertas Florentina*. The consolidation of Florence resulting from its determined defense against Giangaleazzo and, even more, the growth of the Florentine state into a major Italian power, thus became the main theme of Bruni's later narrative.

Of course, even from this changed perspective, the struggle against Giangaleazzo remains the central event in the external history of Florence, and its significance for the preservation of Florentine liberty was not lost. At the beginning of his account of the years 1390 to 1402, Bruni calls the war with Giangaleazzo "without doubt the greatest the Florentine people ever fought," and he tries to make as vivid as possible the danger that Milan's expansion had posed for "all free people in Italy." He tells us how the Florentines became aware as early as 1387 that Giangaleazzo was the archenemy of the republic on the Arno because the Milanese duke believed—as an address ascribed by Bruni to Giovanni Ricci characterizes the situation[17]—that none of his conquests were secure so long as the Florentines, "libera in civitate nati," were able to preserve their independence and give aid to other independent states. But the emphasis in the *Historiae* is clearly on the reward for the persistent and ultimately lonely resistance of Florence.

---

[16] For the dates of the individual books of the *Historiae*, see Essay Three, introductory paragraph, and, for details, *Crisis*, 2d ed., 568f.

[17] *Historiae*, 242–43.

Not long before, it had still been politically one among many Italian city-states; in the struggle against Milan it became a great power, capable of drawing all of Italy, pope and emperor, France, and Germany into its destiny.

For the Villani chroniclers—Giovanni and Matteo, his younger brother and successor as a writer—the Florence of the fourteenth century, as in earlier times, had been merely a semi-autonomous component of a universal community, whose goals were determined by the two leaders of the world, the pope and the emperor. Matteo, who lived to experience the first military confrontation with the Visconti (with Giovanni Visconti in 1350), saw it as nothing other than a struggle under the guardianship of the Church, which held natural right of leadership in the resistance to Milan. The initiative lay with the pope, and Florentine policy was justified because the city, like other Guelph communes, was following his plan. Bruni took as his primary theme what to Matteo would have appeared as arrogance—namely, that Florence was successful in involving the pope and the emperor in its schemes—and he considered this the most glorious claim one could make for his city. He was the first to recognize that by the middle of the Trecento, it was the city-state of Florence and not the Rome of the popes that was most antithetic to the Visconti state, and that Florence represented a political microcosm sui generis, with its own compelling requirements.

In his presentation of the war with Giangaleazzo, therefore, Bruni clearly makes his criterion for Florence's historical maturity its rise to the status of a major power capable of actively influencing other nations. "Not only were swords crossed with our own people [the Italians] in this war, but the Florentines set in motion great armies and powerful generals from France and Germany, and it is a wonder that a single people could muster enough courage and resources for such mighty deeds."[18] In Bruni's analysis, it is the education received from the wars with Giangaleazzo that finally overcame provincial

---

[18] Introduction to Book x. *Historiae*, 247.

narrowness and resulted in the expanded horizon necessary for a great Italian power. With the outbreak of war against Giangaleazzo in 1390, the Florentines began to learn by hard experience that all of Florence's prudence and efficiency in repulsing the Milanese troops in central Italy were not enough; that it would take a more far-reaching policy to gain lasting security. "For the Florentine people understood that they could not protect the city from the devastation of a lengthy war by merely repelling the aggressors from their doorstep. So long as the enemy could live in peace in northern Italy and not feel the effects of war at home, he would be able to provide what was needed for the war in Tuscany. If he were exposed to war in northern Italy, however, he would soon run out of money and would be placed in the gravest jeopardy, since his position of dominance [in northern Italy] was not a long-established one. It seemed indispensable, therefore, that the enemy should be made to sense the danger of war at home."[19] By itself, Florentine strength was insufficient for this broader strategy: allies had to be found—Germans under their newly chosen king, Rupert, and Frenchmen—and financed in part with Florentine money. To encircle Milan, European politics had to be guided into Florentine channels.

Bruni revealed his value judgments in various ways, most of all in the elaborate speeches made in his narrative by major leaders, Florentine and non-Florentine. These rhetorical harangues do not always tell us what was really said; rather, they afforded the fifteenth-century author a means—as such speeches still did for Machiavelli and Guicciardini a hundred years later—of presenting a more objective interpretation of historical events. Greek and Roman historians frequently put speeches to this use, and Bruni was the first to adopt their method, which he took directly from Livy. This was one of the artistic devices by which Livy had tried to make a multitude of conflicting ideas understandable: as nation after nation in Livy's history loses its independence to Rome, he allows

[19] Ibid., 249.

85

various personae to voice objections to the uniqueness of Rome's claim. In this way Livy gave his readers a basis for evaluating the motives and intentions of Rome's adversaries as well. He thus subtly delineated a perspective that Bruni was able to put to good use in a work whose first book, as we have seen, was critical of Rome's destruction of independent life in Etruria. By 1401, Bruni writes, Milanese expansion in central Italy had advanced so far that only the intervention of a third power—this meant Venice—seemed able to prevent the impending triumph of the Visconti over Florence. At this point, the *Historiae* presents an alleged discussion among Florentine and Milanese envoys to Venice about their respective military goals, the recounting of which, Bruni says, will make it possible for the reader "to weigh the right or wrong of the situation."[20]

In response to the accusation that the Visconti duke was interfering in Tuscany, the Milanese ambassadors are made to argue that their duke had formed an alliance with Siena and Pisa only because he was begged to do so; the real cause of Milanese interference was Florence's long-standing violation of her neighbors. "The Pisans and Sienese would not need anyone's help if they were not wantonly harassed [by the Florentines]. They have now taken refuge with Giangaleazzo because their possessions are endangered. . . . It is more than obvious that Giangaleazzo has not meddled in the affairs of Tuscany arbitrarily but was called in to help. . . . One should therefore rather despise the arrogance of the Florentines against their neighbors than reprove the help offered them by Giangaleazzo."[21] Moreover, add the Milanese envoys, Italy's national interest is being harmed by the Florentine policy of forming European alliances. "Contrary to the custom of our ancestors, the city of Florence has called to Italy Frenchmen and Germans—foreign and barbaric nations, enemies and adversaries of everything Italian; she has thus led them into Italy,

---

[20] "ut iustitiae causa a legentibus examinari possit" (ibid., 284).
[21] Ibid., 285.

willing to have them subjugate Italians, people whom nature herself has excluded by the barrier of the Alps. So blind have they become to prudence that they cannot see the common ruin awaiting all Italians if Frenchmen and Germans are brought across the Alps into Italy. . . . And yet the Roman people earned its greatest praise and glory by destroying the Cimbri and Teutoni during their invasion. . . . But these 'new Romans,' as they call themselves, have brought barbarian and savage nations into Italy—they have even hired them. Such is their restlessness, perversity, and detestable disregard for their *patria* and Italian origins! Surely everyone knows what those who deliver native ground into the hands of enemies ought to be called!"[22]

The Florentine ambassadors do not really refute these accusations. They merely appeal to the right and duty of an independent state to defend itself and assure its survival. Aggression, they say, does not begin with the overt use of military machines against fortress walls. Rather, "one who constructs military machines and prepares them for the assault, even if he has not yet set them into operation against the walls of his adversary," is also an aggressor. "Did not Giangaleazzo just as surely violate the peace when he surrounded Florence by seizing so many cities and towns, thus preparing the siege, as it were, and constructing machines for the assault?" This is all the more true because it was done by a tyrant whose policy of surprise attack had been well known in Italy since his invasion and occupation of Verona and Padua in 1387 and who was known to have "promised himself an Italian kingdom" (*ut regnum Italiae sibi repromittat*). Under the circumstances, preventive countermeasures were necessary, and this justifies Florence's collaboration with the French king and German emperor-elect; the strategy of political and military encirclement employed by Milan against Florence had to be matched by Florence's resistance against Milan. This, and not a false historical analogy, must be used to measure Florence's alleged

[22] Ibid.

guilt. There is a great difference between the 600,000 Cimbric and Teutonic invaders of Roman times and the handful of Frenchmen and Germans brought in by Florence.[23]

This is the ambiguity in the political situation, presented in opposing views, that Bruni wants his readers to see and to use as the basis of a fair judgment. He depicts the emergence of Florence as an Italian power in pragmatic terms, trying to impress upon the reader that developments in Quattrocento Italy were ambivalent and that it is necessary to understand the various interacting, often antagonistic, interests of the time and not simply blame or praise Milan or Florence.

The correctness of this interpretation of the orations in the *Historiae* is not in doubt, because shortly after 1440 Bruni also summed up the motivations and causes of the wars with Giangaleazzo in his memoirs—the *Rerum Suo Tempore Gestarum Commentarius*—and there it is the author himself, not an alleged speaker, who speculates on the origin of the Italian wars. His reasoning follows exactly the chain of propelling events and ineluctable reactions to which the ambassadors of the rival parties refer in the *Historiae*. In the memoirs we read that when Giangaleazzo, whose power was already enormous, annexed to his "imperium" the large possessions of his uncle Bernabò, whom he had violently deposed and imprisoned, and added Verona and Padua as well, Florence was gripped by suspicion and fear at the accumulation of such *immodicae opes*. The Florentines, therefore, "as a precaution prepared remedies and armed themselves." Giangaleazzo, in turn, was put on his guard and forbade the Florentines to frequent the towns in his territories. "At this turn of events, all those in Tuscany who feared or hated the power of the Florentine people became interested in Giangaleazzo, sought his help, and called him to Tuscany, in particular the Sienese." The latter were in violent conflict with Florence at the time, because in the country town of Montepulciano, which had traditionally been subject to

[23] Ibid., 286f.

Siena, a party had arisen that was friendly toward Florence, and in 1390 it succeeded in incorporating the town into the Florentine region-state. As a result, "the Sienese openly began to seek refuge in the power of Milan and even admitted substantial troops of Milanese cavalry into their city. Suspicion and hatred grew and war finally broke out. This war lasted many years, although there were some periods of peace in between. These, however, were so filled with suspicion that arms were scarcely ever laid down and the war was quickly resumed. Not only Tuscany but also northern Italy became involved in various ways, since the Florentines sent military forces there and brought large armies of cavalry from France and Germany into northern Italy."[24] In this description of the causes of the war, the word *libertas* never appears; the key word here is "suspicion," which is considered the natural source of every action taken by the Italian states and the inevitable outcome of the political climate. Its appearance in Bruni's work represents a new and more realistic understanding of the political processes at work in the nascent equilibrium system of the Italian powers.[25]

[24] Bruni, *Rerum Suo Tempore Gestarum Commentarius*, ed. C. di Pierro, in *Rerum Italicarum Scriptores*, new ed. (Bologna, 1926), vol. 19, pt. 3, p. 429f.

[25] The paragraph in the *Rerum Suo Tempore Gestarum Commentarius* reads: when the Florentine people realized that in addition to Giangaleazzo's power "Bernabovis insuper opes ac potentiam accessisse, horrere iam inde tantas vires ac formidare immodicas opes incepit. Quam mox suspicionem auxit Verona primo, deinde Patavium, urbes magnae ac potentes ad imperium additae. Itaque, crescente suspicione, parare iam inde remedia ac se praemunire Florentini pergebant. Et ille vice versa cavere diligentius, ac Florentinos versari in suis oppidis prohibere. Iam per Etruriam quicumque aut formidabant populi florentini potentiam aut oderant; ad hunc respicere ac refugere, et in Etruriam accersere, et imprimis Senenses, tunc infensi maxime Florentinis ob Politiani receptionem." Consequently, the Sienese "coeperunt et ad Mediola-nensis opes se totos convertere magnumque illius equitatum intra urbem recipere. Ita crescentibus suspicionibus atque odiis, tandem bellum exarsit. Id bellum multis duravit annis, quamquam intercessit nonnunquam pax, verum ita suspiciosa, ut vix ab armis discederetur ac resumeretur confestim bellum. Nec per Etruriam modo, sed per Galliam quoque varie fuit id bellum impli-

If Bruni now appears less passionately involved in the cause of *libertas* and concerned primarily with the balance of power in Italy, we may wonder whether the cause was not also that he, like others near the middle of the century, grew more sensitive to general Italian concerns than he had been during the divisive and dramatic internecine wars fought in Italy around 1400. Other late works of Bruni's, written in the same period as the last books of his history of the Florentine people, bear out the affirmative answer suggested by the *Historiae*. In his already cited memoirs, even though these surely show no signs of wavering in his commitment to Florence, we find a striking description of how in the time of his youth, after the long devastation of Italy in the Trecento by non-Italian mercenaries, "the means of making war had returned to Italian hands" (*arma . . . in manus Italorum penitus redierant*). "The Italians began to regain their reputation as cavalry soldiers," and "victory and the hopes of every belligerent state [on the peninsula] came to be vested in the mounted soldiers of Italy."[26] This is a pan-Italian point of view for which one would look in vain in Bruni's early writings, and it is doubtful whether this side of the situation could have been so strongly felt in the Florence of 1400, threatened as it was by Giangaleazzo Visconti's cavalry. Again, in the preface of the *Bellum Italicum Adversos Gothos Gestum*, which is roughly contemporary with the memoirs, Bruni, depicting the rule of the Goths as a misfortune for the entire peninsula, calls Italy his *patria* with almost as much warmth as he usually does Florence; and in a

---

catum submittentibus eo copias Florentinis ac magnos equitatus ex transalpina Gallia et Germania commoventibus" (*Rerum Suo Tempore*, 429–30).

[26] "Arma per hoc tempus in manus Italorum penitus redierant, cum superiore tempore per equites exterarum nationum mercede conductos bella geri per Italiam consuessent. . . . Me puero, primum nostri veterem equestris militiae gloriam reciperantes, magnis Italorum turmis militare coeperunt, crescensque paulatim multitudo usque adeo peritia et audacia praestitit, ut nemo iam exterum equitatum habere vellet, victoria et spes omnis bellantium in italico equitatu reponeretur" (*Rerum Suo Tempore*, 430).

not much earlier letter—a fervent evocation of the love in Virgil's *Georgics* for the beauty of Italy and the humane manners of its inhabitants[27]—Italy is celebrated both as a *natio* and as a *patria*, terminology that had been natural to Bruni during his earlier years only in reference to Florence and a few other city-states.

To give another example, about 1440 Bruni was forced to defend himself against an accusation that during his tenure as one of the Florentine *Ten of War* he had not been a strong enough advocate of war in the conflicts with other Italian states. His justification appeared in the form of an historical work—the *Commentarium Rerum Graecarum*—in which, following Xenophon's *Hellenica*, he surveyed the ruin that overtook the city-states of Greece as a result of their internecine wars. Thus, in the period when he was writing the latter part of the *Historiae*, Bruni's analyses, in harmony with the subtle movement toward a stable Italian states-system that was taking place under Cosimo de' Medici's leadership, included all three of the focuses of interest needed for an awareness of Florence as a major Italian power: the politics of inter-Italian and European scope characteristic of the nascent region-states; the fatal effect of that politics on many of the small medieval Italian states; and the city's growing involvement in the destiny of the Italian peninsula as a whole.

When Bruni first began working on the *Historiae*—the *prooemium* was written between 1415 and 1419[28]—he characterized Florence's rise from a commune to a power with European interests as one of the significant points of comparison with the history of Rome; in the proem, this comparison appears together with the historical parallel between the significance for Florence of the destruction of Pisa's navy and the significance for Rome of the destruction of Carthage's sea

[27] See Bruni's *Ep.* VII 7 in Mehus' edition, dated by Luiso, 21 August 1436.
[28] See the reference to the time of the preface of the *Historiae* in *Crisis*, 2d ed., 370.

power. Nevertheless, his history of Florence is not merely an attempt to characterize the city's development as the rise of a second Rome. The further we advance into the book, the stronger becomes our impression that Bruni is emphasizing those aspects of his conception of Florentine history which distinguish it from the historical outlook of the Romans and their idea of universal empire. In spite of what he had said in the proem, his observation of the similarities with Rome had taught him something about the heterogeneous structure of Florentine history. What Bruni really wanted to show, and indeed succeeded in showing, was not the growth of an individual city to a position of imperial power, but rather how one city-republic, starting from a local base, could accumulate so much strength that it eventually participated in the European politics of cooperating as well as contending sovereign powers. Bruni's city history not only gives us the earliest systematic historical criticism of the rule of Rome over Italy and the world but offers the first history in which individual cities and states are no longer participants in a game whose outcome is determined by emperor or pope. Instead, each state and each people decides its own course and seeks a place for itself in the sun—as Bruni, during the early phase of his thinking and writing, had so impressively described it in his introductory book.

Thus, the *Historiae Florentini Populi* is of twofold significance for historical thought in Florentine civic Humanism. Its effort to illuminate Florentine growth by comparing the history of the city with that of the *Respublica Romana* makes Bruni's work an ancestor of Machiavelli's *Discorsi* of a century later, in which the suprahistorical *Roma Aeterna* of the Middle Ages was finally transformed into a historical model from which modern states could learn the immutable causes and laws of history. At the same time, Bruni's introduction to the Florence and Italy of his own day affords the earliest example of a type of history tracing the development of individual states or nations from local partners in a provincial power balance into sovereign states, and finally into members of a national and even European equilibrium system. In both respects, this is the first uncompromising modern antithesis in historiography to the medieval view of supernaturally ordained agencies and their alliances and wars.[29]

[29] More recently, an illuminating essay by Louis Green has demonstrated that a similarly directed, though much less revolutionary, transformation from "medieval" to "modern" patterns of thought occurred during the transition from the late Trecento to the early Quattrocento in Florentine chronicle-writing. See L. Green, *Chronicle into History: An Essay on the Interpretation of History in Florentine Fourteenth-Century Chronicles* (Cambridge, England, 1972).

FIVE

The Memory of Cicero's Roman Civic Spirit in the Medieval Centuries and in the Florentine Renaissance*

I

ANYONE who studies the influence of Cicero on later generations must marvel at how differently his historical figure was viewed in successive centuries.

To students of the history of philosophy, it is a matter of course that every period creates its own images of Plato and Aristotle, and that at the heart of each re-creation is a growing awareness of some previously unknown aspect of these two great masters—an awareness which helps that period clarify its own ideas. Cicero's role in the history of Humanism shows a similar pattern. He exhibited different faces to succeeding generations, and each became discernible when humanists or writers arrived at a point where sympathetic understanding of some neglected feature of Cicero's life or work helped them to perceive and strengthen their own identities. Knowledge of such discoveries is important, therefore, not only because they bring to light some lasting truth about Cicero but also because they contribute enormously to our understanding of his interpreters' modes of thought.

Many of the historical images of Cicero, and the use to

* This essay originated as a lecture in 1938 and was published under the title "Cicero and the Roman Civic Spirit in the Middle Ages and the Early Renaissance" in the *Bulletin of the John Rylands Library*, vol. 22 (Manchester, England, 1938). It was reprinted in expanded and revised form in Fredric L. Cheyette, ed. *Lordship and Community in Medieval Europe: Selected Readings* (New York, 1968), and has now been further expanded and thoroughly revised.

which each was put, are well known. As a teacher of rhetoric, Cicero appeared very differently to the humanists of the Renaissance than to medieval students. Although some of his writings served as standard texts for practical rhetorical instruction down through the centuries, in his own day he was a leader in efforts to transform rhetorical training into a general program of studies stressing the indivisibility of thought and expression in all intellectual pursuits. This program was proposed in Cicero's *De Oratore* for cultured men in all walks of life and not merely as a technical training for orators or for those practicing the art of writing. Thus, the author who stood revealed to the humanists of the Renaissance when, during the early fifteenth century, complete texts of the *De Oratore* became known, differed essentially from the mere teacher of rhetoric familiar to the Middle Ages.

Other writings of Cicero likewise evoked varying responses through the centuries. Readers who principally sought guidance on ethical values and moral conduct saw in him a teacher of the cool, rational wisdom of the Stoic school of philosophy; for them one basic text was his *Disputationes Tusculanae*, without which the growth of the Stoic tradition, as it is known in Western thought, would be unthinkable. A different Cicero—the representative of the cultivated life of the Roman aristocracy—came to light during periods in which aristocratic culture called for a master of propriety, humane *temperantia*, and harmonious social mores. The medieval chivalric code of courtly manners was already inspired by some pertinent pages from the corpus of Ciceronian writings, in particular some sections of the *De Officiis*; and in later centuries, Cicero was often viewed as the teacher of an ethics attuned to aesthetic norms and the inexhaustible variety of human individuality. After 1500, when authoritarian doctrinairism was felt to be an obstacle to new tendencies, religious as well as secular, Cicero, as an adherent of the skepticism taught by the Platonic academy, helped readers to free themselves from dogmatism and prejudice. He figured in this capacity during the sixteenth and seventeenth centuries in the rise of a new lay tradition. And in the latter part of the seventeenth and in the eighteenth century, when philosophers and writers strove to create a stable body of ideas and values based on reason—a natural ethics and a natural religion—yet another kind of philosopher seemed to reveal himself to Cicero's readers: a teacher of the identity of human nature in all nations and ages. This last aspect of Cicero's thinking, which reflected a different strain of his Stoic heritage, came to the fore especially in his *De Legibus* and *De Natura Deorum*. In short, throughout the Middle Ages and modern era we find the view of Cicero the man and writer changing, together with the influence of Ciceronian thought, according to the spirit of the times.[1]

Not that we have reason to believe that the historical images of Cicero and uses of Ciceronian thought have all been identified. On the contrary, especially for the complex period of transition from medieval to modern thinking, some of the contemporary images of Cicero are still half hidden from view. It is possible, however, to regain them by examining some of the Ciceronian ideas that acted as ferment for writers of the fourteenth and fifteenth centuries. Above all, we should bear in mind that the first half of the Quattrocento in Italy was the era in which the memory of the ancient city-states— Greek, Roman, and Etruscan alike—was fully resuscitated. In this atmosphere, Cicero was bound to exert a peculiar power—scarcely felt at other times—as soon as it was recognized that he had spent a large part of his life in the service of the *Respublica Romana* and that he had composed some of his greatest literary works to help create a culture suitable for active city-state citizens and a philosophy of dedication to society and the state. This is a facet of the changing Renaissance relationship to Cicero that has rarely been remembered by modern readers.[2] Yet one could find no better framework for

[1] This was brought to the attention of historical students by Th. Zielinski's *Cicero im Wandel der Jahrhunderte*, 4th ed. (1929).

[2] This is true even of Zielinski's excellent work, as well as of A. Hortis, "M. T. Cicerone nelle opere del Petrarca e del Boccaccio," *Archeografo Tries-*

the history of Humanism in the early Renaissance, especially in Florence, than the story of how the aspect of Cicero the Roman citizen and thinker was but timidly recognized throughout the medieval centuries, only to be seized upon in the Quattrocento by humanists as an essential aid in their efforts to break away from many of the assumptions held during the Middle Ages.

II

Few writers from the past were as deeply concerned with the inherent needs of the *vita civilis* as Cicero. At the time when Rome and its empire first came into contact with the culture of the Hellenistic world, a tendency had prevailed among Greek philosophers to seek inner independence through tranquil studies in the privacy of an existence far removed from public cares. A few generations later, in Cicero's day, amid the disappointments and confusion of the civil wars, many in Rome were eager to learn from Greek philosophy that another worthy life existed besides that of a politically active citizen. It was one of the objectives of Cicero's literary work to counteract this trend. His ethics recalled citizens to the *vita activa politica*. He set himself the task of adapting the Greek spirit of philosophical investigation to the needs of Roman citizens, who were enjoined not to shirk their responsibilities to the commonweal.

Whatever expressions of public-spirited philosophy could be found in Greek literature—in Plato, Aristotle, Dicaearchus, and Panaitius of Rhodes—were conscientiously incorporated by Cicero in his writings. This was true for most of his life. The idea of the true "orator," which appears after the period of his great speeches, especially in the *De Oratore*, is developed further in the time of his great political opera (*De Legibus* and

---

tino, n.s., 6 (1879–1880), and a more recent, learned survey of many of the literary sources, W. Rüegg's "Cicero in Mittelalter und Humanismus," in vol. 2 of *Lexikon des Mittelalters* (Munich, 1983), col. 2063–72.

De Republica), finally reaching its culmination in the *De Officiis.* In all these works, Greek concepts of the *vita activa politica* were given a Roman setting whenever possible. Corresponding ideas were ascribed to great Romans of the past—mottoes and maxims revealing Cicero's own bent of mind and incorporating significant changes that he allowed himself to make in his Latin adaptations of his Greek models. In the *De Republica* and the much later *Tusculans*, for instance, he attributes to the elder Brutus and the *pontifex maximus* Scipio Nasica the sayings "the wise man is never a private individual" (*numquam privatum esse sapientem*) and "when the liberty of citizens is at stake, no one should remain a private person." In the *De Officiis* he argues that the virtue *prudentia*, which characterizes the state of mind fundamental to a life of study and philosophical rationalization, is inferior to *iustitia, fortitudo,* and *moderatio*, the virtues of the active life. Anyone who believes the function of a philosopher is to teach disdain for military and state honors deserves blame, not admiration, we read in the *De Officiis*. It may be true in certain cases that withdrawal from public activities for the purpose of studying and writing results in a life of value. But "more fruitful to mankind and more suitable to greatness and renown are the lives of those who apply themselves to statecraft and to great enterprises." And again, "Parents are dear to us; children, relatives, and friends are dear; but only love for our *patria* embraces all others; and what good man would hesitate to give his life for her if by his death he could contribute to her welfare?"[3] Such statements are of the same kind as the famous passage in the *Somnium Scipionis* (the annotated fragment of the *De Republica* preserved during the Middle Ages through Macrobius) in which Cicero insists that "nothing, at least on earth, is more agreeable to the God who rules the universe than assemblies and societies of men associated by the bonds of law—such as are called *civitates*"

---

[3] "Cari sunt parentes, cari liberi, propinqui, familiares, sed omnes omnium caritates patria una complexa est, pro qua quis bonus dubitet mortem oppetere, si ei sit profuturus?" (*De Officiis* I.17, 57).

(*concilia coetusque hominum iure sociati quae civitates appellantur*).[4] Later, when the time and occasion were right, these many manifestations of Cicero's Roman creed were to make a profound impression on the minds of readers.

The study of philosophy was justified in Roman eyes only because intellectual work was itself seen as an "activity," which called not for peace of soul but for an expenditure of human energy no less strenuous than that required by civic life. Such a dynamic conception of intellectual work was not entirely unknown in Greek philosophy. The early followers of Aristotle had already debated the respective merits of the contemplative and the active life. To extol the contemplative state of mind, Theophrastus, who succeeded Aristotle as head of the Peripatetic school, had formulated the impressive paradox that the wise man is never less alone than when he is alone. In solitude his intellect is free to move in all directions; intellectually he can come into contact with the good men of all times. When he is farthest from human companionship, he is closest to the divine.[5] This paradox appears in slightly changed form in Cicero's *De Republica* as the key to true Roman *otium*, which is very different from leisure.[6] There we read that Scipio Africanus Maior, in order to justify his holidays after his great political deeds, said of himself that "he had never been less alone than when he was alone"; "he had never

---

[4] *De Rep.* II.25, 46; *Tusc.* IV.23, 51; *De Off.* I.6, 19; I.21, 70–71; *De Rep.* (*Somn. Scip.*) VI.13.

[5] "Sapiens autem numquam solus esse potest. Habet secum omnes qui sunt, qui umquam fuerunt boni, et animum liberum quocumque vult transfert. Quod corpore non potest, cogitatione complectitur. Et si hominum inopia fuerit, loquitur cum Deo. Numquam minus solus erit, quam cum solus erit." These ideas of Theophrastus have been preserved in Jerome's *Adversus Jovinianum*; see note 17 below.

[6] That Scipio's dictum, reported by Cicero (and before him, in Cato's *Origines*), was suggested by Theophrastus is obvious. It is sufficient to compare Cicero's text (see notes 7 and 8 below) with Theophrastus' words, in the form just quoted from Jerome, and to remember that Cicero was familiar with the dispute between Theophrastus and Dicaearchus as to the respective merits of the *vita activa* and *vita contemplativa*.

done more than when he was doing nothing."[7] From this Cicero concluded that Scipio had found a new source of intellectual energy in solitary philosophic studies.

But Cicero was not content to stop at this. He continued to probe the Roman idea of active leisure. Ten years later, in the *De Officiis*, he conceived a different explanation for Scipio's statement, giving it the form in which it circulated during the Middle Ages and Renaissance, when the *De Republica* was lost. The Cicero of the *De Officiis* persuaded himself that the victor of Zama could not merely have pursued studies in his *otium*. If Scipio engaged in great mental activity in solitude, it could only have meant that he was preparing the vast plans by which he built the Roman Empire: "in his leisure he considered what action had to be taken" (*in otio de negotio cogitabat*). Cicero himself, it is true, did not follow Scipio's example in the enforced intervals between his public activities during the civil wars, but led a life of literary and philosophical *otium* in the silence of his country home. Yet he could boast later that he had not used this solitude merely to forget his unhappy fate or gain inner peace through contemplation. His chief task in his retreat had still been to labor as a citizen for Rome: he had been laying the foundations for a Latin literature and preparing the empire of the Latin language, just as other citizens had built the political empire of Rome. He proudly compared his own literary, but patriotic, *otium* with the statesmanlike seclusion of Scipio. "Leisure and solitude, which serve to make others idle," he said, remembering Scipio's dictum, "acted as a goad in Scipio's case." His readers were meant to understand that he himself had also used leisure and solitude for the benefit of Rome, as became a citizen.[8]

Cicero wanted his fellow citizens to recognize that from the

[7] "Africanum . . . scribit Cato solitum esse dicere . . . de se . . . numquam se plus agere, quam nihil cum ageret, numquam minus solum esse, quam cum solus esset" (*De Rep.* 1.17, 27).

[8] ". . . numquam se minus otiosum esse, quam cum otiosus, nec minus solum, quam cum solus esset. . . . Ita duae res, quae languorem adferunt ceteris, illum acuebant, otium et solitudo" (*De Off.* III.1, 1).

beginning he had lived up to the ideals he had advocated in his writings. In the *De Legibus* he already considered it his task "to bring learning out of the gloomy depths of the study . . . not merely into the sunlight and dust but into the fighting line and the center of the conflict." Still earlier, in the *De Oratore*, he had shown in his examples of great Romans of the past what culture could mean for the daily life of a citizen. Cato Censorius was described as the type of citizen who knew how to unite theory and practice by taking an interest in both private and public matters. Cato's legal studies did not prevent him from being an active lawyer; private business never diverted him from his duties as an orator in the forum or as a member of the senate. Marcus Crassus, the leading speaker in the conversation set forth in the *De Oratore*, did not abandon his practice in the law courts for the sake of his studies, and even so he had been able to bring the latter to maturity. He is pictured as choosing for his model the citizen "who does not give others the impression that he is pursuing philosophical studies and yet is studying." Indeed, such study in the midst of activity remained Cicero's highest ideal of a citizen's education. In later years, when he had to defend himself against those who questioned his capacity for philosophic work after an extensive political career, he boasted that he was well prepared for it because (like Crassus) "I was studying philosophy most earnestly just at the time when I seemed to be doing so least."[9]

During the Middle Ages, when those concerned with problems of conduct and culture were knights, monks, or secular clerics, no part of Cicero's legacy was less appreciated than this Roman craving for a share in political action and the building of a culture accessible to men who lead busy lives. But on the eve of the Renaissance, when citizens of the Italian city-states longed for a lay literature and moral standards befitting men who spent their existence in the *vita activa politica*,

[9] *De Leg.* III.6, 14; *De Oratore* III.33, 135; III.22, 72–83, 89; *De Nat. Deor.* 1.3, 6.

what better ally could they have than the Roman Cicero? The most revealing, and sometimes dramatic, episodes in the history of Cicero's influence were occasioned by this Roman trait in his various writings on the education of statesmen, orators, and citizens: the *De Oratore, De Legibus, Somnium Scipionis,* and *De Officiis.*

III

Historical generalizations are never quite accurate, and the contention that medieval men were insensitive to Cicero's civic traits is not the whole truth. To be sure, the civic world of Rome was virtually forgotten for centuries, and we are often amazed to see how fully the historical figure of Cicero the Roman thinker had passed from memory. But even in clerical or monastic milieus, some unmistakable echoes of Cicero's Roman teachings continued to be heard. Although they were few and far between, they are of great interest because they illustrate both the enduring power of those ideas and the degree to which the Roman legacy was transformed in the Middle Ages.

The disguising of Cicero's philosophy of civic participation—one might call it a mimicry that allowed it to survive and exert a subtle influence in an alien world—began even before Christianity had fully transformed the spiritual and intellectual atmosphere. During the fourth century, largely under the impact of Neoplatonism and particularly of the writings of Plotinus, mystical contemplation and new transcendental values began to exert a strong influence on pagan and still Roman-minded circles. This phase is attested by Macrobius' commentary of about 400 on the *Somnium Scipionis,* which preserved a fragment of Cicero's *De Republica* for the Middle Ages and the Renaissance. Macrobius' intention in presenting the Roman classic to a new audience was to prove that, despite his championship of the active political life, Cicero had been aware that religious contemplation was on a higher plane. Seen through the eyes of a writer of the new age, Cicero appeared to have admitted as much in the passage of the *Somnium Scipionis* which claims that "nihil est illi principi deo qui omnem mundum regit, quod quidem in terris fiat, acceptius, quam concilia coetusque hominum iure sociati quae civitates appellantur."[10] To Macrobius, the parenthetical phrase "quod quidem in terris fiat" was evidence that Cicero had qualified his claim by saying that in the eyes of God a life of service to the state is superior only with respect to earthly matters; in other words, that Cicero had already distinguished between a path leading good statesmen to heaven "per terrenos actus" and a higher one taken by those "who start out from heavenly things themselves" (*qui ab ipsis caelestibus incipiunt*).[11]

Once Cicero had thus been made a denizen of the religious-contemplative age, he was allowed some influence with regard to his civic persuasions. In Plotinus' conception, the active political life formed the earthly ground from which the human mind should ascend as quickly as possible to the vision of the divine and the purification of the soul. Under the influence of Cicero's teachings, Macrobius understood this to mean that the path through the *otiosae virtutes* of contemplation is certainly the higher one, but that the *negotiosae virtutes* can also lead to beatitude. It is thus best to pursue both the higher and the lower path. If Cicero "quite rightly" predicted eternal bliss for the *rectores rerum publicarum*, so runs Macrobius' argument, he must have done so "to show that some attain to happiness through the virtues of leisure and others through the virtues of action." Following Cicero, therefore, Macrobius feels at liberty to seek exemplary lives among the great Roman statesmen of the past—King Numa, the two Catos, and the two Scipiones Africani, all of whom combined wisdom with political action. The younger Scipio Africanus, with his divinely

---

[10] *Comm. in Somn. Scip.* 1.8, 3–12; II.17, 4–9. For a translation of Cicero's dictum, see the text connected with note 3 on p. 98 above.

[11] A similar but more thoroughgoing interpretation of Macrobius' transformation of Cicero's political ethos into a combination of the *vita activa* and *vita contemplativa* is found in Aldo Bernardo's *Petrarch, Scipio, and the 'Africa'* (Baltimore, 1962), 113–21.

inspired dream, belongs most particularly, according to Macrobius' concluding remarks, "to that group of men who both mold their lives according to the precepts of philosophy and support their commonwealths with deeds of valor." That is why, in the *Somnium Scipionis*, the younger Africanus "is charged with upholding the highest standards of both modes of life."

In this fashion, some of Cicero's Roman ideas were carried down to the Middle Ages among the often uncongenial reflections of a Neoplatonic writer. During the twelfth and thirteenth centuries, when the Scholastics were creating a powerful synthesis of religion and the politico-social sphere, one of the major sources of inspiration was Macrobius' political modification of the Neoplatonic flight from life.[12] Finally, toward the end of the Middle Ages, humanistic readers began to sense the true Ciceronian attitude behind Macrobius' commentary and to free the Roman core from its Neoplatonic shell.

Within the Christian sector of the late Roman world, the last heir to the Ciceronian spirit was the lonely figure of Boethius, the Roman consul and statesman at the court of Theodoric the Ostrogoth. One hundred years after Macrobius, we find an echo of Cicero's civic attitude in Boethius' philosophical work. "Although the cares of my consular office prevent me from devoting my entire attention to those studies, it seems to me a sort of public service to instruct my fellow citizens in the products of reasoned investigation," Boethius wrote. "Nor shall I deserve ill of my country in this attempt. In ages long past, other cities transferred to our state the lordship and sovereignty of the world; I am glad to assume the remaining task of educating our present society in the spirit of Greek philosophy. Wherefore this is verily a part of my consular duty, since it has always been a Roman habit to take

---

[12] See H. van Lieshout, "La Théorie Plotinienne de la vertu. Essai sur la genèse d'un article de la somme théologique de Saint Thomas" (diss., University of Fribourg, 1926), 124ff.

everything in the world that is beautiful or praiseworthy and add to its lustre by imitation."

By that time a profound metamorphosis of the Ciceronian heritage had taken place in the literature of the Church Fathers.[13] A transformed Cicero is found in St. Ambrose's adaptation of the *De Officiis* for the use of the clergy. This Christian recasting of Cicero's final guide to morals and conduct is a deliberate effort to extenuate the strongly civic tenor of Cicero's teachings. Written in the second half of the fourth century, the *De Officiis Ministrorum* (*On the Duties of the Clergy*), no longer gives preeminence to the political and social virtues. In direct conflict with Cicero's evaluation, *sapientia-prudentia* is now made superior to all the virtues of the active life. Yet, even in this revision by a father of the Church, a number of original Ciceronian features have survived the changed times. Since Ambrose was, perhaps more than any other patristic writer, a Roman at heart, traces of Cicero's Roman patriotism and civic outlook can be detected in his guidebook for priests. One of these traces is the symbol Cicero created when he defined the *otium* of Scipio. The Ciceronian characterization of true leisure as a means of regenerating man's energy and inner strength found a response in Ambrose. It seemed kindred in spirit to the Christian teaching that solitude should increase one's usefulness to one's fellow men. Like Cicero, Ambrose contrasted an *otium* leading to ceaseless activity of the spirit with the despicable leisure of men "who distract their minds

[13] Among earlier Church Fathers, Cicero had had a fuller and more direct impact, as one learns by consulting Lactantius' works of around 300. I want to illustrate this with one quotation: "Sapientia enim nisi in aliquo actu fuerit quo vim suam exerceat, inanis et falsa est recteque Tullius civiles viros, qui rem publicam gubernent, qui urbes aut novas constituant aut constitutas aequitate tueantur, qui salutem libertatemque civium vel bonis legibus vel salubribus consiliis vel iudiciis gravibus conservent, philosophiae doctoribus praefert" (Lactantius *Divinae Institutiones* III.16, 2).

As for the above quotation from Boethius (from his Latin translation of *In Categorias Aristotelis*), the English text is that given by Edward Kennard Rand, *Founders of the Middle Ages* (Cambridge, Mass., 1928), 158, though with some modifications.

from activity in order to indulge in idleness and recreation."
But eager to surpass the pagan world, Ambrose declared that
it was in fact not Scipio but Moses and the prophets who had
first advocated a leisure of true activity. Even while they appeared to be alone and idle, they were listening to the voice of
God and thus gaining strength to accomplish feats beyond human power.[14]

Ambrose was the first of the recorded readers of the *De Officiis* to find inspiration for the Christian concept of active devotion to the faith in Scipio's tireless "activity" of mind in solitude. In Carolingian times, the abbot Paschasius Radbertus
gave the by then familiar Roman aphorism a place in one of
the fundamental texts of medieval theology: If, Paschasius
wrote in his *Commentary on St. Matthew*, the pagan Scipio was
never less idle than when he was at leisure, because he used his
otium to think about the exigencies of his *negotia*, "how much
less should we, who have been subjected to heavenly discipline, grow weary in our *otium* of meditating on divine matters." To whom, he asked, were Scipio's words more suitable
and necessary than to monks living in the uninterrupted *otium*
of the monastery?[15] The result was an ideal in which monastic
dedication to contemplation and scholarly devotion to an industrious life of study were linked.[16] When we come to Petrarch, we shall find that this train of medieval thought was
still relevant.

As the Middle Ages advanced, however, almost all vestiges
of Cicero's civic outlook on life were lost. Until the twelfth
century, Cicero was usually viewed as if he himself had been
a monastic scholar—a recluse who taught contempt for mar-

[14] *De Off. Min.* III I (Migne, *Patrologia Latina [PL]* 16, 145).

[15] *Expos. in Matthaeum*, Prologus in Lib. XI (*Monumenta Germaniae Historica,
Epistolae Karolini Aevi*, vol. 6, pp. 148f.). Radbertus makes similar use of the
Scipio paradox in *Expos. in Psalm. 44*, Praefatio (ibid., 148, n. 2).

[16] An example from the twelfth century is in Giraldus Cambrensis' *Sym-
bolum Electorum, Ep.* 24 (ed. Brewer, in *Rerum Britannicarum Medii Aevi Scriptores*, vol. 1, p. 281), where the saying "se nunquam minus solum quam cum
solus extiterat esse" is, however, surprisingly ascribed to Socrates.

riage and women and all the passions and burdens of earthly life. The writer who laid the foundation of this early medieval view of Cicero was St. Jerome. In defense of chastity and the solitary life, the father of scholarly monastic humanism in the time of St. Ambrose collected all the classical testimonies— genuine and spurious—against the married state. Jerome ascribed to Cicero the saying that "you cannot devote yourself to a wife and philosophy at the same time" (*non posse se uxori et philosophiae pariter operam dare*). He went back further, quoting Theophrastus' praise of learning in solitude, which Cicero had transformed in the *De Officiis* into praise of ceaseless activity for the community. Jerome thus preserved for monastic humanists of the Middle Ages the original meaning of Theophrastus' dictum that the truly wise man is nowhere less alone than in solitude, because the human intellect comes in contact there with the sages of all times and with the divine. This dictum seemed to Jerome to harmonize with the alleged Ciceronian warning against family life and women.[17]

The two passages—the spurious Ciceronian saying and Theophrastus' dictum—continued to be associated in the literature of the Middle Ages, especially in the earlier part. Until the twelfth century, the medieval Cicero remained a teacher of misogyny and flight from active life. Following Jerome, great scholars of the twelfth-century renaissance, such as John of Salisbury and Walter Map, continued to attribute to Cicero the opinion that the truly wise must live in solitude, away from family cares.[18] Abélard made Cicero an outright critic of

[17] *Adversus Jovinianum*, Lib. I, chs. 47–48 (Migne, *PL* 23, 276ff.); see note 5 above.

[18] Walter Map, *De Nugis Curialium*, ed. M. R. James, in *Anecdota Oxoniensia*, Mediaeval and Mod. Ser., vol. 14, p. 150; John of Salisbury, *Policraticus*, ed. Webb, vol. 2, p. 298. Webb's reference to *De Off.* III.I is a mistake; the entire section of the *Policraticus* is literally taken over from Jerome's *Adv. Jov.*, Bk. I, chs. 47–48. William of Malmesbury, in his *Historia Regum Anglorum* (ed. Stubbs, vol. 2, p. 65: "Lucubrabat [Beda] ipse sibi pernox in gratiarum actione et psalmorum cantu, implens sapientissimi viri dictum, ut nunquam minus solus esset quam cum solus esset"), also obviously had recourse not to *De Off.* III.I, as Stubbs believed, but to Jerome.

the drudgery of the *vita activa*, ascribing to him the observation that "just because something is toilsome [*laboriosum*], it need not be *praeclarum* and *gloriosum*"—impugning with this allegedly Ciceronian quotation the belief that the laborious life of a secular cleric is worthier of reward than the calm contemplation of a coenobite and that the struggle against the temptations of life is more meritorious than monastic seclusion.[19] Even our strongest evidence for the widespread and often enthusiastic interest in Cicero's works during the twelfth century, the well-known *Moralium Dogma Philosophorum*, does not escape this trend. Although it literally repeats the Ciceronian conclusion that *prudentia* is inferior to the other three, more active cardinal virtues, the motive for Cicero's choice remains unperceived. Of the virtues *iustitia, fortitudo*, and *temperantia*, the last is preferred because it has the least connection with public life. By means of temperance, says the anonymous author of the *Moralium Dogma*, man rules himself; by courage and justice, he rules over family and state: "but it is better for man to govern himself than to exercise external dominion."[20]

IV

It was not until the thirteenth century that Cicero slowly began to reemerge as a civic thinker. At first it may seem strange that a fresh appraisal should have begun then. At that time, in contrast to the twelfth century, the appreciation of classical poets and writers was declining rather than growing, as we are aware today.[21] The study of the classical authors was re-

---

[19] Abélard, *Opera*, ed. Cousin, vol. 1, pp. 693f.; vol. 2, p. 621.

[20] *Moral. Dogma Phil.*, ed. J. Homberg, in Arbeten utgivna med Understöd av Vilhelm Ekman Universitetsfond, vol. 37 (Uppsala), 53. The work has been studied more recently by Ph. Delhaye in "Une adaptation du *De officiis* au XIIe siècle," *Recherches de Théologie Ancienne et Médiévale* (1949), but the authorship has not yet been conclusively established.

[21] This has been known since at least the 1920s. See L. J. Paetow, *A Guide to the Study of Medieval History*, rev. ed. (New York, 1931), 442ff., 484ff.

stricted, as it were, to an anteroom of an imposing edifice, the largest halls of which were built to accommodate the new theology, jurisprudence, and finally, science. In ethics and politics, Aristotle, the systematic philosopher, came to the fore, detracting from Cicero's previous authority. On the other hand, the ever-growing intellectual curiosity of the century began to throw a measure of light on the ancient authors. More of them were read than ever before,[22] even though readers in scholastic universities no longer showed the enthusiasm which, in earlier centuries, St. Ambrose and the author of the *Moralium Dogma Philosophorum* had had for such Ciceronian works as the *De Officiis*. In the process of comparing Cicero's moral system with others known at the time—those of Aristotle, the Church Fathers, and recent philosophers—the scholastic readers came to recognize the distinctive, long-forgotten nature of Cicero's ideas.

The process is seen in its inception in the major encyclopedia of the thirteenth century, the widely circulated *Speculum* of Vincent de Beauvais. We still encounter Jerome's allegation that Cicero had said he could not serve both philosophy and women. Moreover, this Jeromian assertion serves as primary evidence of Cicero's personality, about which many misleading statements are made. There is no attempt to comprehend Cicero's teachings by establishing the context and significance of the apparently conflicting utterances in his works. In fact, in order to document praise for both the *vita socialis* and the *vita contemplativa*, Cicero's various sayings are split into two groups and cited respectively in support of one or the other. What is new and valuable in Vincent's encyclopedia is the degree of familiarity with Cicero's works, which goes far beyond that of the preceding centuries. Scipio's paradox from the *De Officiis*, for instance, is referred to both in Vincent's *Speculum Doctrinale* and in his *Speculum Historiale*; and in sup-

---

[22] This was proved by E. K. Rand in "The Classics in the Thirteenth Century," *Speculum* 4 (1929), and "A Friend of the Classics in the Time of St. Thomas Aquinas," *Bibliothèque Thomiste* 14 (1930).

port of the active life, Cicero is quoted to the effect that *otium* may be useful to some philosophers, but "more fruitful to mankind and more suitable to greatness and renown are the lives of those who apply themselves to statecraft and great enterprises."[23]

One reason why renewed attention was paid to passages expressing Cicero's civic attitude was that in the twelfth and thirteenth centuries civic society again began to participate in the literary culture of the time. Although they were usually still clerics, the scholars and popular writers of the period were at last learning to look at the world from the standpoint of the knight or the citizen. The cleric writing in civic surroundings necessarily viewed his studies in a different light than did the writer in a monastic cell. He did not relate his work to contemplation and philosophic speculation, but planned and appraised it as a service to the community—as an intellectual counterpart of the political activity of citizens.

In 1119, or not much earlier, Guido, a clergyman in Pisa—at that time one of the most flourishing maritime cities in Italy—made a compilation of medieval sources on geography, politics, and history (often legends), which he adapted to the Mediterranean interests of the citizens of Pisa. He justified his work by saying that since nature herself had constituted human society, the best part of both *negotia* and *studia* ought to be devoted to the commonweal. This was not only his personal opinion, he said; it was confirmed by the teachings of St.

---

[23] *Speculum Historiale*, ed. Duaci (1624), Lib. VI, chs. 8 and 11, pp. 175, 177; *Speculum Doctrinale*, Lib. V, ch. 41.

It is true that if the copious extracts taken from Ciceronian works by a certain Hadoardus had really been collected during the Carolingian period, as was long supposed, the knowledge of Cicero's writings in the early Middle Ages might have been greater than that shown in the thirteenth century in Vincent de Beauvais' encyclopedia. But as R. Mollweide has proved in *Wiener Studien* (1911–1915), these extracts can hardly have been made in the ninth or tenth century; they must have been compiled in the last period of Antiquity, probably in the sixth century by learned pupils of St. Jerome living in Gaul. See also the confirmation of Mollweide's research by A. Lörcher, in *Jahresbericht über die Fortschritte der klass. Altertumswissenschaft* 203 (1925): 153f.

Ambrose, who in turn had referred to Cicero's *De Officiis* as his major inspiration. Following their precepts, he was trying through his literary work to make a contribution to human society.[24]

A hundred years later, Italian laymen began to give expression to moral ideals in writings of their own. In one of the earliest of these, the *Libro . . . della Dilezione di Dio, e del Prossimo, e della Forma dell'Onesta Vita*, written by Judge Albertano da Brescia in 1238 (that is, a few decades before the publication of Vincent de Beauvais' encyclopedia), we find the Cicero of the *De Officiis* quoted as a decisive authority in the discussion of the two ways of life between which man must choose. All other spiritual and secular authorities, Albertano admits, seem to favor contemplation and flight from active life. Christ's preference of Mary over Martha, the teachings of the Son of Sirach and of the apostles, the Stoic contempt for the material world, and several statements in Cicero's own work, all warn us not to consume our energy in toiling for this transient existence. Only the Cicero of the *De Officiis* is on the opposing side, claiming boldly that an existence spent on "cose comunali e grandi" is "more fruitful" than the easier life of contemplation, and that a noble mind should choose unrest and exertion for the benefit of the world over happiness in untroubled solitude. For the layman Albertano, the teachings of the *De Officiis* alone are sufficient to balance all other authorities. Man, he concludes, can choose freely between the two ways of life;[25] Roman civic spirit and medieval contemplation are of equal value.

[24] Guido's *Historiae Variae*, Lib. I, chs. 1–3, in *Ravennatis Anonymi Cosmographia, et Guidonis Geographica*, ed. M. Pinder and G. Parthey (1860). The background of Guido's work—the struggles and victories of the Pisans in their war with the Saracens for the Balearic Islands, ca. 1113–1118—has now been carefully reconstructed in Craig B. Fisher's "The Pisan Clergy and an Awakening of Historical Interest in a Medieval Commune," *Studies in Medieval and Renaissance History* 3 (1966): 143ff., 177ff. Guido was probably a deacon of the Pisan church (see ibid., 180).

[25] See the concluding chapter of *Il libro . . . della dilezione di Dio, e del prossimo, . . . e della forma dell' onesta vita*.

The revival of Cicero as a Roman philosopher had thus already begun by the middle of the thirteenth century, when scholastic learning reached its zenith. We have a record of the textbooks used at the time for the baccalaureate examination in the arts faculty of Paris.[26] "Moral philosophy" was divided into two sections. For the study of man's inner life and moral self-education, Aristotle's *Ethics* served as text. But in the area where "the human soul lives *in bono aliorum*," that is, in social ethics, Cicero's *De Officiis* was the prescribed guide along with practical study of the *Leges et Decreta*.[27]

The literary work of St. Thomas Aquinas reflects and builds upon this educational plan. In his *Commentary on the Sentences* as well as in his *Summa Theologiae*, the chapters dealing respectively with the importance of contemplation and of the active life cite only the Cicero of the *De Officiis* as champion of the *vita activa*, just as Judge Albertano's book had done a few decades before. Cicero's claim that *iustitia* should be placed at the head of all the virtues and that there is no excuse for disdaining a public or military career puts him in disagreement with the other authorities acknowledged by St. Thomas. But anxious to establish a gradation among competing values, Thomas, the great scholar and theologian, does not consider Cicero's lonely championship of the active life a counterweight to the traditional values. The Ciceronian challenge still has a place in the hierarchy of thirteenth-century scholastic

[26] Discovered by M. Grabmann in a manuscript of the *Archivo de la Corona de Aragón*; see M. Grabmann, vol. 2 of his *Mittelalterliches Geistesleben* (1936), 193f.

[27] The familiarity with Cicero's writings was already impressive in the twelfth century. A list of authors recommended to students, and attributed to the English scholar Alexander Neckham (1157–1217), proposed for Cicero: *De Oratore, Tusculanae Disputationes, De Amicitia, De Senectute, De Fato, Paradoxa, De Officiis*, and *De Natura Deorum*. R. R. Bolgar, *Classical Heritage* (New York, 1964), 198, remarks in reference to this list: "The conclusion is inescapable that the contemporaries of Abélard knew far more about the classical literature than did the contemporaries of Alcuin." On *De Officiis* in medieval universities, see also R. M. Martin, in *Revue d' Histoire Ecclésiastique* 31 (1935): 360.

thought, but it is a subordinate one. A definitive gradation had already been achieved, Thomas decided, by Sts. Augustine and Gregory the Great; by Aristotle, who conceded first place to the *bios theoretikos* in his *Ethics*; and by Macrobius, who combined Cicero's view with Neoplatonic teachings, leaving room for a certain "measure of escape from human affairs."[28] The famous Ciceronian maxim from the *Somnium Scipionis*— nothing is more agreeable to God than the "concilia coetusque hominum iure sociati quae civitates appellantur"—thus loses its civic significance. Its form is taken over, but its meaning is changed by the alteration of the passage to read: no sacrifice is more agreeable to God than the "regimen animarum"; that is, the care taken by the Church in its spiritual rule over human souls.[29]

V

But gradualism did not endure when the pendulum swung back to a strong enthusiasm for Antiquity, an enthusiasm comparable to that which the twelfth-century renaissance had shown for certain ancient authors. What happened to the thirteenth-century hierarchy of values when Cicero again became the object of intense interest and sympathy? In the second half of the thirteenth and during the fourteenth century, the civic world of the Italian city-states found a permanent place in intellectual life, and the Roman statesman-philosopher was in-

---

[28] *Comm. in Sent.*, III, dist. 35, q. 1, art. 4; *Summa Theol.*, 1–2, q. 61, art. 5.

[29] It is true that the situation is complicated. In *Comm. in Sent.*, loc. cit., St. Thomas ascribes the quoted saying to Gregorius Magnus, *Super Ezech.*, *Homil.* XII, but the only relevant sentence found there, "Nullum quippe omnipotenti Deo tale est sacrificium, quale est zelus animarum" (Migne, *PL* 76, 932), does not show any direct relationship to the words of the *Somnium Scipionis*. The term "regimen animarum" does occur, though in a different context, at the beginning of Gregory's *Liber Regulae Pastoralis*, pars I, cap. 1. (My thanks go to Giles Constable for this discovery.) One would therefore conclude that when Thomas cited Gregory from memory, he also remembered, perhaps unconsciously, the striking phrase in the *Somnium Scipionis*.

creasingly accepted as a teacher of civic conduct, and even came to be revered.

By that time the Tuscan cities had succeeded those of Lombardy as the foremost representatives of city-state freedom in Italy, since Lombardy had already fallen prey to tyranny, and there is no lack of revealing information about Tuscan civic thought. About 1300 that information still comes largely from the clergy, in particular from friars residing in urban monasteries. Among them, two Dominicans—the Florentine Remigio de' Girolami and Tolomeo of Lucca, former disciples of Aquinas and highly respected in the Tuscan city-states in Dante's day—allow us to trace in detail how devotion to the community was preached from pulpits and how it influenced contemporary writings on politics and history. The primary source for these Dominicans remained the Aristotelian *Ethics*, which was understood better than ever before in the surroundings of the Italian commune, the counterpart in so many respects of the ancient city-state. But Cicero now began to be recognized along with Aristotle as the most effective guide to civic obligations. When Tolomeo of Lucca asked why God had allowed the pagan Romans of Antiquity to build their world empire, he concluded that more than any other people they had been guided by *amor patriae*. Love of one's country is "the most meritorious of all virtues," he insisted, because "zeal for the common good" tends toward the same end as the divine command to love one's neighbor as oneself. Like God's commandment, therefore, the call of the *patria* admits of no exception. "This is why Tullius [Cicero] says in reference to the *respublica*, that nothing which prevents you from answering the summons of your country must be permitted to stand in your way." In the *De Officiis*, Tolomeo pointed out, "the *respublica* is considered the most gratifying and most valuable of all human associations," because Cicero says that love of relatives and friends, and of anything else, "is encompassed by the love of one's *patria*."[30]

---

[30] "Inde est quod Tullius dicit de republica, quod nulla causa intervenire

Thus, in these urban circles Cicero's civic doctrines at last regained a profound ethical value, and an important aspect of the historical Cicero again became visible. In an anonymous Italian biography of Cicero, probably written not long after 1300,[31] we can observe how much more had been learned by that time about Cicero's personality than the meager information found in Vincent de Beauvais' encyclopedia. Although the details of Cicero's political career were still unknown, in this early fourteenth-century biography he is clearly a Roman statesman as well as an author. "Even though Cicero devoted himself so wholeheartedly to administrative affairs and the protection of the republic," says the anonymous admiring biographer, and even though he was such a busy lawyer "that it is almost impossible to believe human strength could suffice for all his labors, he was also filled . . . with the greatest desire to study and write. It seems a wonder that he could be so enormously active in both these spheres."

This nascent awareness of Cicero the Roman citizen was bound to result in conflict when it encountered the existing medieval preconceptions. It was forced to the surface by the

---

debet, unde propria patria denegetur." "De hoc autem amore patriae dicit Tullius in lib. *De offic.* [the reference is to 1.57; see note 3, above] quod 'omnium societatum nulla est gratior, nulla carior, quam ea quae cum republica perseverat. Unicuique enim nostrum cari sunt parentes, cari sunt liberi, cari sunt propinqui ac familiares, sed omnium propinquitates patria sua charitate complexa est.'" Thus Tolomeo of Lucca, about 1302, in the *De Regimine Principum* (by Thomas Aquinas up to Lib. II, ch. 4, but continued by Tolomeo), Lib. III, ch. 4. As a convenient introduction to the character of Remigio de' Girolami's work, cf. D. R. Lesnick, in *Speculum* 57 (1982): 929f.; for Remigio's admiration of Cicero, see Charles T. Davis in the *Proceedings of the American Philosophical Society* 104 (1960): 665f.

[31] The *Epythoma de Vita, Gestis, Scientie Prestantia . . . Ciceronis* in the famous Cicero codex in Troyes from Petrarch's library, partly printed in P. de Nolhac, *Pétrarque et l'humanisme*, 2d ed. (1907), vol. 1, pp. 227ff. De Nolhac (p. 231) gives reasons why the biography cannot have been written by Petrarch himself in his youth but must be the work of a writer of the early fourteenth century. E. Norden, in vol. 2 of *Die antike Kunstprosa*, 4th ed. (1909), 738f., agrees with these conclusions and enlarges upon the biography's probable Italian origin.

inner struggles of Petrarch, who was heir to the outlook formed in the Italian city-states and to many older medieval traditions. Born and bred in exile, he was descended from a family of Florentine citizens, and during the first half of his humanistic career he preferred an extended sojourn in southern France—in papal Avignon, where he took lower orders, and in the isolated Alpine valley of Vaucluse—to the life of a citizen in Florence. During his early years in Avignon he came in contact with both the Franciscan spiritual movement and the monastic literature of earlier generations. In him the contradictions between monastic persuasions and the reviving memory of Cicero the Roman statesman attained the intensity of a battle. The struggle grew all the fiercer because, in his search for ancient authors and manuscripts, Petrarch discovered a key to a deeper knowledge of Cicero's personality, a key unknown in preceding centuries: his intimate *Letters to Atticus*.

When Petrarch made this discovery in 1345 in the cathedral library in Verona, he came face to face with the historical Cicero for the first time. He saw a Roman who had given up his offices only under the compulsion of Caesar's victory, a citizen who avidly followed political events from his rural retreat and, after the murder of Caesar, returned to the confusion of the civil war and to his ruin. The semi-clergyman and hermit of the Vaucluse was horrified by this discovery. He wrote a letter full of accusation, as strange as it is moving, to the shade of Cicero in Hades. "Why did you involve yourself in so many useless quarrels and forsake the calm so becoming to your age, your position, and the tenor of your life?" he reproached his fallen idol. "What false splendor of glory drove you . . . to a death unworthy of a sage? . . . Oh, how much more fitting would it have been had you, philosopher that you were, grown old in rural surroundings . . . meditating upon eternal life and not upon this trifling existence here below! . . . Oh, would that you had never aspired to the consul's insignia or to triumphs!"[32]

[32] "Quid tibi tot contentionibus et prorsum nichil profuturis simultatibus

However much Petrarch admired Cicero's eloquence, his precepts for a cultivated life, and his independence from dogmatism, superstition, and the errors of polytheism, Cicero's civic bent of mind was to him nothing but an offense against the monastic values which, at least in the 1340s, Petrarch was neither willing nor able to abandon. In the humanistic works written in the solitude of the Vaucluse, he stressed the contrast between the vanity of Cicero's political passions and the fruitfulness of his all-too-brief withdrawals from politics. Cicero appears in Petrarch's *Rerum Memorandarum Libri* and even more in his *De Vita Solitaria* as the historic example of a citizen who became an involuntary witness to the superiority of solitude. Petrarch insists that almost all of Cicero's literary works were written in the *solitudo gloriosa* of his later years. "It was solitude that caused this man's mind to unfold; moreover— this is the strange and wonderful thing—it was a solitude obnoxious to him. What, one may ask, would it not have accomplished if he had desired it? How much should we not long for that which brings such great benefit even to one who is unwilling to endure it?"[33]

The Cicero whom Petrarch admired was Scipio's follower

---

voluisti? Ubi et etati et professioni et fortune tue conveniens otium reliquisti? Quis te falsus glorie splendor . . . ad indignam philosopho mortem rapuit? . . . Ah quanto satius fuerat philosopho presertim in tranquillo rure senuisse, de perpetua illa, . . . non de hac iam exigua vita cogitantem, nullos habuisse fasces, nullis triumphis inhiasse" (Petrarch, *Ep. Fam.* xxiv 3, in Francesco Petrarca, *Le Familiari*, ed. Vittorio Rossi, vol. 4, pp. 226f.).

[33] "Accendit ergo viri illius ingenium solitudo et, quod miraberis, odiosa; quid putas, optanda est que vel nolentibus tantum prodest?" (*De Vita Solitaria*, ed. Martellotti, in *Francesco Petrarca: Prose* [Milan, 1955], 536–38). In the *Rerum Memorandarum Libri*, Petrarch had written: "But what *negotium*, I ask, can be compared with the *otium* of that man [Cicero], what social life with his solitude? However grievously he himself might bewail the ruin of his *patria*, it was the same event that caused the monuments of Cicero's divine genius to reach all nations" (*Rerum Memorandarum Libri*, ed. Billanovich [Florence, 1943], 5: "Sed quod negotium, queso, cum illius otio, que frequentia cum illius solitudine conferenda est? Quam licet ipse casum patrie miseratus graviter defleat, inde tamen ad omnes populos perventura divini ingenii monimenta fluxerunt").

in the praise of true *otium*. Like earlier medieval writers, he adopted St. Jerome's and Theophrastus' description of the "wise man" as one for whom solitude means escape from women, marriage, and communal life. But (also following and developing medieval practice) it is the Scipio of the *De Officiis* of whom Petrarch is most fond. Indeed, in his *De Vita Solitaria* he calls Scipio the "standard-bearer" (*signifer*) of a humanistic *otium*, because for him, too, the highest aim of leisure is intense intellectual activity. Scipio's paradox, set down in the *De Officiis*, is a recurrent theme in the *De Vita*. His words make clear, says Petrarch, what he himself (Petrarch) meant by solitude. He did not mean relaxation or idleness but the concentration of all mental faculties to a higher degree than was possible amid the distractions of civic life. "The body may take its holidays, but the mind must not rest in *otium* longer than is necessary to restore its energy." True *otium*, says Petrarch, is "not inactive and useless but makes use of solitude in service to others"—service rendered by literary activity.[34]

In certain respects, this was both the highpoint of Cicero's medieval influence and the beginning of a development reaching beyond medieval tradition. In his *De Otio Religioso* Petrarch interpreted literary solitude and monastic seclusion from one and the same psychological angle. A quiet, comfortable life, free from anxiety, he said, is as harmful to a solitary man as it is to a man of the world. Struggle and exertion are necessary to test the powers of every human being. The decline and fall of the Roman Empire is lasting proof of the dangers of peace and quietude. When Rome no longer had to struggle for its existence, carefree security and thirst for pleasure and luxury destroyed the energy of the Roman people.[35]

In referring to Roman history as proof of the necessity of inner struggle, Petrarch reveals the subtle connection between

[34] *Rer. Mem.*, 4; *De Vita Solitaria*, ed. Martellotti, 550–58; *Epistolae Seniles* II, 5.

[35] *De Otio Religioso*, ed. G. Rotondi (1958), 20; in *Opera* (Basel, 1581), 301. On the consequences for the humanistic and Renaissance view of history, see Essay Two, pp. 25f.

his conception of active leisure and his idea of the civic world of Rome. Here as elsewhere he is still on medieval ground; but the seeds he has let drop only await a propitious wind to carry them to more fertile soil. Petrarch rejected a life of active involvement in communal and family affairs, but he praised intellectual activity in *otium* more highly than had anyone since Roman times. When this praise finally gained the approbation of active citizens, the time was at hand for a full return to ancient Roman values. At that point, the slow process of medieval change became a rapid transformation.

The old conception of the Renaissance as a relatively sudden break with medieval tradition was not altogether wrong, as we shall see in other contexts as well.[36] But it was wrong insofar as that break was dated too early. A true upheaval in intellectual life did indeed take place, but not until the end of the fourteenth century; not until Petrarch's humanism was finally transplanted to civic surroundings—first and foremost in Florence.

VI

Coluccio Salutati, Petrarch's admirer and an ardent Florentine patriot (chancellor of Florence from 1375 to 1406), was the first of the citizen-humanists. In his youth Salutati had intended to reply to Petrarch's idealization of the solitary life with a book to be entitled *De Vita Associabili et Operativa*. This work was never published, but Salutati's sympathy with the Roman civic spirit soon showed itself on another occasion. Just as Petrarch had unexpectedly found himself face to face with the real Cicero thanks to his discovery of the *Epistolae ad Atticum*, so Cicero was revealed to Salutati in 1392 by the discovery of the *Epistolae Familiares*. But whereas Petrarch's initial joy had quickly turned to disappointment, the Florentine chancellor honored those very Ciceronian traits which Petrarch had considered unworthy of a philosopher. He admired

---

[36] Especially in Essay Seven, pp. 189f., and Essay Nine, p. 226.

Cicero's role in political life, his participation in the civil wars, and his thirst for political renown.

Had Cicero not said that no one ought to remain a private individual when civic liberty is at stake? Salutati understood him well. He justified Cicero's actions during the civil wars by pointing out that, according to the *Noctes Atticae* of Gellius, Solon had decreed in Athens that a citizen who continued to lead a private life in times of civil unrest should be considered unfaithful to his city and expelled.[37] Cicero had thus not been oblivious to the duties of a "wise man" when he took part in the struggle for the liberty of the *respublica*. He had acted as a true philosopher and as a Roman citizen, like Brutus and Cassius, neither of whom thought it permissible to retire into solitude while the world was in flames.[38]

A few years later, one of Salutati's disciples, Pier Paolo Vergerio, wrote a reply, in Cicero's name, to Petrarch's letter of accusation to Cicero in Hades. It was the true voice of a Roman citizen that spoke "from the Elysian fields." "Why did you forsake the calm so becoming to your age, your position, and the tenor of your life?" Petrarch had indignantly asked his master. "The nature of my *otium*, my age, position, and lot," Vergerio makes Cicero reply, "required me to live my life in the midst of activity." Philosophy and culture, Vergerio's Cicero insists, "were not meant to serve my own self-gratifying leisure but to be used for the benefit of the community. It has always seemed to me that the most mature and best philoso-

[37] *Ep.* VIII 7 (1392), in vol. 2 of Salutati's *Epistolario*, ed. Novati, 389; *Ep.* IX 3 and 4 (both between 1392 and 1394), in vol. 3 of *Epistolario*, 25f and 50.

[38] To understand the background of Salutati's thinking, we should recall the following episode: When, about 1377, one of the leading Florentine patricians of Salutati's generation, the jurist Lapo da Castiglionchio the Elder, composed a book of paternal instruction for his son, he referred in the introduction to Cicero-Macrobius' "sentenza" in the *Somnium Scipionis*, which claims that there is a place in heaven "al quale non può andare alcuno nè entrare per alcuna altra virtù, se non solo coloro che la loro Republica consigliano, ajutano e difendono." See Lapo da Castiglionchio, *Epistola a Bernardo suo figlio*, ed. L. Mehus (Bologna, 1753), 2. Concerning the date of Lapo's writing, see Mehus' introduction, viii.

phy is that which dwells in cities and flees solitude [*philosophia quae in urbibus habitat et solitudinem fugit*]." Cicero, writes Vergerio, upheld the doctrine that he is worthiest "who takes upon himself work for the state and the cares demanded by the *salus omnium*." Thus Vergerio's Cicero maintains that he worked for the *respublica* as long as any citizen could work for her. When Caesar established his tyranny, Roman citizens were not allowed to ask whether he was a great man or "full of clemency." They had to face the fact that Caesar had made the state—which "the law and the senate" were called upon to govern—dependent on the clemency or cruelty of a single man.[39]

Shortly before 1415 Leonardo Bruni, Salutati's disciple and Vergerio's friend, composed his biography of Cicero—the standard biography for the Renaissance—on this foundation.[40] The work was entitled *Cicero Novus*, because it was intended to replace Plutarch's *Lives of Demosthenes and Cicero*, which had been translated into Latin some years before[41] and seemed to Bruni to favor the Greek orator. But the title *Cicero Novus* also had a deeper meaning. In contrast to the "old Cicero" of the Middle Ages and of Petrarch, this "new Cicero" of the Florentine Renaissance was no longer assumed to show a contradiction between his political career, full of calamitous passions, and his fruitful philosophic life in a haven of quiet solitude. It continued the trend of thought revealed by the anonymous Italian biographer at the beginning of the fourteenth century. The new conception of Cicero was based on acceptance of the ideal union of political action and literary creation represented by the Roman statesman-writer's life.

[39] Vergerio's *Epistolario*, ed. L. Smith, Fonti per la storia d'Italia, vol. 74 (1934), 439ff.

[40] Bruni must have become familiar with Vergerio's fictitious Cicero letter about the time he wrote his biography, because he writes with amusement in his *Ep.* IV 4, dated Florence, 2 January 1416 (ed. Mehus, vol. 1, p. 111), that "not long ago in Arezzo" he, Bruni, had seen a letter in which Cicero was replying to Petrarch.

[41] By Jacopo Angeli da Scarperia.

"No one who sees Cicero's literary legacy," says Bruni admiringly, "would believe that he had any time for people; and no one who reads about his political activities, his speeches, occupations, and struggles both in public and in private life, would ever imagine that he had leisure for reading and writing."

In Bruni's view, the explanation for this exemplary feat lay in the discovery that Cicero's literary and political activities were two facets of one and the same lifework: the labor of a Roman citizen for his *patria*. One must not look upon Cicero's life, the *Cicero Novus* suggests, as if his political activities had been followed and, as it were, replaced in his later years by philosophical studies in solitude. Rather, one must understand that the Roman statesman was guided in all his occupations by his civic philosophy. "From the selfsame sanctuary of philosophy he took the factual knowledge needed for the administration of the republic and the expressions and phrases used in his writings and teaching." This double engagement gave Cicero his strength. "Despite the great claims made on him by a state that ruled the world," he was able "to write more than philosophers whose lives are spent in leisure and study; and conversely, despite his intense preoccupation with studying and writing, he was able to do more active work than those who are not burdened with literary matters." This is the key to Cicero's place in history. His life was a twofold attainment for Rome: As a consul and orator he served his state, and as a thinker and writer he created a Latin philosophy previously unknown to the Roman world. "Thus he alone, of all men, I believe, has lived up to the two greatest and most difficult tasks."[42]

From this time on,[43] Cicero taught the Italy of the Renais-

[42] "Ita solus, ut credo, hominum duo maxima munera et difficillima adimplevit" (Bruni, in his *Cicero Novus seu Ciceronis Vita*, in *Leonardo Bruni Aretino, Humanistisch-philosophische Schriften*, 114f.).

[43] A scholarly amplification of Bruni's biographical outline—revealing, like Bruni's work, the mature historical consciousness of the fifteenth century—was the voluminous biography of Cicero in Sicco Polenton's *Scriptorum Illus-*

sance two things: that a citizen's primary task is to serve his ✓
community; and that active participation in state affairs need
not diminish his intellectual powers, indeed it may even stimulate them. A generation later, these same concepts were used
by Giannantonio Campano in his biography of Enea Silvio
Piccolomini (who became Pope Pius II) to define the significance of one of the great figures of the century. It is amazing,
Campano tells us, that despite his many papal duties Pius
should have found time to write, and that, conversely, such a
prolific writer should have found time for action. It is a measure of the greatness of this man that "as a writer he accomplished more than others who do nothing during their lives
but write."[44]

It was in civic circles, however, that these ideas called forth
the strongest response. Perhaps more than any other Italian
city, including Florence, fifteenth-century Venice was the
counterpart to the Rome of Cicero's day. Like the latter, the
city-state of Venice was ruled by noble patricians whose lives
were spent in the administration of a vast Mediterranean em-

---

trium Latinae Linguae Libri XVIII, Lib. x–xvi. Taking Bruni's idea of Cicero
as his starting point, Sicco endeavored to collect every single fact concerning
Cicero's career as a writer, orator, and statesman in order to create a biography as comprehensive as Cicero's historical personality. He himself says that
originally he had not planned to include a life of Cicero, because it had been
done so well by Bruni, but finally yielded to the urging of his son and friends.
For Sicco, as for Bruni, Cicero's literary *otium* in his old age was not a haven
he should never have shunned, but one to which he returned "when contrary
winds and waves prevented him from sailing to the destination he had fixed
for himself." The activities of the *forum* and *curia* were then replaced by philosophic studies, "ut scribendo saltem prodesset quibus dicendo, ut soleret,
bene consulere tempora prohiberent" (Polenton, *Scriptorum*, ed. B. L. Ullman, Papers and Monographs of the American Academy in Rome, vol. 6
[1928], xiv, 265f., 407, 408). The final version of the *Scriptorum Illustrium* was
written in 1437 (according to Ullman, p. xxxi).

[44] Berthe Widmer, *Enea Silvio Piccolomini in der sittlichen und politischen
Entscheidung* (Basel, 1963), 20–21, to whom we owe this extension of our fifteenth-century evidence, states rightly that, although Campano's knowledge
of the *Cicero Novus* cannot be proved by external evidence, the influence of
Bruni's view is unmistakable.

pire and who endeavored to combine their political activities with a civic culture. In 1417, Francesco Barbaro, an early patrician champion of Humanism in Venice, observed that a beneficial admiration for the culture and political teachings of Antiquity had begun to pervade the Venetian aristocracy. Even though Venetian citizens might become efficient without being taught, he said, Roman teachings and examples would make them "wiser and more courageous rulers of their state." To a friend who had been appointed governor of Zara in Venetian Dalmatia, Barbaro sent a copy of a letter concerning the administration of Roman provinces which Cicero had written to his brother Quintus. Those of us who read Cicero's writings, Barbaro remarked, will be indebted to the Roman writer, for we will render better service to our republic.[45]

In the following year, when another member of the Venetian nobility, Leonardo Giustiniani, delivered the funeral sermon for a great Venetian statesman, Carlo Zeno, he described the life of the deceased much as Cicero himself would have done. After devoting the best years of his life to the state, Zeno had withdrawn into *otium* and humanistic studies. But in these studies "he exercised due measure, so that he never failed to be available when his counsel was needed by the state or his friends." He applied *otium ad negotia*, becoming perfect in both, so that he remained useful to his community in his old age. It was in this Venetian atmosphere that Barbaro renewed Cicero's formula, proclaiming it the task of Venetian citizen-humanists "to bring philosophy out of the gloomy depths of the study . . . into the fighting line and the center of the conflict."[46]

Florence, the foremost seat of civic culture in the fifteenth century, was to bring the revival of Cicero's Roman influence

[45] R. Sabbadini, ed., *Centotrenta lettere inedite di Francesco Barbaro* (Salerno, 1884), no. 1.

[46] L. Giustiniani's *Funebris Oratio*, in Muratori, *Scriptores Rerum Italicarum*, vol. 19, col. 375f.; *Centotrenta lettere di Barbaro*, no. 95; Card. A. M. Quirini, ed., *Francisci Barbari Epistolae* (1743), Appendix, no. 50. For Cicero's wording as a model, see p. 101 above.

to its climax. Soon after 1400, Florentines of the old stamp began to complain that the younger generation was using Cicero's *De Officiis* to defend the thesis that "happiness and virtue are bound up with political position and reputation." In the eyes of their elders, these younger men were forgetting the philosophic truth that the "perfect life" is one of contemplation and peace of mind.[47] But such protests were of no avail. By the 1430s Matteo Palmieri, Bruni's closest follower among the citizen-humanists, was to re-create the civic attitude of the *De Officiis* in its entirety. As St. Ambrose had done at the beginning of the Middle Ages when he composed a *De Officiis* for use by the clergy (*De Officiis Ministrorum*), Palmieri produced an adaptation of the Ciceronian work tailored to the needs of his own century. This Quattrocento version was entitled *Vita Civile* (*Civic Life*).

It would require too much space to trace in detail the restoration in Palmieri's book of the Ciceronian faith in action and communal values. In brief, he maintains that virtue in the full sense cannot be attained in solitude. It "will never become perfect unless it is challenged; loyalty is recognized not in those who carry no burden but in those to whom great matters are entrusted."[48] Palmieri's concluding chapter, as we have seen in another context,[49] is profoundly impressive, for it combines the vision of the *Somnium Scipionis* with the doctrines of the *De Officiis*. He transfers Scipio's dream from Roman to Florentine conditions. In place of the younger Scipio

[47] Cino Rinuccini, *Invettiva contro a cierti calunniatori di Dante . . . Petrarcae . . . Boccaci*, in A. Wesselofsky, *Il Paradiso degli Alberti* (Bologna, 1867), vol. I, pt. 2, app. 17, p. 314. For more details, see Essay Six, p. 137.

[48] Fuller discussions of the *Vita Civile* will be found in Essays Six and Nine. More recently, a useful epitome of the work has been provided by August Buck's "Palmieri als Repräsentant des Florentiner Bürgerhumanismus," *Archiv für Kulturgeschichte* 47 (1965), reprinted in Buck's *Die humanistische Tradition in der Romania* (Bad Homburg v. d. H., 1968), 253–70. The first words of the *Vita Civile*, in which Palmieri describes the ideal union of a civic and studious life, almost literally repeat, without acknowledging it, the introductory words of the *De Oratore*.

[49] See Essay One, pp. 21f.

Africanus, Dante (who as the wanderer through heaven and hell is best qualified to report on the rewards of souls after death and thus on the ultimate values of life) receives a message from the hereafter. It reaches him on the battlefield of Campaldino, on the day of one of the greatest Florentine victories. This message is nothing but the Ciceronian teaching from the *Somnium Scipionis*. "I saw in heaven [says Dante's fallen friend, returned to life for one short hour] the souls of all the citizens who had ruled their states justly, and among them I recognized Fabricius, Curius, Fabius Maximus, Scipio, Metellus, and many others who for the sake of their country forgot themselves and their possessions." They taught that "no human work is more valuable than concern for the welfare of the *patria*, the maintenance of the *città*, and the preservation of unity and harmony in a rightly ordered community."[50]

From the libraries and studies where Cicero's dialogues were read and adapted to Florentine needs, we step out into the Piazza della Signoria, the center of Florence's political life. There, in 1427, the *capitano del popolo*—a Roman, Stefano Porcari, as we know—delivered an oration before the public authorities. The *capitano* was always a citizen from another city, who occupied his high office for a limited period; nevertheless, Porcari can serve as a spokesman for Florence, because by his own admission his ideas were deeply indebted to his present environment. His speech was full of admiration for the state, the prosperity, and the public spirit of Florence. In such surroundings, said the *capitano del popolo*, a citizen ought to feel that he owes his happiness and his intellectual and material possessions entirely to the community. Even in solitude no good citizen should forget his duty to be grateful. Porcari recalled the example of Scipio Africanus Maior, quoting the paradox of Scipio's tireless activity in leisure as it was handed down by Cicero. In his speech, all the medieval, monastic modifications of Scipio's words are forgotten. The fifteenth-

[50] *Vita Civile*, ed. Gino Belloni (Florence, 1982), 201ff., 208.

century humanist interprets Cicero as follows: Scipio's saying means that in the silence of his solitude "he was wont to think of the incomparable and glorious gifts he had received from the commonwealth. He thus spurred on his energies in order to deserve those gifts by his deeds and persistent efforts."[51]

This uncompromisingly civic interpretation not only went in the direction that Cicero the Roman statesman had indicated, it actually went beyond the ideas expressed in the *De Officiis*. Anyone acquainted with the long historical process we have been reviewing cannot but recognize the advent of an age which was more akin to that of ancient Rome than all the centuries of the Middle Ages. Petrarch's conception of a Scipio discovering after his victories that philosophical studies in solitude have equal or even higher rank for the noble mind than victories and honors, lost its power in the fifteenth century. When it was not interpreted as the paradigmatic story of a citizen returning to his civic duties with renewed strength after a pause for lonely, studious concentration,[52] the old symbol of Scipio's flight into solitude was abandoned altogether in favor of the ideal of a civic culture without need for bookish or contemplative retreat after periods of action but rather thriving amid the activities of daily life.

It was Pier Paolo Vergerio who first directed this challenge against the Ciceronian idea of Scipio's "leisure." In Vergerio's *De Ingenuis Moribus et Liberalibus Studiis Adolescentiae* (the first comprehensive outline of humanistic pedagogy, written in

---

[51] Edited (but attributed to a wrong author) in *Prose del giovane Buonaccorso da Montemagno* (1874), 18. On Porcari's authorship, see G. Zaccagnini, in *Studi di Letteratura Italiana* 1 (1899): 339ff. In another speech on the piazza, Porcari also cited in extenso the dictum from the *Somnium Scipionis* that a special place in heaven awaits those who have acted for their states, because to God nothing is "acceptius quam concilia coetusque hominum iure sociati, quae civitates appellantur" (*Prose del giovane*, 93).

[52] See Guarino da Verona (*Ep.* 681, before 1441, in *Epistolario*, ed. Sabbadini, vol. 2, p. 272): when Scipio and Laelius sought relaxation in the countryside, "nec ut laborem fugerent et inertiae sese dederent eos id factitasse constat, sed ut recentiores et ad novum laborem instauratiores se redderent otiabantur."

1402 after an extended sojourn in Florence), the *otium* of Scipio is cited as an example not to be followed by ordinary men. After a life of exceptional exertion, Scipio Africanus, a man of unique virtue, could retreat into solitude at an advanced age, "yet he who . . . knows how to maintain his solitude amid the turbulence of crowds, his inner calm in the midst of action, does not seem to me to be of lesser worth." Vergerio's advice was to preserve one's natural elasticity within the framework of daily life by gymnastic exercises, hunting, and fishing. If this were done, a retreat into solitude would prove superfluous. The symbol of Scipio, renewing his energy in loneliness, was replaced by that of Cato; for Cato, wrote Vergerio, devoted himself to his studies in the midst of public affairs. He learned to study in the *curia* while the senate was assembling. In this way he made himself fit not only for giving practical advice in questions of the moment but for laying down political principles that would benefit his *patria* for all time.[53]

What was this fifteenth-century humanistic ideal but the old doctrine voiced by the orator Marcus Crassus in Cicero's *De Oratore*? "What cannot be learned quickly," Crassus had said, "will never be learned at all."[54] A citizen should therefore not withdraw from civic duties to scholarly isolation, it was asserted in the *De Oratore*. His fellow citizens should never feel that he was devoting himself to study.

In 1421 a complete text of the *De Oratore* was discovered in the cathedral library of Lodi in northern Italy. From then on Crassus' words, which like many others had been missing from the manuscripts known to the Middle Ages, were read

[53] "Unde nimirum et in rem praesentem, et in omne tempus saluberrima patriae consilia dictabat" (*De Ingenuis Moribus*, ed. A. Gnesotto, in *Atti e Memorie della R. Accad. di Padova* 34 [1918]: 119 and 142). For Cicero on Cato, see p. 101 above. Concerning the date of the *De Ingenuis Moribus*, see my *Crisis*, 2d ed., 494, n. 20.

[54] ". . . ut, nisi quod quisque cito potuerit, numquam omnino possit perdiscere" (*De Oratore* III.22.82–83, 89). For Cicero on Crassus, see note 60 below.

anew.[55] The rediscovery of the complete *De Oratore* not only gave rise to the development of new principles in the pedagogy of the Renaissance but also helped lead to a historical reinterpretation of Dante: Cicero, whose strength lay in his power to evoke the great figures of Roman history, taught Florentine citizens how to contemplate the greatest figure of their own past. Seen in the light of Ciceronian concepts and presented in Ciceronian terms, Dante came to symbolize for the Florentines the highest values in a citizen's life.[56]

To the fourteenth century Dante had been a philosopher aloof from the ordinary world. The chronicler Giovanni Villani[57] had written that he was "presumptuous and reserved because of his learning, careless of graces as philosophers are," and "not very good at conversing with the unlearned."[58] Boccaccio, moreover, had reproached the Florentine poet for not having kept to the retired life of a philosopher. In his biography of Dante, Boccaccio described Dante's misfortunes as those of a philosopher who forgot in the civic atmosphere of Florence "what obstacles to a studious life women are" and that philosophy cannot be at home in a mind made restless by political ambition. Thus Dante had lost his intellectual peace through marriage and had entered the maelstrom of domestic and public cares.[59]

The strong revival of civic ideals in fifteenth-century Florence led Leonardo Bruni to reconstruct Dante's political ca-

---

[55] Paragraphs 18–109 of the third book of the *De Oratore* were unknown during the Middle Ages. See R. Sabbadini, *Le scoperte dei codici latini e greci ne' secoli XIV e XV*, vol. 1 (1905), 100 and 218.

[56] As already sketched briefly in Essay One, pp. 19f.

[57] Giovanni Villani on Dante, in his *Cronaca*, Lib. IX, p. 136.

[58] That Villani's view reflects a typical attitude in the Florence of his time is confirmed by what Trecento writers tell us about Dante's friend, the learned poet Guido Cavalcanti, who in Compagni's chronicle is called a "giovane gentile, cortese, ardito, ma *sdegnoso e solitario e intento allo studio* [my emphasis]"; in Boccaccio's *Decamerone*, novella VI, 9, Cavalcanti appears as "molto astratto dagli uomini."

[59] Boccaccio's reproaches against Dante are found in his *Trattatello in laude di Dante*, as well as in his *Compendio della origine, vita, costumi e studii di Dante*.

reer and his part in the citizen army during the battle of Campaldino. Bruni's *Vita di Dante* (written in 1436) not only stressed these aspects of Dante's life but pointed out that the poet had also had a wife and children, like any true citizen. The greatest philosophers—Aristotle, Cicero, Cato, Seneca, and Varro—wrote Bruni in his *Vita*, had been heads of families and had served their states. Petrarch had lived for himself. Dante's life could teach citizens that true intellectual work need not lead to idle solitude. After the battle of Campaldino Dante "applied himself to his studies with greater zeal than ever; yet he did not neglect intercourse with his fellow citizens. And it was a marvelous thing that although Dante studied continuously, nobody would have got the impression that he was studying."[60]

"And here," said Bruni, "I would like to rectify the mistake of many ignorant people. They believe that no one is a student who does not bury himself in solitude and leisure. Among the stay-at-homes, withdrawn from human society, I have never seen one who could count to three. A lofty and distinguished mind does not need such fetters. On the contrary, the right conclusion is that whatever does not find expression at once will never do so."[61]

Thus, in creating a new image of Dante, Bruni brought back the ideas, and even some of the words, of the *De Oratore*, not merely by imitating a literary model but by extending and transforming them under the influence of the naïve yet powerful self-confidence of fifteenth-century Florence. These reinforced Ciceronian notions about the proper conduct of

[60] We recall that Cicero had reported about Marcus Crassus that he "does not give others the impression that he is studying when he is pursuing his philosophic studies," and that he himself (Cicero) "had been studying philosophy most earnestly at the very time when I seemed to be doing so least." For Cicero, see p. 101 above.

[61] "E era cosa miracolosa, che, studiando continovamente, a niuna persona sarebbe paruto, che egli studiasse. . . . Anzi è vera conclusione e certissima, che quello, che non appara tosto, non appara mai" (Bruni's *Le Vite di Dante e di Petrarca*, in Bruni, *Humanistisch-philosophische Schriften*, 53f.).

citizens would henceforth subtly influence the Florentines whenever they considered their great men. When Poliziano wrote to Piero de' Medici about the qualifications that had made Cosimo great, he praised him not only for never being idle and for doing countless things, but especially for being able to give others the impression that he had "nothing to do."[62]

VII

Not long after Poliziano drew this picture of Cosimo de' Medici, the civic strain in Florentine thought began to weaken under the impact of rising Neoplatonism. During the period in which Marsilio Ficino was the leading philosopher of Florence, the attitude toward Cicero as the acknowledged standard-bearer of Roman values began to change in intellectual circles. In Cristoforo Landino's *Camaldulensian Disputations*, a work with strong Neoplatonic overtones written in the mid-1470s, a life of philosophic contemplation is again prized over involvement in the *vita activa politica*. In comparing the two ways of life, Landino concludes that Cicero's achievements are exemplary by either standard but that the different results obtained in his labors allow us to make a choice. For one cannot deny that humanity is most indebted to Cicero not for his stand against Catilina or Anthony, or for his efforts to restore liberty to his fellow citizens, but for the intellectual work which he performed while living "far from political affairs, entirely preoccupied with important inquiries. . . . The difference between his outstanding actions and his inspired research, then, is evident: With the first he helped only one state, with the latter he has given instruction to all who can read Latin. By his prudent counsel he managed to ward off

---

[62] "Non cessat . . . et cum tam multas res agat, deesse tamen videtur quod agat" (in a letter published in Angelo Fabroni's *Magni Cosmi Medicei Vita*, vol. 2 [Pisa, 1788], 251).

momentary dangers; but what he wrote as a result of his meditations and inquiries is relevant to all ages."[63]

In Landino's eyes—and probably in the eyes of many members of Ficino's circle—Cicero's life teaches us "that those who spend their time in action are certainly useful, but only to contemporaries or at most for a short time. Those, however, who bring to light the hidden nature of things will always be useful. Deeds do not outlive their authors, but thoughts live on through the centuries; they are immortal and have the flavor of eternity."[64] What is remarkable in this reaction of a late Quattrocento Florentine writer is his failure to ask whether Cicero's experiences as an active statesman and citizen did not condition the Roman's thinking and give his writing its peculiar strength and depth. It is as if Landino were talking about two different people. For the first time, a serious regression threatened the long historical progress that had been made toward a fuller grasp of human nature as it reacts to the challenges of life.

Neoplatonism, a constant element of Renaissance thought from that time on, never wholly dominated the Florentine or broader Italian scene. Indeed, the generation of Machiavelli reacted violently against the Neoplatonic depreciation of the

[63] "At vide, quid inter illas praeclarissimas actiones et has divinas speculationes intersit! Illis enim uni civitati profuit, his vero omnibus, qui latine norunt, praecepta tribuit; illis, quae consilio et prudentia egit, maxima quae tunc urgebant pericula propulsavit, quae autem investigando litteris mandavit, in omne tempus prospiciunt, ut non modo praesentibus et qui tunc vivebant consuleret, sed et iis, qui hactenus per tot iam saecula fuerunt, et iis, qui posthac futuri erunt, ad bene beateque vivendum praecepta reliquerit" (*Quaestiones Camaldulenses*, "Liber primus de vita contemplativa et activa," ed. Peter Lohe [Florence, 1980], 43–44). Cf. also the perceptive discussion of these passages in E. Garin's *L'Umanesimo italiano: Filosofia e vita civile nel Rinascimento*, new ed. (Bari, 1964), 101f.

[64] "Quapropter ex his sic universus locus concluditur: qui in actionibus versantur, prodesse quidem, sed aut ad praesens aut ad breve tempus, qui autem naturam rerum in obscuro abditam in lucem nobis proferunt, eos semper profuturos. Actiones enim una cum hominibus suum finem sortiuntur. Speculationes autem cuncta saecula vincendo inmortales perdurant et aeternitati aequantur" (*Quaestiones Camaldulenses*, loc cit.).

world of action and social obligation. The traditions of early Quattrocento Humanism were at no time totally abandoned, and in particular, Dante's life and work remained for Renaissance readers and writers the epitome of what the Ciceronian ideal of the citizen seemed to teach. Bruni's biography of Dante was circulated more widely and used more frequently than any other writing of the early Renaissance. Almost every biographer of the poet leaned heavily on Bruni during the fifteenth and sixteenth centuries: Giannozzo Manetti in the age of Cosimo, Giammario Filelfo and Cristoforo Landino in the very period of Florentine Neoplatonism, and Alessandro Vellutello of Lucca, the well-known commentator of the *Divina Commedia*, during the first half of the sixteenth century.[65] All of these writers accepted the conception of Dante as a symbol of union between thought and action, studious and civic life; all were dependent, through Bruni, on Cicero's *De Oratore*.

After fifteen centuries, the ideal Cicero had established for Roman citizens was thus restored, re-created in fifteenth-century Florence in the image of the Florentine poet.

[65] According to Vellutello, Filelfo had simply reproduced Bruni, Landino had had too much confidence in Boccaccio's "leggerezze," but Bruni had formed his judgments "da vero istorico." Indeed, Vellutello followed Bruni so closely in his *vita* of Dante—as Michele Barbi judged (*Della fortuna di Dante nel secolo XVI* [Pisa, 1890], 81)—"da trascriverlo poco meno che a parola dal principio alla fine."

SIX

The Florentine Revival of the Philosophy of the Active Political Life*

I

WHAT set the Florentine humanists apart from most of those outside Florence was not so much their memory of Cicero's civic spirit as their revival of the entire ancient philosophy of the active political life, a revival which sometimes went even beyond the Greek and Roman models in its consistency. This process began with the generation after Petrarch, in which Coluccio Salutati was the leading Florentine figure.

To say that Salutati was the first to give literary expression to the thought that a life spent in civic and political activity was equal in value to the *vita solitaria et contemplativa* would be an exaggeration.[1] For this would slight the fact that Salutati's vindication of the *vita activa politica* failed to become an integral part of his philosophy and does not appear in the appropriate places; that is, in his treatises on morals. Instead, we encounter it in his letters, on occasions when literary adversaries or friends too insistently adhered to the traditional ways

---

* Originally written in Italian and published under the title "La Rinascita dell'etica statale romana nell'umanesimo fiorentino del quattrocento," in the periodical *Civiltà Moderna* 7 (Florence, 1935). That version included six introductory pages on the memory of Cicero from late Antiquity through the early Renaissance, now omitted as redundant after the more extensive presentation of the same topic in Essay Five. The last eight pages, dealing with the memory of Cato of Utica from the Trecento to the Cinquecento, have similarly been excluded from the present English version, which is a translation of most of the remainder of the essay, at times differing in emphasis or formulation but otherwise reproducing the original as it was initially conceived.

[1] What follows modifies somewhat the view of the historical position of Salutati given in the Italian version of this essay in 1935.

of thinking.[2] Nothing demonstrates the limitations of his defense better than the knowledge that in 1372, while Petrarch was still alive, Salutati began to compose a treatise *De Vita Associabili et Operativa*, either in opposition to Petrarch's *De Vita Solitaria* or with the intention of enlarging the horizon of Petrarch's work. Presumably because the religious preference for contemplation and the traditional identification of religious contemplation with the philosophical views of medieval Stoicism still carried much weight, Salutati never finished this book and instead produced, in 1381, a totally different piece of writing entitled *De Saeculo et Religione (On the Secular Life and the Religious Life)*. Since it was composed as a spiritual guide for a friend who had entered a monastery, it cannot be taken as characteristic of the values Salutati considered valid for a layman's existence. Nevertheless, one generation later no Florentine writer of rank would have thought it necessary, or even admissible, to describe the secular and civic world in tones of utter contempt, as Salutati did, in order to exalt by contrast the quietude and unshakable peace of mind found in monastic separation from the *saeculum*.

Such hesitations and reversals show that in essential respects Salutati was a pre-Quattrocento writer, or at least a transitional figure.[3] This should not, however, make us underrate the fact that his correspondence exhibits the first strong opposition of a citizen in an Italian city-state to the old practice of arguing in favor of the *vita contemplativa*. Salutati's rejoinders to adversaries and to the admonitions of friends were meant even more seriously than Petrarch's youthful nibbling at traditional values.[4] Very instructive, for instance, is an oc-

[2] I have pointed out the various, serious limitations of Salutati's apology for the *vita activa politica* in the second (1966) edition of the *Crisis*, in a section added to the chapter dealing with Salutati and Cino Rinuccini, esp. pp. 106ff.

[3] He has now been masterfully described as such in Ronald Witt's *Hercules at the Crossroads: The Life, Works, and Thought of Coluccio Salutati* (Durham, N.C., 1983).

[4] See my later evaluation of such examples from Petrarch's youth, in *Flori-*

casion on which a friend of Salutati's, a notary in Siena, was grieving over the loss of six sons in an epidemic and voiced his desire to leave the misery of this world and become a monk, despite his having been called by the commune of Siena to serve in public office. Do not give way to a momentary impulse and abandon your past activites, Salutati advises. You would be wrong to assume that the peace of monastic solitude will necessarily lead to God along a surer and straighter path. It may be true that the cloistered life has proved the right choice for certain monks who were impelled to it by Christian charity, rather than by weariness and desperation. Yet many others have found a way no less safe, indeed even safer, in the "negociosa et associabilis vita." Honorable activity seems to Salutati to remain "something holy and holier than idleness in solitude [*sanctum forte et sanctius quam solitarium ociari*]. For holy retirement to the countryside benefits only oneself, as the Church Father Jerome says, but active holiness shapes the lives of many by setting examples for a multitude."[5] A few years later, when Pellegrino Zambeccari, a chancellor of Bologna and disciple of Petrarch's who had remained a firm adherent of fourteenth-century Stoicism, tried to persuade his Florentine colleague that even from a moral point of view a superior kind of life could be led in *solitudo*, Salutati countered with a question: Since according to the Christian faith man was meant to gain eternal beatitude, why would nature have created him a social and political animal if life in the company of his fellows were incapable of providing another path to salvation?[6]

On the threshold of the new century (in 1401), Salutati defended humanistic secular culture in his correspondence along the same lines. The Camaldolensian monk Giovanni da Sam-

---

legium Historiale: Essays Presented to Wallace K. Ferguson (Toronto, 1971), 28f. and 30ff.

[5] "Sancta quippe rusticitas solum sibi prodest, ut ille [St. Jerome] ait. Negociosa vero sanctitas multos edificat" (Salutati, *Epistolario*, ed. F. Novati, Fonti per la Storia d'Italia, vol. 2, p. 453; *Ep.* VIII 19).

[6] Salutati, *Ep.* IX 4 (1392–1394), in *Epistolario*, vol. 3, p. 50f.

miniato had objected to the new studies from a monastic point of view. With your proclaimed "sancta rusticitas," Salutati replied, you are useful only to yourself and to a few of your brethren. My objective is to be useful to a wide circle of fellow citizens. Retreat from life may be the "safer" way inasmuch as in the *saeculum* the soul finds itself among things spatially removed from God; but God can be close to man in the midst of worldly activity, in pagan writings, in every place where there is a glimmer of truth, even though it is buried amidst many errors. By fleeing from secular life, a man serves only himself.[7]

When one examines this unusual reaction of a chancellor of Florence on the eve of the Quattrocento, one senses that after the passage of a thousand years an age has reappeared capable of responding to the call to activity and respecting the reality of a life that exemplifies the ethic taught in the *De Officiis*. Indeed, we catch an early glimpse of the revival of interest in the ideas of the *De Officiis* in the generation of Leonardo Bruni, which came into its own at the beginning of the new century. Some young members of that generation believed that Cicero's dialogue taught that happiness and true virtue could be attained by a life of participation in the offices and honors of the community and that it was not necessary, therefore, to forgo worldly possessions and sensuous pleasures. We have already encountered this reaction in the reprobations directed by Cino Rinuccini, a representative of the moral and intellectual attitude of the older generation, against a humanistic circle of younger men who thought that this was precisely the position expressed by *De Officiis*.[8] They seemed to have forgotten, Cino warned, that "human felicity . . . does not lie in riches, honors, or physical delights but in the operation of perfect virtue, in the perfect life that applies itself to contemplation, once the passions have been restrained, and is sufficient unto itself. . . ."[9]

[7] Ibid., 542f.; *Ep.* xII 20 (21 September 1401).
[8] See Essay Five, note 47.
[9] "felicità umana . . . non è nelle richeze nè negli onori nè ne' diletti cor-

The new ideas of life spread despite their incompatibility with long-accepted values, and with them spread the philosophy of the active political life as expounded in the *De Officiis*. Thirty years after Rinuccini, the Ciceronian civic ethic was revived in its entirety by Matteo Palmieri, whose Florentine guide to civic morality, appropriately entitled *Vita Civile*, was patterned after *De Officiis*. Thus the *vita civilis* once again became the model, instead of the ideal of the philosopher-sage. As Palmieri's dialogue puts it, the objective of the *vita civilis* was "the proven life of those virtuous citizens with whom man has often lived on this earth in the past and [with whom he] will be able to live in the future."[10] Exactly as in the *De Officiis*, this "proven life" of citizens engaged in communal affairs refuted the philosophical conceits of Plato. Already in his preface, Palmieri lays down the following principle: "I decided not to describe the imagined perfection of citizens who have never been seen on earth and who, as Plato and other noble minds portrayed and judged them, are perfect in virtue and wisdom because they have been depicted generically and in the abstract rather than having been seen in the flesh."[11]

But what, then, should be done with the Neoplatonic concept of a hierarchy of virtues handed down to early Renaissance humanists through Macrobius' *Somnium Scipionis* and

---

porali, ma è nell'operazioni della virtù perfetta, nella vita perfetta, nella quale, modificate le passioni, attende poi alle contemplazioni, che è contenta di se medesima compognendo leggi a ben vivere" (Cino Rinuccini, *Invettiva contro a certi calunniatori di Dante . . . Petrarca . . . Boccaci*, in A. Wesselofsky, *Il Paradiso degli Alberti* [Bologna, 1867], vol. 1, pt. 2, app. 17, p. 314). On Cino Rinuccini, we now have G. Tanturli's informative paper "Cino Rinuccini e la scuola di Santa Maria in Campo," *Studi Medievali*, 3d ser., 17, 2 (1976): 625–74.

[10] "l'approvata vita de' civili virtuosi coi quali più volti s'è vivuto et potre' vivere in terra" (Palmieri, *Vita Civile* [autograph], Cod. Firenze Bibl. Naz. Centr. II, IV, 81 fol. 2a; now edizione critica by Gino Belloni [Florence, 1982], 7).

[11] "Diliberai non volere fignere la immaginata bontà de' non mai veduti in terra cittadini, i quali, da Platone et più altri nobilissimi ingegni considerati et fincti di virtù et sapientia perfecti, più tosto sono per specie et figura dipincti che mai in carne veduti" (ibid.).

138

accepted in Petrarch's *De Vita Solitaria*? Palmieri learned from this concept that there are other valuable kinds of human existence besides the community life he wanted to revalue; that one must not only distinguish "four qualities of virtue" but must arrange these on an ascending scale: "civic virtues, purgatorial virtues, virtues of minds already purified, and exemplary or truly divine virtues." But he went far beyond the line of thought Petrarch had tried to follow.[12] The stage of "virtù d'animo già purgato," the *Vita Civile* declares, is "like supernal things and not appropriate to man"; it may be excluded, therefore, from practical decisions. Similarly, Palmieri argues that even though the solitary life, the breeding place of the "purgatorial" virtues, raises the spirit and makes us "conoscitori delle cose divine," it also alienates us "from all public action" and trains us to be "of no use in the society of mortals" and "to be concerned only with [our] own salvation." Seen in this light, the Neoplatonic concept of a hierarchy of virtues does not merely allow the conclusion that any of the various ways of life and states of the soul can lead to happiness and the divine—this had already been concluded by Petrarch—it also shows that the civic life must precede any ascent to the virtues of contemplation. One might say, therefore, that the contemplative life ranks *below* civic commitment, because it is "postposta a questa." Palmieri concludes by making the words of the *Somnium Scipionis* his own: "The fact remains that one can do nothing on earth that is dearer or more pleasing to God than to rule justly and administer the congregations and multitudes of men who are united by justice. It is for this reason that God promises to just governors of cities and conservators of the *patria* a distinct place in heaven, where they will live in eternal bliss together with his saints."[13]

---

[12] See my comment on Petrarch and Plotinus' hierarchy of the virtues, in *Florilegium Historiale*, 29.

[13] Palmieri, *Vita Civile* (autograph), fol. 21b–22b; ed. Belloni, 54f. As for the date of the *Vita Civile*, there can be little doubt that it was composed in the latter part of the 1430s. The older hypothesis of Vittorio Rossi—1431–1432—was modified in the first edition of the *Crisis* by the suggestion that the

The parallel between Florentine and Ciceronian thinking does not end here. Cicero, to use his own simile, had wanted to bring study and philosophy out of the scholar's den and into the forum in order to eliminate the split (*dissidium*) between philosopher and statesman, and had eventually devised a program for intellectual culture that came close to satisfying the needs of Rome's active citizens. The Florentine humanists of the Quattrocento attempted something similar when they freed early Humanism from its limitation to an exclusive group of scholars and literati: Humanism was to be an education for the citizen as well as a discipline and method for the scholar.

Let us look at a characteristic application of this idea of educating citizens through study. It is found in a source dating from the time shortly after Bruni's appointment as chancellor of Florence—a source we have already made use of in other essays. About 1428, Buonaccorso da Montemagno, who was born in neighboring Pistoia but became a Florentine both legally and in spirit, undertook the task of depicting the exemplary citizen in an altercation (*Disputatio de Nobilitate*) depicting the rivalry between a valiant plebeian and a high-born, idle patrician in ancient Rome. The victor in this dispute, the plebeian, reports that intellectual and moral stimulation were first provided for him by his library. The study of philosophy taught him, he says, that a man who is intellectually prepared must at some point feel driven to take on the commitments of the active political life. Buonaccorso's plebeian victor acts accordingly, convinced that "the talents of mortal men will be-

---

correct date falls "between 1432 and 1436," the fourth book having been added "not much earlier than 1437" (*Crisis*, vol. 2, pp. 583f.). More recently, Gino Belloni showed that it is probable "che nel '37 il terzo libro della *Vita Civile* fosse composto, e che solo tra il '38 e il '40 il trattato fosse terminato [with the fourth book] e dato ai copisti" (in Belloni's "Intorno alla datazione della *Vita Civile* di M. Palmieri," *Studi e Problemi di Critica Testuale* 16 [1978]: 58f.).

come more excellent if they are used for the common-wealth."[14]

Palmieri, as he tells us, learned something similar from history when he searched the classical authors for a clue to the condition of human life that could best give *stabilità* and *costante fermeza* to the mind. His studies taught him that one may regard as "perfect" only the lives of those "who in some excellent republic attain to such a degree of virtue that they can live in the midst of their affairs with dignity, without error or danger, even if they are considered to be idlers [*ociosi*]."[15] In other words, *otium*—which to the humanist means freedom for study and literary pursuits—is not deemed worthy by these citizens of Florence (any more than, centuries before, it had been by Cicero) unless it is part of an existence in which virtuous activity in the community has generated a respect that can make *otium* safe from its inherent dangers.

In Florence, as we have seen, the first important indication of this school of thought had been Bruni's *Cicero Novus*, which depicts Cicero as the historic model of a fruitful union between Roman statesmanship and literary creativity. In this depiction of Cicero's life and work, Bruni had traced Cicero's greatness to his ability, despite his many exertions on behalf of the greatest state in history, to pursue more literary activities of importance than most philosophers manage to do in a lifetime of peace and leisure.[16] The implications of this attitude for a citizen's education have been discussed in the essay on

[14] "praeclariora tum fore mortalium ingenia cum ad rem publicam accommodantur" (Buonaccorso da Montemagno, *De nobilitate tractatus*, in *Prose e Rime de' due Buonaccorsi da Montemagno*, ed. Manni [Florence, 1718], 74f.; Manni's reading "tantum fore" should be corrected, in accordance with the majority of the manuscripts, to read "tum fore"). I have referred briefly to Buonaccorso da Montemagno as a source in Essay One, note 19.

[15] "che in alcuna optima republica tale grado di virtù ritengono che ne' loro facti sanza errore o pericolo, et ociosi, riputati con degnità, possono vivere" (Palmieri, *Vita Civile* [autograph], fol. 1a; ed. Belloni, 4).

[16] H. Baron, ed., *Leonardo Bruni Aretino, Humanistisch-philosophische Schriften* (Leipzig, 1928), 115.

141

the memory of Cicero's Roman civic spirit and need not be reiterated here.

II

One unfinished task left by Cicero to later centuries was the strengthening of his claim for the superiority of the *vita activa politica* by anchoring it firmly in the observation of human conduct. If the equality, or indeed greater desirability, of the active way of life is accepted, must not the value of psychological stimuli also be accepted? Put differently, must not the revaluation of the active political life encourage a sympathetic appreciation of human emotions, appetites, and passions?

In the age of Cicero such a sympathetic appreciation was already at hand thanks to the ethical writings of Aristotle and, sometimes even more effectively, the works of the less doctrinaire Stoics such as Panaitius and Posidonius.[17] But anyone who accepted the Stoic "sage" as a model would have found it difficult to emphasize these psychological aspects of human behavior, because one of the essential marks of the wise man was his dispassion ("apathy") and emotional tranquillity ("ataraxy"). In the *De Officiis* Cicero focused on the "sage" less than he had in his earlier philosophical writings and was much readier to take the civic view of life into account. But this was not the result of a gradual development in his philosophical reasoning. Only a year or two earlier, in his *Tusculans*, he had expressly rejected most of the arguments that Aristotle and the Peripatetic school had put forward for the life of action. What had changed since then was Rome's political situation and with it Cicero's personal situation, due to the assassination of Caesar. Thus, while the *De Officiis* is not a document espousing withdrawal and philosophical leisure, and while it expresses more of the typical Roman values than

---

[17] See Max Pohlenz, "Poseidonius' Affektenlehre und Psychologie" and "Plutarchs Schriften gegen die Stoiker," in Pohlenz, *Kleine Schriften*, vol. 1 (Hildesheim, 1965), 140–71 and 448–80.

do Cicero's other philosophical works except the *De Repub-lica*, its increased emphasis on the active life and its motivations do not bring it into closer relationship with the Aristotelian school. The Peripatetics are still neglected or rejected; that is, high esteem for the role of emotions and passions is still lacking, as well as the Peripatetics' recognition that material possessions may be used for ethical ends.

In contrast to Cicero, fifteenth-century Florentines were keenly aware of the part played "in real life" by psychological forces, as we observed in our analysis of new historical and psychological ways of thinking.[18] The causal explanation of political processes given by Florentine humanists from Bruni onwards depended on this awareness.[19] In addition, the humanistic literature of the early Quattrocento, again with the Florentines in the forefront, is characterized by a continuing polemic against moralistic judgments, insofar as they disregard the demands of "human nature." After 1400, for example, there was frequent criticism of the traditional admonition—always identified with the doctrine of the Stoic school—not to weep or to allow cool reason to be obscured by grief over the deaths of close relatives and friends. Such rationalistic requests, it was argued by the younger generation, first in Florence and later elsewhere in Italy, reveal a lack of *humanitas* as well as of Christian love. And what would we have of the many exemplary deeds which enrich Roman history, that generation asked, if those who performed them had sought ataraxy and, in accordance with doctrinaire philosophy, had tried to suppress justifiable hatred and wrath, ambition, and desire for power? If passion was to be excluded as a moral force, what would become of the warrior's bravery and the will of citizens to oppose injustice or make great sacrifices for their community?

If we wish to understand the humanists of the Florentine Quattrocento, we must explore the motives of the reasoning

[18] See Essay Two, p. 27.
[19] See Essay Two, pp. 29f.

to which they felt compelled when they encountered dispar-
agement of emotional incentives among the ancient authors,
Church Fathers, and those medieval writers who adhered to
the doctrine of the "sage's" obligation to strive for apathy and
ataraxy.

In this connection, let us look more closely at what we
noted previously; namely, the gradual restoration of Cicero's
ranking of the cardinal virtues.[20] In Bruni's and Palmieri's
writings, *iustitia* is once again judged to be the greatest of the
virtues, for the same reason Cicero had advanced: because it
was a community-oriented ethic. This does not mean, however, that the Florentines were merely reiterating what Cicero
or other Roman authors had said. In their writings we find a
striking revaluation of another of the cardinal virtues, that of
fortitudo.

In conformity with the beliefs of late Roman patrician
statesmen, Cicero had never doubted that political and diplomatic action was more suitable to the noble mind and of
greater ethical value than military activity and valor. He
plainly believed that physical courage may equip men for subordinate positions but it is the intellectual activity of the diplomat that guides the affairs of nations.[21] Since armies of Roman citizens were still protecting the republic, Cicero was
here probably following not popular Roman sentiment but
the convictions of Hellenistic philosophy, especially of the
Stoic school, which declared dedication to things of the spirit,
including the intellectual activity of the diplomat, to be unquestionably superior to the soldier's trade.

---

[20] See Essay Five, pp. 98, 105, 108, 112.

[21] "Sed cum plerique arbitrentur res bellicas maiores esse quam urbanas,
minuenda est haec opinio. . . . Vere autem si volumus iudicare, multae res
exstiterunt urbanae maiores clarioresque quam bellicae" (*De Off.* 1.22, 74);
"Sunt igitur domesticae fortitudines non inferiores militaribus; in quibus plus
etiam quam in his operae studiique ponendum est" (ibid., 77–78); "Omnino
illud honestum, quod ex animo excelso magnificoque quaerimus, animi effi-
citur, non corporis viribus. . . . Quare expetenda quidem magis est decer-
nendi ratio quam decertandi fortitudo . . ." (ibid., 23, 79).

Among Florentine humanists of the fifteenth century, the situation was curiously reversed. After the middle of the fourteenth century, Florentine citizens no longer went to battle themselves but sent mercenary troops under famous condottieri hired by the republic. These hired troops had to be kept under close Florentine supervision, and from about 1380 to 1440, when Florence was fighting decisive wars for independence against the state of the Visconti of Milan and against the expansion of the south Italian kingdom while gradually building up its own Tuscan region state, the planning of these wars and control of the hired Florentine troops was given high priority by those serving in the leading offices. Almost to the middle of the Quattrocento, the "Ten of War" (*Dieci della guerra*) was the most respected, and at times the most powerful, office of the republic, and Florentine *commissarii della guerra*, usually members of the foremost families, accompanied the troops, occasionally sharing their life in camp and battle. The fame of some of the best-known Florentines of the period (above all Gino Capponi and Rinaldo degli Albizzi) depended on their military expertise even more than on their diplomatic achievements. It was under the influence of this state of affairs that during the first decades of the fifteenth century there arose in Florence, at least in the stratum of society educated by humanists, a nostalgic admiration for precisely that basis of healthy republican life which was lacking in the Florence of the Renaissance: a militia fighting for its own country.

Along with the ideal of citizens-in-arms, which was widely discussed and extolled by Florentine humanists in those decades,[22] there emerged a belief in the high value of *fortitudo* as a civic virtue. In his oration of 1428 commemorating the Florentine patrician Nanni degli Strozzi, who had died in the previous year while commanding the Ferrarese troops allied with Florence in the Milanese wars, Bruni said that valor is the vir-

---

[22] See *Crisis*, 2d ed., 430ff., and C. C. Bailey, *War and Society in Renaissance Florence: The "De Militia" of Leonardo Bruni* (Toronto, 1961).

tue "which more than any other endows men with glory," and he asserted that "the affairs of war incontrovertibly rank higher than the arts of peace." "Est enim fortitudo splendidissima virtus, ac nescio an supereminentissima virtutum ceterarum, plena spiritus, plena vigoris, plena iustissimae animositatis, mascula profecto quaedam atque invicta."[23] And in 1433, when Palmieri was conceiving his *Vita Civile*, Bruni, who was then chancellor, made the following bold statement in a speech in the Piazza della Signoria: "Learning, literature, eloquence, none of these is equal to glory won in battle. The great philosopher must yield the palm to the great captain; Plato is not to be compared with Alexander, or Aristotle with Caesar. . . . Nor would the birth of Plato in Rome have been of as much benefit to the Romans as was the birth there of Marcus Furius Camillus. . . . Nor would the Italians have benefited as much from Aristotle's birth in Italy as they did from the birth there of Gaius Marius, the great general whose military art and martial virtues put to rout and annihilated the Cimbri and Teutoni."[24]

It would be a mistake to consider these pronouncements merely pompous expressions inspired by a solemn occasion. It was not by chance that such hyperbole, which so visibly conflicted with Cicero's evaluation, should have been ex-

[23] ". . . quae homines magis illustrat quam ulla virtutum ceterarum" and "res bellicae pacis artibus sine controversia praeferuntur" (Bruni, "Oratio in Funere Johannis Strozzae," in Stephanus Baluzius, *Miscellanea*, ed. Mansi, vol. 4 [Lucca, 1764], 5 and 7).

[24] "Né scientia né licteratura né eloquentia alla gloria dell'armi è pari o equale. Ciede il sommo filosafo al sommo capitaneo; né Platone ad Alexandro, né Aristotile a Cesare sono da essere comparati. . . . Né tanta certo utilità sarebbe stata ai Romani Platone esser nato a Roma, quanta fu l'esservi nato Marco Furio Camillo. . . . Né tanta utilità sarebbe stata all'Ytaliani Aristotile in Ytalia nato, quanta fu esservi nato Gaio Mario, dal quale sommo capitano y Cimbri et Teutoni . . . con arte militare et con virtù bellicha furono profugati et spenti" (Bruni, *Ragione detta in presentia della magnifica Signoria et di tutto il popolo in sulla ringhiera, quando si diè il bastone a . . . Nicolò da Tolentino . . . capitano di guerra la mattina di S. Giovanni Batista MCCCCXXXIII*; according to Cod. Laur. 42, c. 10, fol. 18b, which has been compared with other Florentine manuscripts).

pressed by a citizen of Florence. As we have already seen, it was not only practical experience or political judgment that prompted Cicero to value the statesman more than the captain but also, perhaps primarily, the Hellenistic and especially Stoic trend of thought that admired reasoning unaffected by emotion and belittled military life dependent on physical prowess and fervent passion. Under the impact of this attitude, which reflects the evaluation of an intellectual writer, Petrarch in his letter "Qualis esse debeat qui rempublicam regit" still took it for granted that one could philosophically determine the inferiority of the soldier "to the man of civilian affairs"—the very teaching of the *De Officiis*. On this basis he urged Duke Francesco of Ferrara to give his highest favor to jurists and men of letters instead of to military men.[25]

It was in Florentine Humanism that opposition to the Stoic and Ciceronian preference came to the surface, a result of the widely accepted ideal of the active citizen under obligation to serve and defend his state. Assisted by an environment little concerned with traditional and formal philosophy, the Florentine humanists were ready to draw conclusions neither Cicero nor Petrarch had been willing to draw. The rationalism of the Stoic philosophy, which Cicero had accepted to a limited degree, was finally called in doubt by the Florentines. Some of them openly defected from time-honored ways of thinking, seeking a vindication of those appetites and passions without which, as they believed, *fortitudo* and civic zeal could not gain their necessary strength.

Coluccio Salutati, in spite of his own strong leanings toward Stoicism, was the first to suggest that the rigid concept of the *ataraxia* of the sage failed to take into account the needs of civic life. He became conscious of this in regard to the role played by anger (*ira*), the passion that "rational" judgment is bound to find least justifiable. Ever since classical times, Stoic

---

[25] Petrarch, *Ep. Sen.* XIV 1, in *Op. Omnia* (Basel, 1554), vol. 1, p. 433; Italian translation in G. Fracassetti, *Lettere senili di Francesco Petrarca* (Florence, 1870), vol. 2, pp. 375f.

rationalism had protested vehemently against anger. Indeed, during the Middle Ages it was regarded as one of the Seven Deadly Sins. No passion was more repugnant from the viewpoint of the *sapiens* than this momentary excess of emotion which obscured reason. Petrarch, Salutati's revered master, had frequently condemned anger as the passion that destroys free will.[26] What gave the Florentine chancellor the courage to disagree with such authoritative opinion was first of all his Christian conscience. He stressed more than Petrarch the gulf that ought to separate the heart of a Christian from Stoic indifference to the outside world. He felt supported, he once said, by the authority of St. Paul. For in his *Epistle to the Ephesians*,[27] Paul does not forbid Christians to fly into a passion, but merely considers it a sin to allow the sun to set before the anger has been appeased.[28]

Salutati thus became sensitive to the fact that not all philosophers of Antiquity had been opposed to anger. He grew keenly aware of a dispute on this score between the *Stoicorum dogma*, shared by Cicero, Seneca, and Posidonius,[29] and the doctrine of Aristotle and the whole Peripatetic school—the doctrine that it is natural and defensible if, at the right moment and in the right place, we allow ourselves to be impelled by anger; for "not to be angry when it is appropriate seems the conduct of a fool" (*non irasci in quibus oportet, insipientis videtur esse*). Clearly, Salutati found himself in a dilemma and

[26] Especially significant examples are *Ep. Fam.* XII 14 (1352); *Ep. Fam.* XX 14 (1359); sonnet 232, "Vincitore Alessandro. . . ."

[27] In the Epistle to the Ephesians, 4:26.

[28] ". . . dixit Apostolus: irascimini, et nolite peccare: non occidat sol super iracundiam vestram. . . . An autem irasci possimus absque peccato . . . nemini dubium debet esse quod sic. Nam qui rationabiliter commovetur ad iram, secundum viam iusticie et ex iusticie zelo desiderando vindictam omnino non peccat; et qui in fervore iniurie commovetur, sed secum recogitans illi motui non consentit, etiam mortali crimine non tenetur" (Salutati, *Epistolario*, ed. Novati, vol. 2, pp. 309–10). Salutati's observation was later revived by Cristoforo Landino, though without reference to Salutati (see Landino's *De Vera Nobilitate*, ed. M. T. Liaci [Florence, 1970], 108; cf. note 38, below).

[29] His source of information here is Macrobius' commentary.

tried to escape along the same route Palmieri would choose a few decades later: perfect freedom from passion—which Cicero demanded in some of his major writings and which, according to Macrobius, was also Seneca's and Posidonius' guiding norm—must be regarded as an ideal that perhaps no one on this earth, "praeter Salvatorem nostrum," has ever been able to attain. "We can say, therefore, that the latter [the Peripatetic observers of the real world] have spoken according to the general condition and way of mortals, while the former [the Stoics] have come nearer to the truth."[30]

As in all the controversies concerning the *vita activa politica*, the first humanist to tackle this dilemma systematically was Bruni.[31] In his Peripatetically oriented *Isagogicon Moralis Disciplinae* we find an emphasis on fortitude and on the concern needed by those who are responsible for public life. Bruni asks how *fortitudo* and *pietas* could take root if one were never impelled by the passion of *ira*. "Infuriated eyes and trembling lips, incoherent speech, a wild gesticulation of the arms, frantic movements": let the opponents of human emotion paint anger in such colors, but let no one forget what would happen, Bruni warns (as would many a humanist afterwards when appraising *fortitudo* and the social virtues), if this anger, so often reviled, should be weak at those moments when the community and the lives and honor of our loved ones are at stake. Woe to him "who is so insensitive and apathetic that he neither suffers grief nor feels depressed when humiliation is inflicted upon our country, our parents, our children, and others who should be dearest to us." In direct contradiction to the Stoic faith in *ratio*, Bruni believes that "stimuli quidam et motus animi vehementiores, . . . qui nos ad pietatem fortitu-

---

[30] "Unde dicere possumus secundum communem mortalium condicionem et cursum hos locutos; illos autem ad rei veritatem propius accessisse" (Salutati, *Epistolario*, ed. Novati, vol. 2, pp. 309–10).

[31] We resume in what follows the analysis of the role played by anger (*ira*) in the ethical reflections of the Florentines from Bruni onward; this distinctive feature of civic thought was first mentioned in Essay Two, pp. 29f.

dinemque impellunt" in such cases are sometimes helpful and appropriate.[32]

From this point on, while humanists outside of Florence long continued to inveigh against anger on the grounds that it obscures and destroys reason,[33] Florentine writers tended to praise this passion as an indispensable aid to the virtues that are most admirable and important in civic life. We find Bruni's disciple Palmieri distinguishing between a blind fury that serves no purpose and the great and beneficial passion that every soldier needs in battle. "The anger which may arise in the course of a deed—since it is virtue that has made us choose danger—can be of great help to valor. So the rear troops of an army, indignantly moved to anger by the sight of the vanguard fleeing, sometimes impetuously attack with great daring and fierce courage, giving new heart to the retreating vanguard and striking terror into the enemy while they demonstrate their own valor."[34] After Bruni's death, Poggio Bracciolini attempted to trace the roots of Bruni's defense of great passion to his powerful personality. In his speech commemorating the death of Bruni, Poggio honored his late

[32] See *Isagogicon Moralis Disciplinae*, in *Bruni, Humanistisch-philosophische Schriften*, 33f., and my comment there on the function of *ira* in the *Isagogicon*. Concerning the date of the *Isagogicon* (between December 1424 and May 1426, probably between December 1424 and December 1425), cf. my reasoning in "The Date of Leonardo Bruni's *Isagogicon Moralis Disciplinae* and the Recovery of the *Eudemian Ethics*," in *Yearbook of Italian Studies* 1 (Montreal, 1971), 64–74.

[33] Not everywhere, however, because Eugenio Garin has meanwhile shown that the defense of passion as a necessary stimulus to social virtue spread through the humanistic literature of Quattrocento Italy and set the tone for some of the most original works in humanistic moral philosophy from the second half of the century onward. See Eugenio Garin, *Italian Humanism: Philosophy and Civic Life in the Renaissance* (New York, 1965).

[34] "L'ira che in su il fatto venisse, poi che con virtù è fatta l'electione del pericolo, può assai aiutare la forteza, come alle volti le seconde schiere, veggendo fuggire le prime, per sdegno commosse a ira, con migliore ardire empetuosi et fieri più che gagliardi assaliscono, rifrancando le schiere perdenti et mettendo terrore a' nimici, colla dimonstratione della loro valentìa" (Palmieri, *Vita Civile* [autograph], fol. 33a; ed. Belloni, 76).

friend by saying that the capacity to feel anger and great passion is the mark of a man whose *virtus* makes him truly wise and outstanding.[35] Conversely, a rigid, uncompromising control of emotion, which had been the undisputed standard for fourteenth-century humanists, including Petrarch, is the sign of someone "mutilated and dull" (*trunci potius ac stipitis*), evidence of a "slow and stupid mind" (*tarditatis mentis ac stupiditatis*), if not of slyness and pretense. "For agitated *ingenia*, quick-witted, vigorous, and fresh, cannot help but be stirred up on occasion by the timidity, unfairness, or error of others, so that they become excited by a kind of indignation." We must, therefore, draw the conclusion, said Poggio, that a passion "which does not harm anyone is not to be reproached but recommended. For it rouses the mind and usually makes it more perspicacious."[36]

In Aristotle's philosophy, Bruni—and after him Palmieri—believed that he had found a powerful support for his defense of anger against the severity of the Stoics, and Aristotelian thought seemed to him profoundly akin to the communal sentiment of fifteenth-century Florence.[37] Half a century later (in the ninth decade of the Quattrocento), Cristoforo Landino endeavored to make *ira* acceptable to rising Neoplatonism by insisting that Plato, in this respect like Aristotle and Christian teaching, had not disputed its legitimacy as a stimulus to moral vigor. From this later phase of Florentine thought two similes of Landino's are revealing. Just as Hercules, after killing the lion, kept its skin for himself, runs the first, so one

---

[35] Poggio Bracciolini, *Oratio Funebris* on Bruni, in *Leonardi Bruni Arretini Epistolarum Libri VIII*, ed. Lorenzo Mehus (Florence, 1741), vol. 1, p. cxxii.

[36] "Nam excitata ingenia, prompta, vigentia necesse est commoveri quandoque ad breve tempus; et aut aliorum timiditate, aut iniuria, aut errore subita quadam indignatione excitari, id magis naturae ingentis ac perspicacitatis esse videtur. . . . Non autem subita effervescentia, et repentina quaedam indignatio, quae nemini noceat, est vituperanda, sed potius commendanda. Excitat enim animum, et ingenium solet reddere perspicacius" (ibid.).

[37] I first noted Bruni's Aristotelianism and its importance for Florentine Humanism in my preface to *Bruni, Humanistisch-philosophische Schriften*, xviii–xxiv.

must subdue anger in such a fashion that "those seeds, which are the greatest benefit nature has given to man, will be used by him to suppress injustice." In the second simile, he claims—as a result of what he has learned from Cicero's *Academica Priora*—that nature, in accordance with the doctrine of the Platonic Academy, bestowed the emotion of anger upon man as a spur, not in order to extinguish the light of reason but "to preserve fortitude, as we see a whetstone sharpen the iron" (*idem ad fortitudinem praestare, quod ad ferrum acuendum cotem praestare videmus*).[38]

Little by little an interest in the effects of *ira* took root in Humanism outside Florence as well. One finds the initial stages of this process in the political writings of a Sienese humanist, Francesco Patrizi, a descendant of a patrician family who participated in the public life of his native Siena in his younger years and suffered the typical fate of exile, until after 1461 he found refuge as bishop of the city of Gaeta.[39] In the earlier of Patrizi's two widely studied treatises on politics, *De Institutione Reipublicae*, dedicated "ad Senatum Populumque" of Siena more than a generation after the beginning of the Florentine controversy over the psychological needs of the man of action, Patrizi still continued to defend the "sage" without any concession to the doubts that had arisen during

[38] Cristoforo Landino, *De Vera Nobilitate*, Cod. of the Bibl. Corsiniana di Roma 433 (dedication copy), fol. 78; ed. Maria Teresa Liaci (Florence, 1970), 108. The second simile given above undoubtedly follows Cicero's *Acad. Priora* II.135. This simile—anger as the "cos" of "fortitudo"—has also been handed down by Cicero, in almost the same words, in *Tusc.* IV.19.43, but as an opinion of the Peripatetic school, not, as in the *Acad. Priora*, as a doctrine of the Platonic Academy, and it is this latter attribution which is the basis of Landino's admiration for it. Differently from Landino, Patrizi (see note 40, below) drew the same simile from the *Tusculanae*, regarding it, in consequence, as a Peripatetic creation.

[39] The basic biography is Felice Battaglia, *Enea Silvio Piccolomini e Francesco Patrizi: Due Politici Senesi del Quattrocento* (Siena, 1936). Patrizi's two political works, *De Institutione Reipublicae* and *De Regno et Regis Institutione*, were completed respectively between 1465 and 1471, and between 1481 and 1484. Both enjoyed an enormous distribution and translation into several languages during the Quattrocento and Cinquecento.

his century. As he then put it, although "some Peripatetics" claim that *ira* ought to be valued as a "whetstone" for valor, "one should not believe them, because the wise man can act bravely without being in a rage."[40] Even in later years, when he composed his second work, the *De Regno et Regis Institutione*, a treatise of equally wide circulation, Patrizi tried to remain loyal to the ideal of the sage; but his own doubts had meanwhile brought him to a point where he was nearer to Aristotelian reasoning than to Stoic dogma. He now discussed the arguments on both sides at great length—those of the Peripatetics as well as those of the Stoics—and tried to reconcile them, although in principle he did not dare to break away from the Stoic norm. He wondered whether repression of all outward signs of anger was not perhaps better than complete freedom from it, "since that could be a sign not only of dignity but also of sluggishness."[41] He further maintained that one ought to distinguish two kinds of fortitude, that of warriors who are courageous in battle (the "fortes bellatores") and that of valiant leaders and commanders ("fortes duces atque imperatores"). For the former, bodily strength, boldness, and fury may indeed be indispensable, and we may have to agree with Aristotle that "anger has sometimes been the cause of an honorable vengeance" (*iram aliquando honestae ultionis causam extitisse*). Perfect *fortitudo*, free from anger in the Stoic sense, is in any case conceivable only as an unattainable ideal. The Stoic norm of the sage could not be fulfilled even by the Stoics' own leaders, philosophers like Zeno or Chrysippus who, according to the Stoics themselves, were only *magni et venerabiles viri*, not true *sapientes*. So, after all, Patrizi admits,

---

[40] "Nec arbitrandum est iram cotem esse fortitudinis, ut nonnulli Peripateticorum affirmant, sed sapientem etiam sine stomacho fortiter agere posse" (Patrizi, *De Institutione Reipublicae* [Paris, 1534], fol. 71b).

[41] ". . . quum illud [i.e., absolute freedom from anger] non solum gravitatis, verum nonnunquam lentitudinis esse possit" (Patrizi, *De Regno et Regis Institutione* [Paris, 1531], 156f.). See ibid., 279–87, for what follows in our discussion.

the notion of a "sage" without irascibility is really nothing but a *prima idea vel ficta quaedam imago*—an "imaginary picture."

The necessity for *ira* received its most precise and effective formulation toward the end of the century from the great humanist writer and courtier Gioviano Pontano of Naples. Having grown up outside Florence, he too had to liberate himself during his earlier years from the traditional scorn for the strongest of the *affectus*. When he became the educator of the younger Alfonso of the royal family of Naples, for whom he wrote a sort of "mirror for princes," he taught his pupil that whoever wants to rule others must first learn to control himself; that is, must strive for freedom from all emotion and passion—especially from *ira*. But when Pontano wrote his famous dialogues many years later, each devoted in great detail to one of the major virtues, he discovered in his analysis of *fortitudo* that he had to question the doctrine of *ataraxia*. His verdict on the necessity of *ira* was now: "It is natural for man to become angry; through anger a certain vigor is communicated to the spirit, which generates a vivaciousness that is not insignificant for a readiness to attack difficult things and conquer them"—always assuming that, in order to retain the fruits of his anger, the valiant man will not go against reason and that his anger has a just cause.[42] This was an unequivocal judgment, free from the hesitation that is so striking in Patrizi, widely read during the early sixteenth century, and heeded, one may assume, both in Italy and north of the Alps; but it came more than two generations after the Florentines Bruni, Palmieri, and Poggio had brought forth the first revaluation of *ira* and other *affectus* necessary for the active life.

One question still has to be answered. The Quattrocento references to Peripatetic teachings are summary in character and do not cite chapter and verse of the Aristotelian writings.

---

[42] "Naturale est homini irasci, ac per iram vigor quidam animo subministratur, qui alacritatem gignit illam, in qua non parum est ad res arduas aggrediendas easdemque superandas momenti" (Pontano, *De Fortitudine*, Lib. I ["De fortitudine bellica et heroica"], ch. 28, "De pugnantibus ob iram vel dolorem").

Is the psychological recognition of anger really present in the ancient models in the form it takes in the humanistic writings of the late fifteenth century? More specifically, were the Quattrocento humanists simply restoring the Aristotelian doctrine or do we find that here as elsewhere in their work, contact with the classical past, whether consciously or not, actually modified the historical heritage?[43]

In the *Nicomachean Ethics* the justification of *ira* as a stimulus to *fortitudo* is part of a general evaluation of the types and causes of courageous behavior. In Aristotle's context, however, this is basically intended to distinguish and unmask those attitudes which, from a philosophical point of view, as he says, are erroneously called *fortitudo* (ἀνδρεία). All such psychological aids, after all, "force" man to be brave. "But a man should be brave because fortitude is a virtue and because it is beautiful to be virtuous." By the same token, if "anger," instead of merely acting as a support for rational judgment, becomes a primary stimulus, it can at best lead only to a desire to fight and not to true bravery, "since [in this case] the stimulus to action is neither the beauty [of virtue] nor reason, but passion, even though the result bears a certain resemblance [to bravery]. Neither are those who are sustained by well-founded confidence 'brave.' " At the critical moment, it will be seen that these pseudo-forms of *fortitudo* merely appear to be, but are not "virtue."[44] In spite of his realism, therefore, Aristotle does not wish to efface the boundary line between ethics and psychology.

In his *Vita Civile*, Matteo Palmieri keeps close to the discussion found in the *Nicomachean Ethics*. But the original direction of Aristotle's text is altered: the psychological and other natural foundations of fortitude acquire a more positive significance in the presentation of the Florentine writer. It is true that Palmieri, who in this case has taken both his material and its

---

[43] This takes up in somewhat greater detail a discussion already outlined in Essay Two, p. 27.

[44] Aristoteles *Eth. ad Nic.* III.9 (ed. Bekker, ch. 11).

arrangement from Aristotle, initially says, like Aristotle, that courage which arises under especially favorable conditions cannot be called *fortitudo* in the true sense. But he immediately adds that those "other kinds" of valor, even if they are not "true valor," are yet "very much like it"; that frequently they are of great benefit "agli huomini non perfecti, co' quali comunemente si vive." Anyone familiar with Palmieri's work[45] knows the importance of such phrases: it is Palmieri's specific intention to write about "the proven life of virtuous citizens with whom man has often lived on this earth in the past and [with whom he] will be able to live in the future." Anything beyond that is considered by him a sort of philosophical chimera which could never exist in real life, any more than could the citizens of Plato's *Republic*, who "are depicted generically and in the abstract rather than having been seen in the flesh."[46]

Thus, the Florentine citizen has transformed the Greek philosopher's cautious distinction between perfect virtue and its pseudo-forms, which are devoid of beauty and genuine moral value, into a realistic analysis of the true nature of courageous behavior. In contrast to the drift of Aristotle's thought, he reflects that it is in battle, not elsewhere, that man learns to be valiant. "For on the battlefield shame makes him face dangers he would not willingly face merely for the sake of doing the right thing. But because he sees the faint-hearted disgraced and the brave esteemed and honored, he endures in order not to be considered a contemptible coward."[47] Moreover, the example of those whom such a man would emulate, or the fear of punishment, awakens in him the strength to die gloriously rather than live in shame. The brutal coercion of warfare may have a still more powerful effect. For "at times necessity gives man courage and makes him fight bravely when all other hope of salvation is lost and the only safety lies in his arms and his outstanding *virtù*." So it is with sympathy that Palmieri recalls

---

[45] See p. 138 above.
[46] See ibid.
[47] Palmieri, *Vita Civile* (autograph), fol. 32b; ed. Belloni, 74.

Catiline's speech to his troops during their final battle, when, according to Sallust, "necessity" prompted Catiline to impress upon his fellow soldiers that their only choice was victory or death.[48]

In argumentation and tone, this is quite unlike what is said in the *Nicomachean Ethics* but very similar to what Machiavelli was to argue in Florence more than two generations later.[49]

[48] *Vita Civile*, ed. Belloni, 75.
[49] See Essay Two, note 5.

Franciscan Poverty and Civic Wealth in the Shaping of Trecento Humanistic Thought: The Role of Petrarch*

I

EARLY Humanism took shape during the fourteenth century in a world spiritually determined by the mendicant friars—in particular, the Dominicans and Franciscans—and one cannot understand the view of life of the earliest humanists without knowing the historical background created by the activities and teachings of these two orders. Being "mendicants," they placed voluntary poverty at the center of their conception of true Christian conduct, a pious tendency that had already been prepared for in the lay religiosity of the eleventh and twelfth centuries.[1] But from the early thirteenth century onward, it was the Franciscan order that carried the

---

* Essays Seven, Eight, and Nine were first written and published in 1937–1938 as one large paper spanning both the Trecento and Quattrocento ("Franciscan Poverty and Civic Wealth as Factors in the Rise of Humanistic Thought," *Speculum* 13 [1938]). In the early 1970s, I decided that the Trecento part, dealing with a transitional period and a major figure, Petrarch, demanded more in-depth analysis than had been feasible in combination with the Quattrocento part. The portion devoted to the Trecento—the present Essays Seven and Eight—was therefore significantly enlarged and completely rewritten. (Some introductory pages dealing with the nature of the Italian Renaissance from the perspective of the early 1930s have been omitted.) Essays Seven and Eight now appear essentially in the form of the early 1970s and replace the first half of the original paper.

[1] More recently, no one has shown better than Herbert Grundmann, in his *Religiöse Bewegungen des Mittelalters* (Hildesheim, 1935), that the ideal of poverty was already the heart of medieval lay religiosity during the eleventh and twelfth centuries. See also "La povertà nelle eresie del sec. XI in Occidente," in Cinzio Violante's *Studi sulla Cristianità Medioevale* (Milan, 1972).

ideal of *paupertas voluntaria* to the masses as well as to the cultivated circles of society, including the early Trecento humanists. In comparison, the Dominicans, who were more involved in the scholarship of the medieval universities, had less popular appeal. The ideas that rocked the late thirteenth century and the whole of the fourteenth in the name of *paupertas* were therefore felt by contemporaries to be chiefly of Franciscan origin, and we are not being arbitrary when we speak of "Franciscan poverty" as the force that increasingly molded conceptions, values, and spiritual struggles.

This impact had not yet gained full strength by the middle of the thirteenth century, a generation or so after St. Francis and St. Dominic, when scholastic education and scholarship were at their zenith. Leading intellects in the universities did not feel driven to denigrate possessions and affluence, despite their religious esteem for voluntary poverty. This was, of course, especially true of Thomas Aquinas, the great Dominican whose evaluation of worldly goods held firmly to the balanced and judicial view in ethical matters he had acquired from the Greeks through Aristotle. Although as a theologian and friar he was profoundly convinced that an essential element of evangelical perfection must be sought in *paupertas voluntaria*, as a philosopher he accepted the view of Aristotle and his Peripatetic school that material possessions are not only permissible to sustain bodily life but must be considered a necessary "aid" (*adminiculum*) to the maturation of moral life, as is evident in the case of such virtues as liberality.[2] St. Thomas was not ignorant of the fact that the Stoicism of late classical philosophy, in apparent conformity with mendicant ideals, had frequently advocated *paupertas*, but in his *Summa Theologiae* he expressly protested against the "unreasonableness" of

---

[2] Cf. A. M. Orlich, "L'uso dei beni nella morale di S. Tommaso," *La Scuola Cattolica*, 4th ser., 24 (1912): 218ff., and A. Fanfani, "Le soluzioni tomistiche e l'attegiamento degli huomini dei sec. XIII e XIV di fronte ai problemi della ricchezza," *Rivista Internazionale delle Scienze Sociali e Discipline Ausiliarie* 39 (1931): 574ff.; O. Schilling, *Die Staats- und Soziallehre Thomas von Aquinos*, 2d ed. (Munich, 1930), 261ff. and 267f.

the Stoic doctrine that neither temporal goods nor misfortune should have any essential meaning for a true sage. Moreover, Christian belief in the harmony of a divinely created world provided Thomas with a standard for judging the relationship of the spirit to material things. In accordance with the Peripatetics (Aquinas states in his *Summa Theologiae*), Augustine teaches that for human beings, who consist of body as well as mind, material possessions can be real goods—though of "very little value" compared with spiritual goods.[3]

In his day the attitude of lay citizens was hardly different from that of St. Thomas. One of the oldest literary expressions of the Italian civic spirit was the *Libro . . . della Dilezione d'Iddio, e del Prossimo, e della Forma dell'Onesta Vita*, written in 1238 by Judge Albertano da Brescia (already known to us as an early follower of Cicero's *vita activa* philosophy[4]), a writer for whom the problems of civic wealth and civic instincts still overshadowed strong Franciscan inclinations. This early thirteenth-century north Italian citizen made the same assumptions Aquinas would make a few decades later in his *Summa Theologiae*. The enjoyment of riches is permitted by God, he says. "Surely, according to the commandments of God and his saints, you can rightly acquire and possess riches. For we find many saints who had much and [even] great wealth, among them the holy Job. And in the Gospels one reads of Joseph of Arimathea, who was a gentleman, rich and just, and a disciple of God." The civic jurist concludes: "So you are allowed to acquire and possess riches, though you must not put your heart into them." A man may even love his possessions if he has acquired them through care and labor and if he possesses

---

[3] Against the Stoic doctrine "nullum malum posse accidere sapienti. . . . Sed hoc irrationabiliter dicitur. Cum enim homo sit ex anima et corpore compositus, id quod confert ad vitam corporis conservandam aliquod bonum hominis est: non tamen maximum . . ." (*Summa Theol.*, Ia IIae q. 59 art. 3); against the Stoics, "qui ponebant bona temporalia non esse hominis bona," both Augustine and the Peripatetics can be quoted, Aquinas said (ibid., IIa IIae q. 125 art. 4).

[4] See Essay Five, p. 111.

his treasures rather than being possessed by them. But if riches are to be loved, all the more worthy of love are the arts by which possessions are obtained. Love these arts and teach them to your children so that they may help themselves if you become poor or they meet with misfortune. Such is the explicit advice given by this layman of the early thirteenth century.[5]

In the second half of the century, however, the general direction of opinion finally turned toward the sweeping demands inherent in the ideal of Franciscan poverty. This ideal had originally seemed to set a standard only for religious orders and sometimes for other ecclesiastical circles. But now that chivalry had ceased to be the determining factor in Italian medieval life, it began a victorious procession through all ranks of society. While bitter controversies concerning the right of the mendicant orders and other church members to corporate possession of worldly goods engrossed religious authorities right up to the pope, lay associations ("Tertiaries," adjunct to the regular orders of the Franciscan Friars and Poor Clares) were formed, especially in urban society, whose aim was to realize the ideal of Franciscan poverty outside the walls of religious houses. Among the orders of friars, the Spiritual Franciscans emerged as the most rigorous defenders of poverty, repudiating all compromises agreed to by earlier religious movements. Finally, a heretical and even revolutionary sect, the "Fraticelli," demanded that not only the order but all segments of the Church should submit to the rule of absolute poverty. Meanwhile, within large segments of the population

---

[5] Albertano's treatise, written in Latin, was soon circulated in at least three distinct forms of "volgarizzamento," evidence that it was a typical and widely influential work. I have used the "volgarizzamento fatto nel 1268 da Andrea da Grosseto," ed. F. Selmi (Bologna, 1873), in the Collezione di opere inedite o rare dei primi tre secoli della lingua, especially the chapters "Come tu dei acquistare e conservare le ricchezze" and "Come si debono amare le ricchezze." On the personality of Albertano and his versatile services for Brescia, see the article by P. Guerrini in vol. 1 of the *Dizionario biografico degli Italiani* (Rome, 1960).

of the Italian communes, the Franciscan ideal came to be seen as the remedy for an age growing ever more affluent and commercialized. Under its influence, though within a Christian framework, the doctrines of ancient Stoicism were revived in intellectual circles (which included most early poets and writers in the expanding urban world of Italy). These doctrines taught that a life of poverty is necessary for a wise man's independence of mind—a recrudescence of the school of thought so emphatically rejected by Thomas Aquinas in his *Summa Theologiae.*

In the generation before Dante, an early encyclopedia of knowledge for lay citizens—the *Trésor,* primarily a compilation of scholastic knowledge, written about 1265 by the Florentine chancery notary and diplomat Brunetto Latini—revived the distrust of riches shown by medieval Stoics before the full rise of Scholasticism in the thirteenth century. While Thomas' followers held to the Peripatetic approval of wealth,[6] the Florentine layman Latini copied almost verbatim from a work of the twelfth century—the *Moralium Dogma Philosophorum*—a section in which selected passages from Cicero, Seneca, Horace, and Juvenal appear to demonstrate that all riches are a danger to virtue. Money brings nothing but trouble, the *Trésor* says, and fills mankind with a greed that has brought many to ruin. "Diogenes was richer in his poverty than Alexander in his greatness," as Latini quotes Cicero. In his quotations from Juvenal, Latini, like the *Moralium Dogma,* stresses those satires which describe the rich man as devoured by abject fear of thieves while "he who has no possessions marches past the thieves singing."[7]

The same negative attitude toward wealth appears in Guit-

---

[6] For Egidio Romano, cf. his *De regimine principum,* Lib. II, pt. 3, chs. 5ff.; for the attitude of Antonino of Florence, see B. Jarrett, *St. Antonino and Mediaeval Economics* (London, 1914), 59f.

[7] *Trésor,* Livre II, pt. 2, ch. 100; in Giamboni's vernacular adaptation, the *Tesoro,* Lib. VII, ch. 70. This agrees almost literally with the section "De peculio, thesauro, ornatu," in the *Moralium Dogma Philosophorum,* ed. J. Holmberg (Uppsala, 1929), 59–64.

tone d'Arezzo, the poet most widely read before Dante in the patrician society of the central Italian towns. He was the first to circulate artfully composed letters in the Tuscan vernacular, one of which, largely a compilation of quotations from available sources, stresses the general accord of ancient Stoics and Christian writers in their warnings against riches. Written to a friend who had lost a large sum of money, this noteworthy letter of consolation—more or less coeval with Latini's encyclopedia—commiserates with the addressee's despair, but not because of the loss itself, which should be regarded rather as an occasion for joy (*matera gioiosa*). For, an inexhaustible number of pagan authorities, among them Seneca, Cicero, and even allegedly Aristotle, and many biblical and later Christian writings, demonstrate that he who loses his property is rid of one of the primary sources of avarice, since wealth never makes a man content with his lot; rather, the greater the riches, the more desperate the toiling for ever greater wealth. Our Lord teaches that "nessuno può servire Dio e moneta." As Seneca says, "avarizia non se sazia, ma cresce cupidità," and St. Paul, "radice di tutto male è avarizia." The really poor person, therefore, Guittone insists, is not the one who owns little but the one who owns much and yearns for more.[8]

About 1300 this line of thought was not foreign even to Dante. To be sure, as a follower of Thomas Aquinas, the poet never loses sight of Aristotle; yet in his half-Franciscan, half-Stoic enmity toward riches, he reveals the great change in sentiment that has taken place among the citizens of the Italian communes after the generation of Aquinas. In the "Paradiso" of the *Divina Commedia*, the simple old days of Florence are contrasted with the materialistic present, its restlessness and covetousness; St. Francis is praised with affectionate warmth, and in many passages curses are uttered against the wealth of

---

[8] Cf. Marti's critical text of Guittone's letter, in *La prosa del duecento*, ed. C. Segre and M. Marti, La Letteratura Italiana: Storia e Testi, vol. 3 (1959), 37–52, esp. 37–41.

the Church.[9] In the *Convivio* the poet attacks a definition of nobility attributed to Emperor Frederic II, along with the Aristotelian notion the emperor had tried to modify. Frederic was reported to have said that nobility is based on a combination of good breeding (*antiqui boni mores*) and inherited *divitiae*—a variation of the Aristotelian statement that *virtus* and old wealth combine to create nobility. Dante objected to the part played by wealth in both definitions. Criticizing the emperor's dictum, he asserted that nobility can have its origin only in *virtus*. The picture of true *nobilità* shown in Dante's *Convivio* is therefore, like Latini's view in the *Trésor*, founded on the Stoic precept that riches cannot contribute to "nobility" because they fill us with an insatiable lust for possessions and at the same time with a constant fear of losing what we have.[10]

In all of this, the leading minds of the Italian Trecento were propelled as well as limited by an intellectual current of largely religious inspiration.[11] Christian spirituality and Franciscan renunciation of worldly goods seemed to combine with an in-

---

[9] *Paradiso*, canto XV: Cacciaguida's glorification of ancient Florence in contrast to its current condition; canto XI: praise of St. Francis.

[10] *Convivio*, trattato IV, deals with the inferiority of all riches; capitoli IV, 8 and 10, contain polemics against Aristotle and Frederic II; capitolo IV, 12, borrows literally from Boethius: "Si quantas rapidas flatibus incitus . . . Humanum miseras haud ideo genus cesset flere querelas" (*Consol.*, Lib. II, metr. II), and also borrows from Cicero's *Paradoxa* 1.6: "Numquam mehercule ego neque pecunias istorum neque tecta magnifica neque opes . . . in bonis rebus aut expetendis esse duxi, quippe quum viderem homines rebus circumfluentes ea tamen desiderare maxime, quibus abundarent. Neque enim expletur unquam nec satiatur cupiditatis sitis, neque solum ea qui habent libidine augendi cruciantur, sed etiam amittendi metu."

[11] For the influence of the philosophy of poverty on the citizens of Florence up to the second half of the fourteenth century, compare the well-known letters of the notary Lapo Mazzei (characteristic quotations in A. Fanfani, *Le origini dello spirito capitalistico in Italia* [Milan, 1933], 139, 141) and the statements in Boccaccio's consolatory letter to the exile M. Pino de' Rossi (in Boccaccio's *Lettere*, ed. Corazzini [Florence, 1877], 78f.), and in his speech in praise of *paupertas* (Boccaccio, *De Casibus Virorum Illustrium* I, 15), as well as *De Casibus* III, 1, "Paupertatis et Fortunae Certamen," and ch. 17, "In Divitias et Stolidam Vulgi Opinionem."

herent tendency of the Stoic mentality to assure the sage's independence from the vagaries of fortune. Even before Petrarch began his work, this alliance had become firmly established in the surroundings in which his mind was formed. Our best witness is no less than the head of the Italian Guelphs, King Robert of Naples, whom Petrarch had looked up to in his earlier years as a friend and as the sponsor in 1341 of his coronation as poet on the Roman Capitol. The treatise *De Paupertate Evangelica*, written in Robert's entourage as early as about 1320, possibly by Robert's chancellor, and which favored the claims of the Spiritual Franciscans, may give us some idea of the context and form in which the all-pervading interest of the century in *paupertas* must have reached Petrarch.[12]

The argument of the treatise begins with an assertion that contempt for wealth and treasure was not unknown to pagan authors and to many a great man in Antiquity. After this has been illustrated, the discussion turns to the precepts of the Bible and of Christian writers and, with that, to the real purpose of the treatise: the theological scrutiny of evangelical and mendicant poverty. From the viewpoint of humanistic erudition, there is little new in this discussion of the meaning of Franciscan poverty. What it does show us is that the Franciscan view of life forms the background to this Stoic evaluation of *paupertas*. Although the author of the Neapolitan pamphlet was evidently unacquainted with Sallust and Livy (soon to be the humanists' major guides to the legendary poverty of early Rome), his sources, which were those commonly available to medieval writers—three moral treatises by Seneca and a few examples of ancient conduct taken from Valerius Maximus[13]—were thought sufficient to prove that the Fran-

[12] Printed in G. B. Siragusa, *L'ingegno, il sapere e gl'intendimenti di Roberto d'Angiò* (Palermo, 1891), Appendix, pp. xvif. It was written between 1319 and 1324 (cf. W. Goetz, *König Robert von Neapel* [Tübingen, 1910], 28), probably 1320 to 1322 (cf. S. Brettle, "Ein Traktat Roberts von Neapel 'De evangelica paupertate,' " in *Festgabe für H. Finke* [Münster i. W., 1925], 204).

[13] Piur's assertion (which I accepted in the first version of this essay) that

ciscan faith in poverty was paralleled in Antiquity by the convictions of men engaged in a righteous secular life. In Valerius
Maximus, the author of *De Paupertate Evangelica* tells us, we
find a sympathetic picture of the early Roman statesman
C. Fabricius, who could not be corrupted by gold and silver
and stands as an example of those many ancient leaders "who
scorned riches and were aroused almost to the point of indignation by the thought of possessing them." In Greece (also according to Valerius Maximus) Democritus and Socrates
taught that compromises in the possession of wealth would
not suffice; that it is indeed difficult to have *divitias et virtutes*
in one's house at the same time. Finally, Diogenes—the sage
who drank from no cup but the hollow of his own hand and
who gave a proud reply to Alexander (too famous to need
quoting) when he was offered a gift from Alexander's vast
riches—shows in all his conduct how it is possible for man to
live in such a way that "nothing can be torn from him" by
Fortuna, and how the loss of all material possessions would
only make his life "less impeded." Thus, writes the author of
the Neapolitan pamphlet, the common assumption that security can be expected from affluence is wrong: men frequently
perish precisely because they have great wealth, whereas poverty can be counted on to bring security and happiness.[14]

No other document gives us as striking a picture of the alliance between the religious and classicistic ideals of *paupertas*
in the first decades of the Trecento. This alliance was to last
for a century, until the first decades of the Quattrocento,
when a completely different outlook on life and human nature
came into existence. This does not mean, however, that ideas
remained frozen for a century. To an attentive observer the
beginnings of a new way of thinking are unmistakable from
the middle of the Trecento onward. But they clearly betrayed

---

the treatise refers to Livy and "enumerates a long series of examples of poverty from the great time of Roman history" is misleading (a single example is
mentioned, as noted in the text above). See P. Piur, *Petrarcas 'Buch ohne Na-
men'* (Halle a. S., 1925), 70.

[14] *De Paupertate Evangelica*, ed. Siragusa, xv–xviii.

their origination in a period of transition and did not immediately yield lasting results. This will not come as a surprise to those who have followed the uncertain course of the memory of Cicero and of the philosophy of the active life during the Florentine Trecento.

There are two methods for collecting and evaluating the Trecento evidence of ideas concerning poverty. One is to reconstruct the progress of the greatest and most independent intellect of the period, Petrarch. The other is to trace the vicissitudes of *paupertas* ideology in the hands of Florentines and other Tuscan citizens during the later Trecento. We need to explore both of these avenues.

II

There was little in the world of Petrarch's formative years to make him reject the accepted high evaluation of *paupertas*. After spending his boyhood and early adult years in the surroundings of papal Avignon, in exile from his ancestral Florentine home, he found a retreat from 1337 onward in the secluded valley of the Vaucluse in the French foothills of the Alps. For a decade and a half it provided him with a refuge for his writing, which he took up in the Vaucluse each time he returned from journeys to the outside world. From the first, he viewed this frugal and idyllic existence in the midst of nature, where he felt his creative powers as a poet and writer nourished, as a semiclaustral escape from the suspected perils of the world of material riches. In one of his letters from the Vaucluse, he states that he feels himself to be a Stoic and not a Peripatetic because, he says, he is aware of the unhappiness of everyone who seeks the good things of life not merely in *virtus* but also in the gifts of Fortuna. Once riches are admitted and prized, everything in our existence becomes uncertain, and true happiness is no longer possible.[15] At that time, Petrarch

---

[15] Petrarch, *Ep. Fam.* III 6. Even if this letter is as late as 1351–1352, as Billanovich and Rico have made probable (see Francisco Rico, *Lectura del Secre-*

167

thought the Stoic contempt for those possessions which are subject to the whim of fortune was pervasive and self-evident, and he was inclined to find it in all the classical authors he esteemed, even when they took into account—as Cicero does in his *De Finibus Bonorum et Malorum* (known to Petrarch since 1343)—the Aristotelian view that riches are an "aid" to the exercise of active virtues.[16] In those years, when Petrarch occasionally describes his studious life amid the beauties of the Alpine scenery as a happy *mediocritas* equally far from oppressive poverty and overabundant riches, he immediately adds that if there were no middle road he would judge that even bitter poverty is preferable to the glitter of wealth, because it leads to greater calm and independence of mind.[17]

The key feature of all Petrarch's depictions of his little paradise is the assumption that his life there is good because it represents the state of *paupertas*. "If you wish to be healthy, live like someone who is poor. . . . If you wish to chase away gout, chase away sumptuousness; if you wish to remove evil, drive away wealth!"[18] In an early description of his life in the Vaucluse, he talks about the frugality and rural simplicity of his days spent in walking over the hills with pen and paper in hand. The only companions in his solitude are his dear friends

---

tum [Padua, 1974], 52, n. 32), it still expresses Petrarch's thinking during his stay in the Vaucluse and cannot be of an even later date. I am using Petrarch's *Familiares* in Vittorio Rossi's edition in the Edizione Nazionale delle opere di Francesco Petrarca, vols. 10–13 (Florence, 1933–1942).

[16] "Si sententiam extorques, absit a me non modo summum sed—quoniam et in hac opinione stoicus quam perypateticus . . . esse malim—ne aliquod quidem bonum in divitiis aut in voluptate reponere" (*Ep. Fam.* III 6). The letter then condemns a sort of "felicitas, ad quam non modo forma corporis et prosperior valitudo sed divitiae etiam admittuntur seu potius exiguntur," as being "nimis furum insidiis exposita, nimis denique solicita semper ac trepida, quo nichil est a felicitate remotius." Further on, Petrarch remarks that others may think what they please but for his part he would refer to Cicero's book *De Finibus*, "quem cum legeris, nescio an quicquam vel auribus vel ingenio relictum sit quod requirendum putent."

[17] *Ep. Fam.* III 14. Most of the letters in Book III are no later than the early 1350s, as G. Billanovich has shown.

[18] *Ep. Fam.* III 13.

of many centuries ago, the ancient authors, because friends of flesh and blood are repelled by his coarse food and rustic dwelling. This picture is drawn entirely from the perspective of the material modesty of the Stoic sage. It begins with Petrarch's affirmation that he now lives in harmony with poverty—a "golden poverty," not a sordid or oppressive one, to be sure. He would not want to own any inherited wealth or landed estate, except for his little garden plot, because possessions are merely chains to the mind and the cause of all evil. As long as Fortuna does not grudge him his tiny house with its beloved books, he will be well satisfied. The emphasis in this depiction of his life is clearly on its distance from wealth; to characterize it, he even uses the word *egestas*, which signifies indigence, want, and unmistakable poverty.[19]

The interruption of Petrarch's solitary existence by his coronation as poet on the Roman Capitol (1341) and the impressions of a subsequent journey through Italy did not shake this firm belief in the value of poverty and self-sufficiency. Hardly had he returned to his rural refuge when he was again extolling poverty, in the Trecento manner, as the true way to a spiritual existence. Many people praise *paupertas* yet strive for wealth, he writes, and consequently they arouse suspicion of their love of poverty. Admittedly, such love is a special "gift of God" and is "understood by very few people"; no wonder, he observes, that those who find great examples of poverty in early Roman history, such as could help them to suppress their avarice and cupidity, quickly forget what they have read. Yet these Roman examples are in harmony with Christ's own *sacra et humilis paupertas* and with the pious example of the Apostles, who wandered through the world hungry and poorly clothed. They are also in agreement with the words of Solomon and St. Paul, which tell us that "when we have what

---

[19] ". . . absit inanis / gloria; nil cupio, contenta est vita paratis. / Hoc primum placitis mecum concordat egestas / aurea federibus, non sordida nec gravis hospes. / Si libet, exigui fines michi servet agelli / angustamque domum et dulces Fortuna libellos; cetera secum habeat . . ." (*Ep. Metr.* 1 6, 1338).

we need to feed and cover ourselves we ought to be content."[20] In concept and tone, this line of reasoning is not dissimilar from that of the early tract *De Evangelica Paupertate*, written at the court of King Robert of Naples.

It is no exaggeration to say that the linkage of classical and Christian values persisted in Petrarch's thinking as long as the Vaucluse served as his home and refuge. In his *De Vita Solitaria*, the literary monument to that period (composed in 1346), he includes a chapter intended as a warning against the admission of any kind of acquisitive spirit into the life of solitude. It is not easy to decide how much of the argument offered there is the product of humanistic psychology and how much the expression of a spiritual, Franciscan concern. "People will come," Petrarch writes in this chapter, "who will show us the way to great riches. But this is nothing more than the teaching of avarice. . . . To someone occupied with such thoughts let us say, 'Consider, rather, how to escape from the desire for riches.' "[21] The same convictions prevail in most of the letters describing Petrarch's life of solitude after each return to the Vaucluse. To the very end of his sojourn in the valley, he believes that the absence of avarice is the secret of his happy existence there. Why should he try to acquire more than is necessary to pay for a modest shelter, food, and the cost of his library? To do so would be avaricious, and "avarice is insatiable. . . . Avarice is a constant thirst; it devours everything; it is bottomless. The cupidity of man requires no external penalties"; he will pay for it even if he does not suffer material loss. For by bringing restlessness into man's life, cupidity is "its own punishment." This is the soundest wisdom, although it is "hateful to most men."[22]

---

[20] *Ep. Fam.* VI 3 (May 1342).

[21] *De Vita Solitaria*, in *Francesco Petrarca, Prose*, ed. Guido Martellotti et al., La Letteratura Italiana: Storia e Testi, vol. 7 (Milan, 1955), 572 and 570.

[22] *Ep. Fam.* XVI 3 (28 March 1353). The translation is by Ernest H. Wilkins, in *Petrarch at Vaucluse: Letters in Verse and Prose* (Chicago, 1958). Another testimony that Petrarch felt himself to be far removed from avarice in the years before 1353 is *Ep. Fam.* VIII 4 (in its missive version of May 1349), in which

Yet even during the years shaped by his experiences in the Vaucluse, we see the first signs of a change in attitude whenever he comes in contact with Italian life. In the autumn of 1343 he was sent to Naples on a papal errand, and on his return he interrupted his journey in Parma at the invitation of the ruling family of the Da Correggio, with whom he had already spent about eight happy months after his Roman coronation two years before. This time he settled in Parma until 1345, and in 1348–1350 he returned there once more from the Vaucluse. During these two long Parmesan sojourns, he built a home for himself in the city. In 1346 he had received a well-endowed canonry in Parma (he had taken the lower orders), and this sinecure, to his way of thinking, put him beyond the reach of real *paupertas*. From 1348 onward, additional prebends in northern Italy gradually raised his economic level to one of moderate affluence.

He had set one foot at least on new ground, and if my supposition that the milieu in which he lived always had a decisive effect on him is correct, his growing attachment to an Italian tyrant court must have affected his Vaucluse philosophy of simplicity and *paupertas*. The keen insights into his own nature found in some of his *epistolae metricae* allow us to trace his feelings at the very time when he was building his comfortable and beautiful new house, strikingly different from his simple dwelling in the Vaucluse (even his food became more refined in such surroundings, he tells us). Now he did not refrain from using expensive materials to construct it. Once, while it was going up, he found himself dreaming of the still more precious marbles glittering in mountain quarries, and suddenly he was reminded of man's fragility and those famous small, modest houses of Cato and other early Romans. He felt ashamed of his new undertaking, but then he saw in his mind's eye the proud towers of ancient cities reaching into the clouds and challenging the skies. So "I scorned all little estates,

---

he declared "Quod ad me attinet, cupiditatibus *metam fixi*" [emphasis added]. Rico, *Lectura*, 168, n. 154, has drawn attention to this statement.

and my fickle mind wandered along tortuous paths without end. . . . From those peregrinations it returned, ready to admire modesty and fly into passionate hatred of pomp and splendor. Thus starkly contrasting views of my life endlessly alternate with one another . . . and it seems to me that I am in the midst of tempestuous floods."[23]

In the same Parmesan environment, after the Black Death had come to an end in 1349, he conceived a plan to establish a common household with three surviving friends (a plan that foundered only because one of the selected participants met with a tragic accident). In his letter of invitation, he compared the advantages of settling with his companions in his new house in Parma to those of living in the Vaucluse. His grateful recollections of his *solitaria quies* in the Vaucluse, he wrote, would never die, and if men could live on meadow flowers and pure streams alone, like *animae felices*, his wish would be to return to the Vaucluse with his friends. If it were put in its proper perspective, his Alpine solitude might be a welcome antidote when they became sick of too many urban pleasures, but in the long run the lonely valley was a place for "summer days" and not for the necessities of life. Human nature demands more than meadows and streams. Even when occupied with philosophy and poetry, man has needs that cannot be ignored. " 'Man's nature is not of itself sufficient for the exercise of contemplation,' Aristotle says. 'Our body must also be healthy, and nourishment and other necessities must be provided.' "[24] By the time Petrarch revised this letter for inclusion in the book edition of his *Epistolae Familiares*, a few years later,

---

[23] *Ep. Metr.* II 18. This quotation probably dates from the Parma period of 1348–1350, because the phrase "now friendly Fortuna" (in the introductory verses) seems to point to the time after he received the benefice of 1346. The alternative would be that Azzo da Correggio had helped him out in 1343–1345, but such a gift would hardly have caused Petrarch to talk of a change in fortune. From the standpoint of the questions we are asking, it does not make much difference in which Parmesan period the house was built and the poetical epistle written.

[24] *Ep. Fam.* VIII 3 (1349), preserved in its missive version and printed by Rossi, vol. 2, pp. 194–203, esp. 197–99. The reference is to *Eth. ad Nic.* x.8.9.

he had become more fully aware of the humanistic motive behind this agreement with Aristotle, and he added to his avowal
of the Peripatetic point of view the explanation that "the vul-
gar crowd, to be sure, believes that philosophers and poets are
unfeeling and made of stone; but they are made of flesh, they
retain their *humanitas*. . . ." So he was eager to choose for his
home with his friends not the Vaucluse, with its solitude and
poverty, but "Italy's pleasant, flourishing cities."[25]

Various reasons kept Petrarch from permanently transfer-
ring his residence to Italy before nearly another quinquen-
nium had passed (the most important being that his patrons,
the Da Correggio of Parma, were among the small tyrants
whose local states became part of the region-state of the Visconti of Milan), and at the beginning of the 1350s, when he
was once again under the spell of the secluded charm of the
Vaucluse, his love for rural solitude and simplicity became
stronger than ever. Since the project of a common household
in Parma came to naught, his inner struggle did not become
acute until the summer of 1353, when he accepted the invitation of Archbishop Giovanni Visconti of Milan to settle permanently in a house on the edge of the city. There, after the
first shock of the change from Vaucluse solitude to urban life
had passed,[26] Petrarch began to think of his new life as a closer
approach to "the golden mean." He had occasionally talked of
mediocritas as his ideal in former descriptions of his life; now,
however, this concept became the center of a balanced philos-

---

[25] "Philosophos quidem et poetas duros ac saxeos vulgus existimat, sed in
hoc fallitur ut in multis; carnei enim sunt, humanitatem retinent, abiciunt voluptates" (*Ep. Fam.* VIII 3, final version, ed. Rossi, vol. 2, p. 159).

[26] At the end of 1353 Petrarch had still clung to his earlier convictions that
the rich man is greedier than the poor and that he, Petrarch, ought to live in
solitude, not in cities. See *Ep. Fam.* XVII 3 (13), of September 1353 ("deme
divitias: avaritie subtraxeris fundamentum; pauper enim nonnisi necessaria
vite cupit, que sunt pauca; dives, qui iam nummorum cumulos vidit didi-
citque immensa et inutilia mirari, protinus aureos montes et argentea flumina
cupida sibi meditatione componit"), and *Ep. Fam.* XVII 10 (26), of 1 January
1354 ("Ita ego a prima etate tantus amator solitudinis ac silvarum, iam senior
in urbibus et odiosa frequentia laboro, et male michi est").

ophy of life. Nearly all human beings, he wrote in April 1354 in Milan, are fascinated by extremes. At one end are the insatiable, such as Alexander and Caesar, for whom the world is too small. At the other end are men like Diogenes and Amiclas, who are happy only under the most restricted conditions, fearful of occupying a spacious house or even of touching a coin, "as if it were not enough to avoid avarice, as if it were our duty to succumb to its opposite by declaring war on riches." These are remarkable comments in a century shaken by the revolt of the Franciscans against worldly possessions. And Petrarch makes it very clear that he has their "war" in mind, because to his somewhat impetuous description of Diogenes and Amiclas as philosophers who fear a spacious house and the touch of a coin he adds: "There are many others of this sort, especially among our own [Christian] people, who, following a leader who was poor, have zealously made poverty their best friend and consequently live in the clefts of rocks or in desert caves." Thus a humanistic idea of *virtus* began to replace *paupertas* as the sole standard. "If it is a sign of imbecility to avidly desire riches," Petrarch continues, "the inability to live with them denotes an enervated mind." But different from those at the extremes are the few "who are satisfied in all things by *mediocritas*. To them I wish to belong."[27]

[27] After referring to Alexander and Caesar, Diogenes and Amiclas: "Multos quoque alios praecipue ex nostris, qui pauperem ducem nacti omni studio fecerunt sibi familiarissimam paupertatem, in scissuris lapidum atque in desertis specuum habitantes: sic et in reliquis invenies. . . . Itaque nummos alii non quasi fallax et fragile mortalis vitae praesidium, sed quasi fratres aut filios amant, saepe plus etiam quam se ipsos, quando ut nummis parcant fame pereunt. Horum alii contactum ceu contagiosum aliquid evitant, et quasi non sufficiat avaritiam declinasse, nisi in contrarium relabatur, bellum indixere divitiis, quas ut valde optare imbecillis, sic non posse pati enervati animi est. . . . Sunt quibus in rebus omnibus mediocritas placet. Horum ex numero esse velim" (*Ep. Variae* 64, in vol. 3 of *Epistolae De Rebus Familiaribus et Variae*, ed. Fracassetti [Florence, 1863], 481–82). For the date, ca. 25 April 1354, see Arnaldo Foresti, *Aneddoti della vita di Francesco Petrarca* (Brescia, 1928), 316–18, and Ernest H. Wilkins, *Petrarch's Eight Years in Milan* (Cambridge, Mass., 1958), 69–71.

From the latter part of the 1350s onward, Petrarch, now permanently settled in Milan, began to feel that he had reached this goal. In 1357, in a résumé of his first four years in Milan, he repeats that in his judgment "the best condition" with regard to material goods is "the greatest possible distance from either extreme." "This safe, sweet, and comfortable *mediocritas* has now become mine," he continues; "at least it seems so to me, although I may be wrong."[28] Undoubtedly, this kind of *mediocritas* was rather different from the one he had sometimes written about in former years. Not only by comparison with his previous material conditions in the Vaucluse but by any standard he was now a man of means. His income in Milan was so substantial and his style of living so lavish that in 1357 he had to deny rumors circulating among friends that he had become wealthy and was no longer leading a life of *mediocritas*.[29]

But it is the fact that he was so close to being rich and was aware of it that gives added significance to his psychological observations on his reaction to increasing prosperity. In his own words from 1357: "On this score, I dare to attribute something singular to myself, though rather not to me but to Him from whom every good in man really stems. What I might have done, and what my reaction might have been, under conditions of really substantial wealth I do not know; but so far I have found that the greater my means grow, the less I long for more; the greater my substance becomes, the more tranquil my life and the less my greed, solicitude, and restlessness. It is not hard for me to believe that things might have developed differently if I had been very rich . . . but unless I

---

[28] ". . . optimus et ab extremis distantissimus est modus: procul miseria, procul inopia, procul divitie, procul invidia; tuta vero dulcis ac facilis mediocritas presto est: ita michi videor; fallor forte" (*Ep. Fam.* XIX 16 [12]). For the date, see Ernest H. Wilkins, *Petrarch's Correspondence* (Padua, 1960), 80.

[29] By the 1350s, he had obtained more and richer ecclesiastical benefices than he had ever wanted during the early 1340s. For the importance of the benefices of 1346, see Ernest H. Wilkins, "Petrarch's Ecclesiastical Career," *Speculum* 28 (1953): 760f. and 774.

deceive myself, *mediocritas* has so far not defeated me, although I think that many people will see . . . this as a very rare, even incredible, case."[30] "Incredible" because, according to the rigid psychology of emotions (*affectus*) adopted by medieval Stoics and professed by Petrarch himself, every step from poverty to wealth was bound to increase human desire, greed, passion, unrest, and misery. Thus it was Petrarch's experience after his transplantation from Avignon and the Vaucluse to northern Italy that undermined his faith in the medieval Stoic teachings. And this experience worked in another direction as well: He discovered that he had mastered the art of "achieving solitude and leisure in the midst of city life" (*in mediis urbibus ipse mihi solitudinem atque otium conflare didicerim*).[31] He was not a changed man.

For all this, Petrarch did not regard himself a Peripatetic in his moral reflections; he never really gave up the ideal of the sage who is oblivious to material things. Even in the second half of his life, when he concerned himself with the problems of *avaritia* and *paupertas*, he would sometimes write lengthy passages virtually reiterating what he had written during his years in the Vaucluse. Typical are the diatribes against *avaritia* in two of his letters, *Epistolae Seniles* VI 7 and VI 8, which, like almost all the *Seniles*, can hardly be earlier than the 1360s. In them his sweeping condemnations of *avaritia* are followed by the insistence that they should not prevent anyone from accepting the wealth offered by Fortuna. What he wants to teach, he says, is not that one should try to escape wealth but that one should not possess it "with an avaricious mind."[32] Ex-

[30] *Ep. Fam.* XIX 17 (4–5).

[31] *Ep. Fam.* XX 10 (2 and 4). Petrarch's achievement of this state of mind, probably in 1358, was mentioned in my *From Petrarch to Leonardo Bruni* (Chicago, 1968), 80.

[32] "At ne forte divitias ultro oblatas abiciendas et non potius avaritiam secludendam crederes, sequitur: Divitiae si affluent, nolite cor apponere" (*Ep. Sen.* VI 7, in *Opera* [Basel: Henricpetri, 1581], 549 [as a "De avaritia vitanda . . . Oratio"]). The novelty of this admonition will not be overrated if we remember that something very similar had been written in Italian cities before

cept for this remark, however, Petrarch's arguments in these letters do not go beyond the common thinking of the Franciscan-oriented Trecento. Despite his experiences of the first ten years or so after his return to Italy, he reasons that wherever possessions exceed man's immediate needs, the resulting affluence will be a breeding ground for vice; it will never bring greater peace of mind. Given man's nature, the more numerous our possessions, the greater will be our demand for more.[33] The burden of the second letter (*Ep. Sen.* VI 8) is to show—with stupendous erudition—that classical authors and biblical writers alike, though well aware of this danger, have helped to incite human greed for gold and wealth by using the terms "gold" and "golden" for things they thought to be noble and valuable.

But we should turn to the last years of Petrarch's life. There is, of course, a common human tendency with advancing age to revert to the values of one's formative years. Yet the extent of Petrarch's reversion during the last five years of his life to many of the mental habits of the period when he was a recluse in the Vaucluse is unusual. After spending more than a decade and a half in urban surroundings in or near Milan and Pavia (the two capitals of the Visconti state), the Republic of Venice, and the Padua of the Carrara princes, he decided in 1369 once more to establish a small home in rural solitude, this time in the village of Arquà in the Euganean hills, within the state of the Carrara. We know especially from his literary exchange with Lombardo della Seta, his closest friend among the Paduan humanists, that decisive aspects of the philosophy of life which had guided him in the Vaucluse were then revived, and more strikingly than ever. In Petrarch's admiring comments (in *Ep. Sen.* XV 3) on a little treatise of Lombardo's, *De Bono Solitudinis*, the former lover of solitude, disdainful of any

Franciscan influence reached its climax. See the reference to Judge Albertano of Brescia in note 5, above.

[33] "Caeterum mali huius una radix est, quod qui plura habent, pluribus indigent." ". . . certus nunquam se egentiorem fore, quam cum multa possederit" (ibid., 548).

compromise with city living, seems to have come back to life. The scorn for marriage and family life, which had always loomed behind Petrarch's ideal of the *vita solitaria*, sounds as shrill in this *epistola senilis* as it does in the writings of any of the medieval ascetics. To be sure, Lombardo della Seta, who opens the exchange, sets the tone of the conversation, but Petrarch in turn draws upon the most uncompromising utterances in *De Vita Solitaria* and *De Remediis Utriusque Fortunae* and in his answer supports his friend's ascetic maxims with even harsher words. Lombardo's hatred of city life, as he presents it in *De Bono Solitudinis*, is shared by Petrarch. According to his introduction, during the early months of 1369, before Petrarch had established his home in Arquà, Lombardo had been anxious to visit him in Padua and had actually arrived at the city gate, when abhorrence of the noise and dirt of the city streets and the viciousness of city life so overpowered him that he felt unable to enter the town and finally fled in terror. The scene described by Lombardo presents Petrarch with the opportunity for a special encomium: a loathing of city life that supersedes even the longing for an intimate friend deserves unusual commendation, he writes. City life, he agrees, is the source of all sin, for there the rich lead their contemptible, luxurious existence while the poor suffer. In the countryside, on the other hand, happy frugality and parsimony reign, as they once did in the golden age. In the solitude of nature, bread and water can still offer sufficient nourishment, bringing satisfaction as they did to Epicurus and to Attalus, the Stoic who taught Seneca the appreciation of *paupertas*.[34]

A second occasion for Petrarch's enthusiastic praise comes in his defense of Lombardo's frugality and lonely country life against visitors who ridicule the conviction that a solitude spent reading the great works of the past is the opposite of loneliness. His visitors, says Lombardo, are disgusted by rural

---

[34] According to Seneca *Ad Lucilium* CX. 14–20.

primitiveness and insist that, in any case, the need for marriage and family life cannot be eliminated from human nature. In Lombardo's eyes, next to flight from city life, it is the very absence of women and children that makes possible spiritual communion, in the Petrarchan sense, with the great men of past ages. In order to prove that a female companion can never be a partner (*comes*) to a man leading a life of study, Lombardo revives all the arguments in favor of the monastic tradition of misogyny and all the diatribes against family life heard from the time of St. Jerome to that of the medieval humanists: accusations against the female character, which invariably drives peace of mind from the house; complaints about the ugliness of the female form; the tremendous expense of raising a family; the disappointment caused by most of one's children; the parent's awareness that someone is waiting for his death in order to come into his inheritance; and, if the son should prove better than his father, the awkwardness resulting when the achievements of an offspring overshadow the name and memory of the father. Petrarch again commends Lombardo's wisdom without qualification, while accentuating the tone of hermitlike withdrawal. Philosophy and married life will never come to terms, he says, given the character of women and the ingratitude to be expected from one's children. "If God permits," he tells Lombardo, "we [Petrarch and Lombardo] will preserve our names for posterity not through marriage but through the achievements of our minds, not by the work of a woman but by that of virtue, and with the assistance not of children but of our books." This, Petrarch adds, is what the lives of the great intellects of Antiquity teach us. "What would the names of Plato and Aristotle be today, or those of Virgil and Homer, if they had tried to procure their standing through marriage and children?" We can congratulate ourselves, Petrarch tells his younger friend, "that in spite of the preference of the crowd, you and, like you, I myself, who have wavered so often in other affairs, have so far both remained *immobilis* in this resolve from our youth to the present day."[35]

In Milan, Petrarch's increasing ability to insulate himself against the distractions of the city—in his own words, "to achieve solitude and leisure in the midst of city life"—had induced him to turn away from the Trecento ideal of poverty. His subsequent return to conditions more closely resembling those in the Vaucluse shows that the profound changes of his Milanese sojourn did not permanently transform his attitude toward life, and this helps us to understand why praise of solitary *paupertas* and diatribes against *avaritia* continued to appear in the letters he wrote in his later years.[36] When trying to define Petrarch's historical place in relation to the Quattrocento, we shall need to keep these reversions in mind.

III

The most accurate interpretation of Petrarch's position from his Milanese years onward is perhaps the following: by studiously avoiding true integration into whatever society he joined in Italy, by never establishing permanent roots anywhere and consequently always retaining a certain instability even in his way of thinking, he left the way open to an eventual return from his houses and gardens in Italian cities to a Vaucluse-like solitude on Italian soil. In Arquà, where he finally again lived in "solitude," he embraced much of his initial philosophy of withdrawal.

Apart from this lack of consistency in Italy, however, how different from his earlier thinking in the Vaucluse were Petrarch's ideas in his Milanese period and in the following years? In his youth and when he was in the Vaucluse, faith in

[35] *Ep. Sen.* xv 3 (counted as *Ep. Sen.* xiv 4 in *Opera* [1581], 936). The 1369 dating of this exchange, which makes possible its use as a source for the last phase of Petrarch's life, is owed to the chronological analysis in Ernest H. Wilkins, *Petrarch's Later Years* (Cambridge, Mass., 1959), 163f.

[36] For instance in *Ep. Sen.* vi 7 and vi 8, to which I have already drawn attention in notes 32 and 33, above.

poverty had been for Petrarch what it was for many, if not most, late-medieval Italian writers: a philosophical and spiritual dogma that gave a sense of direction but also narrowed the intellectual horizon. It is characteristic of those writers that they read more Stoic and semi-Christian opinions into their favorite ancient authors than were actually there. One of the most significant points on which the ancients and Christians were supposed to agree was *paupertas*; there seemed to be no doubt that it was appropriate for both ancient and Christian sages to praise poverty and scorn wealth. At the same time it could be insisted—and Petrarch did so from the very beginning—that voluntary poverty did not need to be sordid or abject, and that riches were not evil in themselves but only a potential source of evil because they created insatiable avarice. After leaving the provincial isolation of the Vaucluse, Petrarch became more aware of the ambivalence of the ancients regarding poverty and wealth. Hence he was now prepared at times to reappraise moral and spiritual problems created by faith in *paupertas*.

In the late 1350s and the 1360s, Petrarch clearly recognized that Cicero and Seneca had not made unqualified protests against the wise man's possession of *divitiae*. "Seneca's opinion, which rephrases that of Cicero," Petrarch remarked in this period, "is that augmentation of a person's means, provided it does not injure or harm anyone, is permissible even for a philosopher who wants to respect the limits of the good and the dutiful."[37] As is shown by his correspondence, Petrarch was able with his quickened understanding to discover new dimensions in familiar historical examples. Diogenes is famous for his poverty, he wrote in 1362, yet Democritus' reputation has not suffered because of his wealth. The Virgil who grew rich from Augustus' gifts was no worse than he had been as a penniless exile. As a result, a subtle rivalry began in

---

[37] "Audisne sententiam Ciceronis Senecae verbis expressam, ut opum amplificatio, non iniuriosa nec nocua, bono et officioso viro ac Philosopho etiam sit permissa" (*Ep. Sen.* II 2 of 1362, *Opera* [1581], 757).

Petrarch's mind between the two sets of values. Objections to
overrating the worth of poverty for the sage occasionally led
him to put limitations on strict Franciscan standards. He
maintained that St. Ambrose and St. Gregory, great scholars
and ecclesiastical leaders who accepted *divitiae atque honores*,
stood side by side with and were no less holy than St. Francis,
the man of humility and poverty. Not even Pope Sylvester, he
said, was less holy a priest after receiving Constantine's donation than he had been "when he lived, poorly and shabbily
clothed, in mountain woods and caves." Though Sylvester's
acceptance of the emperor's gift may have spelled misfortune
for the Church in later centuries—this was the great complaint
of the Trecento *Spirituales*—he remained a holy man of great
renown.[38] Eventually Petrarch vowed that if the *mediocritas* he
aimed for was unobtainable and he was forced to choose between the two extremes, he would choose wealth over sordid
poverty and unsatisfied needs, for the latter are bearable only
for those who follow a life of poverty in the name of Christ.[39]

[38] "Neque vero, tametsi rerum labentium contemptores iure optimo lau-
dentur, idcirco vituperandi sunt qui necessariis usibus illas quaerunt modo id
caveant, ne habendi studio iustitiam, modestiam, pietatem verecundiamque
posthabeant. Quanquam enim Diogenes Cynicus, effracto ad fontem vase
ligneo, naturali poculo contentus et versatili domo habitans clarus sit, nihilo
tamen obscurior aut Democritus inter divitias multas, aut ex nostris duo illi,
quibus exprobari opes novimus, Cicero et Anneus." "Sed magis ad nostros ut
veniam, an ne ideo quod Francisci clarissima sit paupertas atque humilitas,
divitiae atque honores Ambrosii aut Gregorii minus clari sunt? Quorum alter
opulentissimae urbis Episcopus, alter Episcoporum omnium princeps erat."
"Nunquid ergo aut Virgilius, multo auro ditatus a Caesare, fuit obscurior
quam dum rure primo depulsus exul atque inops Romam peteret? Aut Sylvester immenso Constantini munere minus sanctus, quam dum pauper, nudus
in nemoribus ac cavernis montium habitaret? Nocuit successoribus suis for-
sitan ea largitas nocebitque, sibi nil penitus abstulit sanctitatis aut gloriae"
(ibid.).
[39] "Demum ne semper philosophemur in nubibus, sed e latebris erum-
pentes aliquando nos et intelligere valeamus, et intelligi de se quidem alii ut
libet, apud me optimus vitae modus est mediocritas. Hinc si cogar ad extrema
deflectere, malim certe dives esse quam pauper, de paupertate loquor anxia ac
deformi, quam tristis indigentia et luridae praemunt [premunt?] sordes. Nam
ut paupertate, si facilis atque honesta contigerit, nihil est dulcius, sic ultima

Here the point of conscious differentiation between the role of poverty in a life devoted to religion and the meaning of poverty for the life of a layman or humanist philosopher seems to have been reached. The latter, Petrarch argues, should judge poverty as philosophers have long proposed: wealth should be praised or disapproved not as a doctrine but as a human condition "neither to be fervidly desired nor arrogantly disdained."[40] Even during his years in Arquà, when Petrarch described his life-long aversion to *divitiae* in his *Letter to Posterity*, he avoided calling poverty a standard that ought to be followed; he expressly stated that he had embraced it out of natural inclination, not on principle: "I have always had extreme contempt for wealth. Not that I had no desire for riches, but I hated the anxiety and toil that are invariably connected with them. . . . Nothing displeases me more than display, for not only is it bad in itself and contrary to humility, but it is troublesome and distracting."[41]

The best definition of the component added in Petrarch's later years to his attitude toward *paupertas* might be: an increased aversion to dogmatism, and therefore a diminished dependence on Franciscan and Stoic tenets. The aversion is noticeable in Petrarch's now more frequent leaning toward Peripatetic views. "Let us forget those high-sounding words" (that is, those of the Stoic dogmatists), he writes on one occasion, "and talk instead like other people, especially since those [Stoic precepts] are neither generally accepted nor in accordance with good sense, and because there is an opposing philosophical school under Aristotle's leadership that loudly

---

nil molestius egestate, unam excipio, quae propter Christi nomen assumpta esset" (ibid.).

[40] "Postremo haec nodi huius resolutio brevis sit, divitias nec ardentius appetendas nec insolentius respuendas: eas denique nec laudandas nec vituperandas quidem, sed, ut spentibus placet, inter indifferentia numerandas. Idem plane de paupertate censeo, huius autem atque illarum usum laude seu vituperio dignum esse" (ibid., 757f.).

[41] For the date of these late insertions in the *Letter to Posterity*, see Wilkins, *Later Years*, 268, and P. G. Ricci's note in *Francesco Petrarca, Prose*, 1161f.

disagrees with them."[42] A distaste for doctrinaire obstinacy influences Petrarch's preference on another occasion as well,
when he explains his dislike for extremes. Even though Diogenes in his poverty may have been happier than Alexander,
he writes, he would rather propose as a model of true "moderation" the philosopher Xenocrates, who when rich King
Alexander offered him fifty talents accepted thirty minas in
order to avoid disappointing the messengers and the appearance of an intentional affront to the king.[43]

Petrarch's reactions are even more interesting on occasions
when his references to the established doctrine of the superiority of poverty are replaced by realistic psychological observations. For example, we have his response to the complaint
that his affluent life in Milan has made him lose interest in the
company of his poorer companions. Quite the contrary, he
answers: he would always prefer to associate with people who
are not wealthy. This claim is not substantiated in the customary Trecento way; that is, by assigning the highest value to
poverty and stressing the unanimous agreement on this score
among classical and Christian writers. Rather, Petrarch points
to his own disdain for rich people whom he had admired
when they were poor. "Not because wealth must be scorned
on principle," he says, "or because *paupertas* is something

---

[42] *Ep. Fam.* XXIII 12 (6), of 1359–1360.

[43] *Ep. Sen.* XIII 13, *Opera* (1581), 927. For the date 1371–1372, see Wilkins,
Petrarch's Correspondence, 106. Whether the ascription to Socrates instead of
Xenocrates in Fracassetti's Italian translation of the *Seniles* (vol. 2, p. 320)
points to a mistake made by Petrarch is impossible to determine in the absence
of a critical edition of the *Seniles*. *Opera* (1581) has Xenocrates. *Ep. Sen.* XIII
13 is also interesting because it confirms that Petrarch remained loyal to his
ideal of moderate wealth to the end of his life: "Scito igitur et compertum
habe, nihilo magis me magnis operibus gavisurum quam honesta paupertas
animum quietaret, hunc mediocritas non quietabit? Ea vero mihi semper af-
fuit, unde usque ad hoc tempus sat liberaliter vixi." The best example, he says,
is the one "continentissimi Xenocratis, qui de quinquaginta talentis, quae sibi
inde miserat Alexander, ne donum regium spernere videretur ac nuncios con-
tristaret, triginta minas tantum, magni muneris exiguam partem, coepit
[cepit?]" (*Opera* [1581], 927).

more pleasing . . . but because long observation has taught me that for many people adversity is a school for virtue and prosperity a school for vice."[44] On the other hand, as late as in *De Remediis Utriusque Fortunae*, composed between the mid-1350s and mid-1360s, he explains that one should not jump to the conclusion that wealth should be shunned because so many are defeated by its inherent perils. "For just as being enamored of wealth is the sign of a petty mind, he who abhors wealth shows that he is insecure, that he has little confidence in himself and fears he may succumb to the lure of gold."[45] This indicates the same tendency to free himself from self-deception that we observed in Petrarch's insistence during his Milanese years that "if it is a sign of imbecility to avidly desire riches, the inability to live with them denotes an enervated mind."[46] The consequence of his years spent in Milan was thus a mode of thinking marked by a decidedly psychological approach to ethical values and a deliberate effort to reject prejudice—a combination one seeks in vain in the recluse of the Vaucluse.

IV

May we conclude from all this that Petrarch anticipated some of the insights of the Quattrocento humanists; that, looking at it from the other end, humanists a generation or two after him developed essentially the values and standards that he had seen from afar? At first glance this seems indeed to be the obvious conclusion.[47] One is inclined to argue that Petrarch was ahead

---

[44] *Ep. Fam.* xx 8, of 1359.

[45] "Ut amare enim pusilli animi, sic pati non posse aurum infirmi est parumque sibi fidentis atque auro succumbere metuentis" (*De Remediis* II, 13); see Klaus Heitmann, *Fortuna und virtus: Eine Studie zu Petrarchs Lebensweisheit* (Cologne, 1958), 186, n. 206.

[46] See p. 174 above.

[47] As I inferred—drawing on a narrower store of information as far as Petrarch is concerned—when I first published this essay nearly fifty years ago. Since there is some validity to this point of view, I will reiterate my initial

of the actual course of events, as a genius or leading mind often is; if Humanism in general had immediately taken the middle course so judiciously pointed out by him at the highpoint of his Italian period, the sudden and radical rejection of medieval attitudes toward the world and worldly goods that occurred about the turn of the century would, so to speak, not have been necessary. But as it turned out, Petrarch's first adherents failed to move in the direction pointed by their master. And indeed, in a century in which the authority of St. Francis and Stoic morality still reigned supreme, how could Petrarch, with his partial alienation from the ideal of *paupertas* for the sage, have gained anyone's confidence? One should rather admit, therefore, that the broad stream of Humanism continued to flow for a number of decades along the same traditional course which Petrarch himself had followed before he transferred his home to the cities of northern Italy. In fact, as we shall see, the generation of humanists that succeeded him clung more firmly than ever to the ideal of poverty in which Antiquity and medieval Christianity seemed to have met and become reconciled. It was not until after 1400 that the reaction against the values of the Trecento set in, first and foremost in the civic world of Florence. When it came, it was a sweeping revolt with incomparably greater momentum than Petrarch's own limited experiences could ever have generated.

We must also ask to what extent a humanist with Petrarch's style of living and *forma mentis*, writing in the middle decades of the Trecento, can at all be thought to have moved in the direction taken by humanists inside and outside Florence after the general revolt that began about 1400. Because more than half a century separates Petrarch from Bruni's, Poggio's, and Alberti's generations, any effort to detect the rudiments of Quattrocento attitudes toward wealth in Petrarch—to see him as a "precursor" of the Quattrocento—may well distort the more complex historical relationship. In analyzing Petrarch's

reasoning here, before discussing some additional and, as I now think, equally indispensable aspects of Petrarch's historical position.

struggle against the psychology of *avaritia* accepted in the Trecento, we have in fact failed to find any anticipation of the
leitmotif commonly encountered in the Quattrocento: the
reasoning that both the health of the community and the self-
fulfillment of individuals require ample material goods and
thus call for a value system that does not make poverty the
ultimate standard. But if there is nothing substantial here to
link Petrarch's appraisal of his experiences with the guiding
ideas of the Quattrocento humanists—and how could we forget what he revealed to Lombardo della Seta about his ultimate values—what, in the final analysis, is Petrarch's role in
the transition from Franciscan persuasions to Renaissance values?

The greatest obstacle to regarding Petrarch's wavering ideas
on poverty and avarice as a direct prelude to the attacks that
occurred at the turn of the century lies in the realization that
his scattered observations on the inadequacy of *paupertas voluntaria* for those engaged in civic and political life were never
crucial to his thinking. His limited toleration for material
prosperity amounted to nothing more than the delighted recognition, from his own experience, that avarice need not exercise its long-assumed pernicious effects in the case of the
rare, exceptional poet or philosopher. Petrarch, in other
words, was concerned with questions that touched a few independent minds; he did not concern himself with the general
problems that were to reverse the meaning of poverty in the
Quattrocento. As a consequence, few humanists of the following century were directly influenced by him in their thinking about the moral and psychological implications of material wealth.

Moreover, in his own time Petrarch had been known as an
adherent, rather than a doubter, of Franciscan poverty. During
the same 1350s in which he tried to work out a humanistic
defense for his own affluence, he wrote and published as a passionate partisan of the belief that strict *paupertas* was the only
salvation for the world—although in his eyes this prescription
applied in full only to the Church and its full-fledged ecclesi-

astical members, high prelates as well as friars and monks. Instead of turning the results of his own introspection into criticism of a universal call for *paupertas*, Petrarch remained loyal to the religious Trecento faith in poverty, acting as one of the most outspoken pamphleteers in the fight of the Franciscan Spirituals against the Church's use of gold and glitter in cult and ceremony, as his *Epistolae Sine Nomine* testify.

Finally, there is another area in which one must beware of overrating the proximity of Petrarch's life and thought to the post-1400 humanistic world of Italy. In view of his long sojourns at the courts of Parma, Milan, and Padua, he has often appeared to modern scholars as the archetype of that group of Quattrocento courtier-humanists which is epitomized in the second half of the century by such outstanding figures as Gioviano Pontano of Naples. Among these humanists, an active life of administrative and diplomatic service to the state produced an intellectual climate in which the ideas that first flowered in the civic milieu of Florence found a congenial echo at the courts of the Renaissance. But again, too many qualifications would be necessary to make Petrarch a "precursor" of this type of public servant. At Parma, Milan, and Padua, he was never a "courtier" or high official in the Quattrocento sense. He never exposed himself to the social pressures of courtly life; nor did he help to create an ethos of service to the state. For this reason, he appears as an associate rather than a member of some of the north Italian tyrant-courts. Living almost entirely on ecclesiastical prebends, despite the fact that he never took higher orders and never accepted a position that would have obligated him to participate in the priestly ritual or the cure of souls, his only real patron was the pope. And although the princes in whose states he lived helped him to obtain the ecclesiastical benefices he desired, he still did not become their client. He was willing to accept the gift of a house on the outskirts of a city on condition that this would not impose on him any regular official duties. Although he occasionally used his pen to the advantage of a princely friend and exercised his eloquence as an ambassador extraordinary, he met his prince virtually as an equal. He never shrank from delivering what he considered to be appropriate criticism and from conversing with his prince not in the manner of a subject but as a famous man converses with a royal friend.

This background of Petrarch's later years helps to explain the apparent paradox that, while in the history of Renaissance individualism he looks very much like a counterpart to the Quattrocento humanists, he failed to make a crucial contribution, commensurate with his genius, to the intellectual transition from Franciscan and Stoic Trecento thought to the ideas of Quattrocento Humanism. Leading as he did a life unparalleled in his day, Petrarch had little to offer any social group or movement in matters of conduct and moral aspiration, even after his return to Italy. Although he spoke out in favor of a philosopher's "Stoic" poverty, he had nothing in common with the many poor humanist teachers and secretaries who typified this trend of thought during the latter part of the Trecento. When he put his pen at the service of north Italian despots, he did not become a permanent member either of their states or of their bureaucracies. And except for a brief connection with Venice that ended in disappointment and finally confirmed his innate antipathy to life in republics, he refused to settle in any free city-state and thereby closed himself off from personal contact with those intellectual circles which his writings on human conduct could have benefited most.

Thus, as in other related areas,[48] Petrarch's penetrating analysis of his own experiences and his "inner struggles" concerning the problems of poverty, avarice, and wealth inspired neither his contemporaries nor his successors in the final transition from the belief in Trecento *paupertas* to the revaluation of wealth and material prosperity that began at the end of the Trecento. More precisely, when the transition eventu-

---

[48] For parallels, see H. Baron, "Petrarch: His Inner Struggles and the Humanistic Discovery of Man's Nature," in *Florilegium Historiale: Essays Presented to Wallace K. Ferguson* (Toronto, 1971), esp. 44ff.; and now my monograph *Petrarch's "Secretum": Its Making and Its Meaning*, Medieval Academy Books, no. 94 (Cambridge, Mass., 1985), esp. 171ff. and ch. 8.

ally occurred, it took the form of a development in two stages, as was earlier suggested in the essay dealing with the memory of Cicero.[49] First, during the latter part of the Trecento, the formative influence of Franciscan poverty and of medieval Stoic philosophy continued, receiving an ever-warmer reception from the laymen of the Italian cities and, finally, from the early humanists. Then, about the turn of the century, the long emphasis on one (by then thoroughly explored) human propensity—the *avaritia* syndrome in the psychology and social outlook of the Trecento—suddenly gave way, at least in Florence, to the exploration of other facets of human nature that had been ignored in the Trecento.

The preparation for, and the phases of, this protracted intellectual process, so out of tune with what Petrarch experienced in his atypical life, will be delineated in the essay that follows.

[49] Essay Five, p. 119.

EIGHT

Franciscan Poverty and Civic Wealth in the Shaping of Trecento Humanistic Thought: The Role of Florence*

I

THE domination of Trecento humanistic thought by the ideal of *paupertas* came to a climax during the last third of the fourteenth century. By that time familiarity with classical literature had increased greatly. But the ancient authors were read with real sympathy only when they seemed to agree with contemporary thinking on *paupertas*.

Petrarch had become aware of his own bias in the course of his development as a humanist, and as we have seen, he corrected his initial misreading of some of the available sources.[1] During his time in the Vaucluse, he had regarded even Cicero's basically Peripatetic *De Finibus* as a plea for Stoic *paupertas* and the self-sufficiency of *virtus*. But in his later Italian years he eventually recognized that there were fundamental qualifications of the Stoic point of view in both Seneca's and Cicero's works; that neither of these authors always opposed the wise man's augmenting his material resources, or even becoming wealthy. Since the relevant works of the two writers were fully known and widely read during the Trecento, no one capable of seeing more than one side of the problem should have doubted the complexity of their attitudes. Yet Trecento authors continued to embrace the idea of Franciscan poverty for two generations after Petrarch, and it would be

---

* See the preliminary note to Essay Seven.
[1] See Essay Seven, p. 181.

difficult to detect even a gradual loosening of its hold on them before the sudden intellectual transformation of about 1400.[2]

Why did the new humanistic values fail to evolve more rapidly during the second half of the Trecento? The major cause would seem to be the trauma of the terrible epidemics that ravaged Italy in and after the middle of the century. Seldom before in the Middle Ages was so much written concerning the *miseria* of human life; the history of Tuscan painting during these two generations shows a clear parallel to this.[3] The adherents of Petrarch's humanism made especial contribution to such writing.[4] These authors sought in the complex ethical reflections of the ancient authors only those features confirming their own pessimistic view of human nature, thus adding a further stimulus to the Trecento depreciation of worldly goods.

The social position of humanists in this period must have helped to foster such views. Many of them had not yet found

[2] There is no doubt that the attitudes of Cicero and Seneca changed. Some of Cicero's remarks on wealth and greed are entirely Stoic in tone, especially one long passage in his *Paradoxa* I.6, the major guide for Dante's attacks against the inclusion of wealth among the marks of *nobilitas* and a source for Petrarch's persistent condemnation of avarice. But in his *De Finibus* (especially IV.10.25f.), Cicero gave a detailed argument against the Stoic doctrine of poverty and found a better solution in the Peripatetic view of material possessions as an "aid" to virtue. As for Seneca, he too dealt with two different aspects of the problem, each in one of his best-known works. In his *De Tranquillitate* (chs. 8–9) the psychological perils of great riches are at the center of his discussion, and he finally concludes that it is better to own nothing than to live like a rich man who constantly fears or actually experiences the loss of his wealth. But in his *De Vita Beata* (chs. 21–23) he had written earlier in his life that "nobody has condemned wisdom to poverty. . . . The wise man has a better means of developing his intellect in wealth than in poverty." It is important only that he should take possessions "into his house but not into his heart"; that is, he should remain inwardly as independent of their gain as of their loss.

[3] As shown in Millard Meiss' *Painting in Florence and Siena After the Black Death* (Princeton, 1951).

[4] The most characteristic is the gloomy fragment *De Miseria Humane Vite* by Giovanni Conversino da Ravenna, in Cod IX, 11, fol. 55v–57v, in the Querini-Stampaglia Library in Venice.

their proper place in the society of the early Renaissance. Most of them were itinerant teachers or secretaries forced to seek a living by traveling from town to town, and they often had to be satisfied with material rewards that scarcely raised them above the level of indigence. There were of course exceptions (the one discussed most often in recent years being Salutati, a newcomer from the Florentine territory who virtually became chancellor for life and an unofficial member of the ruling group); also, it would be rather banal to assume that every individual judged poverty and wealth according to his economic circumstances.[5] Even so, these conditions surely had their effect on the values of a generation in which the newly emerging intellectual class was still largely in a position of inferiority and instability. We must keep this general situation in mind when we examine the reactions of individual Trecento humanists. Did they, in part at least, cling so long to the Stoic ideal of inner independence from material possessions because they found it a consolation for their own kind of existence and a stimulus to their acceptance of it?

The increasing hold of the ideal of poverty on humanistic thought can be traced in the work of all of Petrarch's pupils and intimates, beginning with the most faithful friend of his later years, Lombardo della Seta of Padua, in whose treatise *De Bono Solitudinis*, as we have observed, frugality and indifference to material wants form the basis of the humanistic philosophy of life.[6] As late as the end of the century, wherever the available sources afford a look into the structure of humanistic thought, we find the supremacy of the ideal of poverty unshaken. An informative document is the unfinished *Dialogue Between Franciscus and His Disciple* (written between 1404 and 1409),[7] which reflects the life-long experiences of a native

---

[5] In spite of his affluence, Salutati did not become a defender of material resources and wealth, as we shall presently see.

[6] See Essay Seven, p. 178.

[7] This unpublished dialogue, or rather only the *Prologus* and the first chapters, is in Cod. Vatican. lat. 5223, fol. 31r–37r. The manuscript concludes with the scribe's remark that death has taken the pen from Antonio da Ro-

of northern Italy, Antonio da Romagno. The influence of social position is discussed here with blunt honesty. As a secre-
tary, sometimes in the service of clergymen, sometimes in
small communes in northern Italy, Antonio da Romagno was
dogged by want all his life. He was therefore forced, he writes,
to find some way of making peace with this enemy. Not destined by nature or opportunity to participate in public life and
always oppressed by domestic cares, he felt it his mission to
tell those enmeshed in the affairs of this world how valueless
was all their striving after worldly goods.[8] He offers them the
old consolation that poverty, exile, pain, and death are "evils"
only to the shortsighted and tells his readers that the first step
towards their conquest is education in the love of *paupertas*.
When he began work on his dialogue, says Antonio, he was
deeply impressed by the pure and simple heroes of early Roman times, Curtius, Fabricius, and Attilius. He chose St.
Francis as his teacher, however, because the saint had not only

---

magno's hand (fol. 37r). That Antonio had planned a comprehensive book on
paupertas, of which the completed pages are only a fragment, is also shown by
the remarks on its arrangement inserted between the prologue and the text of
the dialogue, fol. 33r: "Incipit dyalogus inter Franciscum et eius devotum. Et
proponitur criminatio [wrongful accusation] paupertatis, ostendendo induc-
tive quot malorum effectuum tam circa bona fortune quam circa animam
causa est, cum tria bonorum genera omnino tollat." Moreover, on fol. 33r,
we find the intimation that St. Francis' doctrine of poverty is conceived as an
absolute authority, and all Antonio's objections to it are only a method of
procuring an opportunity to confute any doubts regarding the value of poverty. In 1404 Antonio began to devote himself entirely to his philosophical
studies, and in 1409 he died. His work on the dialogue falls between these two
dates. Cf. for this and for the other known facts of Antonio's life, R. Sabbadini, "Antonio da Romagno e Pietro Marcello," *Nuovo Archivio Veneto*, n.s.,
30 (1915): 207–15.
    [8] "Michi non tam laborum fuga quam errorum conscientia ad hanc [sc. phi-
losophiam] traducto vel eo maxime ignoscendum credidi, quod ego quidem
cum a natura muneribus publicisque rebus gerendis non fere satis accomoda-
tus tum a fortuna, licet parum blande familiaribus curis exoneratus, non in-
veni quo pacto possem reliquias vita . . . consumere iocundius. . . . In eo
michi precipue elaborandum existimavi, ut huius vim mali magis repri-
merem, quod me tristius urgeret. Itaque paupertatem ut commune omnibus
sic privatim michi domesticam ab incunabilis pene hostem experiri volui, an
forte possem vel michi pacatiorem reddere vel me sibi" (fol. 31v–32r).

borne poverty but had voluntarily taken her as his bride and had always remained faithful to her.[9] As late as the early fifteenth century, Stoic and religious ideas of poverty were still so closely knit in Humanism that once again we find the Roman heroes and St. Francis placed side by side.

Antonio da Romagno has not been entirely neglected by historians of Humanism, because during the very years in which he was writing his apology for *paupertas* he was one of Guarino da Verona's correspondents.[10] Guarino was one of the first of those humanists who attained lasting fame through the restoration of Greek studies. But his example demonstrates that contact with Greek literature did not in itself have the power to shatter the Trecento ideology of *paupertas*. Before he became tutor to a prince at the court of Ferrara, Guarino had been an itinerant teacher in typical fourteenth-century style, and in his letters of that time he had upheld the same Stoic ideas advocated in Antonio da Romagno's dialogue. In 1408 Guarino sent a message from Constantinople to one of the most distinguished patricians of Venice, Francesco Barbaro, who afterwards became the pioneer champion of civic Humanism in the Republic of San Marco. Never regard possessions and wealth as valuable, the itinerant humanist admonished the Venetian patrician. Even a citizen should pattern himself after "Solon the Wise," who told wealthy men that it is the sage who is truly "rich" because wisdom is a more permanent possession than material goods. "Contempt for riches" is the sign of true *sapientia*, of greatness of heart and courage.[11]

Next to Guarino and Leonardo Bruni, the scholar most in-

[9] "Occurrebant sane preclara illa Romana nomina, Curius, Fabricius, Attilius et item alii, quibus non parvis auctoribus defendi paupertas posset, sed maiori neminem vel auctoritate vel fide susceptutum putavi paupertatis causam quam illum, qui paupertati non modo venienti non fores clusit, sed et ultro quesite nec exiguo quidem precio certo matrimonii federe se despondit, eamque semel adamatam nunquam . . . a suis abire passus [est] amplexibus" (fol. 32r).

[10] Cf. R. Sabbadini, *Epistolario di Guarino da Verona*, vol. 3 (Venice, 1919), 122 (= Miscellanea di Storia Veneta, 3d ser., vol. 14).

[11] Ibid., vol. 1 (1915), 9ff. (= Miscellanea, 3d ser., vol. 8).

fluenced by the new Greek studies at the turn of the century
was Pier Paolo Vergerio. But like Guarino, he firmly upheld
the Stoic doctrine of poverty. It is easy to see from the letters
written by Vergerio's intimate friend Sancto de' Pellegrini that
this ideal dominated the circles in which Vergerio grew up.
When Sancto at last made his fortune after suffering great privation, he felt it necessary to justify his success by saying that
his new happiness was founded not on his recently obtained
wealth, external honors, or enjoyment of family life but rather
on the independence of mind he had achieved by following the
precepts of Seneca. He was free from the cares of indigence,
he wrote Vergerio, but he was also mindful of Lucan's remark
that "poverty is fruitful" (*foecunda virorum paupertas*) and that
need induces virtue. He knew, he wrote, that no one who has
always been rich ever attains to the summit of knowledge.[12]
Similar views came to the fore in Vergerio's work when he
began to lead the life of a scholar in Bologna and Padua, after
his first visit to Florence. Once, *paupertas* oppressed me, Vergerio consoled himself, but now it is my "nurse," my "gentle
guest."[13] In the presence of this guest, the Stoic depreciation
of external life, belief in the self-sufficiency of virtue, and renunciation of possessions and social reputation gained ever-
increasing ascendency in his mind. Henceforth, when he had
to congratulate friends who had attained to high positions, he
frequently could not refrain from adding that all material ac-
quisitions are valueless and that the true sage remains independent of changes in fortune or status. The Stoic precept
from the fifth book of the *Tusculan Disputations*—"virtus per
se sufficit ad bene beateque vivendum"—became Vergerio's
standard. Riches and power may occasionally be an "adorn-

---

[12] "Da michi a principio divitem in summo scientie fastigio collocatum;
necessitas pauperes sollicitat ad virtutem" (in the letter to Vergerio of 1389,
printed as no. 14 in Vergerio's *Epistolario*, ed. L. Smith, Fonti per la Storia
d'Italia, vol. 74 [Rome, 1934], 27). On Sancto de' Pellegrini, cf. A. Hortis, in
Archeografo Triestino, n.s., 8 (1882): 401ff., and Smith in his edition of Vergerio's *Epistolario*, 6.
[13] Vergerio, *Epistolario*, no. 15 (1389), ed. Smith, 30.

ment" to life, he admitted, but virtue, which is self-sufficient and independent, does not need them in order to grow.[14]

The question that is central to the historical appraisal of this tenacious Trecento attitude concerns Florence. On the face of it, it would seem that even the Florentine humanists accepted the doctrine of *paupertas* without making any attempt to bring their Stoic conceptions into harmony with the sentiments of the affluent citizens who surrounded them in the most flourishing industrial and commercial city of Italy. One is struck by the discovery that the author of the *Decamerone*, whom one would least expect to find in this role, is our major witness to the strength in Florence of the Trecento claims for *paupertas*. In his biography of Dante he yielded to the Stoic tendencies in Trecento thought by castigating marriage, family, and participation in public life.[15] When we look through his letters and Latin works, we find that like the itinerant teachers and chancery humanists, Boccaccio was a firm adherent of the doctrine that honorable poverty is the best stimulus for moral and intellectual energy; that he emphasized the enervating effect of riches; and that he insisted, like Petrarch in his earlier years, that we may sometimes find riches useful but that we "can bear a life of honest poverty much better than a life of riches because to the poor every small gain is great," whereas even the greatest gain is insufficient for the rich. Poverty is "free and unburdened," whereas riches only mean "worry and apprehension."[16] Boccaccio calls poverty "the mother of all praiseworthy intellectual activity," the only guarantee for peace of soul on earth, and the only protection for mankind against the dangers of sensual lust. Like other Trecento humanists, he celebrates Diogenes in his barrel, "contemplating

---

[14] Ibid., no. 40 (1392), throughout; no. 45 (1395), 104; no. 74 (1396), 175.

[15] See Essay Five, p. 129.

[16] Boccaccio, in his consolatory letter to the exile Pino de' Rossi (in Boccaccio's *Lettere*, ed. Corazzini [Florence, 1877], 78f.). See also *De Casibus Virorum Illustrium*, Lib. III, ch. 17, where he says with Latin terseness "longe tolerabilius divitiis paupertas," and Lib. I, ch. 15, which contains a speech in praise of *paupertas* (quotation follows in the text).

celestial things with a calm spirit." In the words of a rhetorical Latin eulogy that he addressed to Paupertas, "Tibi stabilitas, tibi immunitas, tibi si qua est quies in mundanis concessa est. Tu artificiosa, tu ingeniosa, tu studiorum omnium laudabilium mater egregia es!" How beautiful it is in your company, Poverty, he concludes "to choose rural places, to live in strict solitude, to . . . contemplate heavenly things under the shade of trees by silvery streams."[17]

At first, we might be tempted to argue that the poet Boccaccio, who had lived in Neapolitan courtly society for a long time, was not a typical Florentine citizen and that he elaborated thoughts current in circles outside the Florence of his time. But we then perceive that in his defense of *paupertas* he also made a "civic" contribution—one, however, that lay within a specifically fourteenth-century context. Most of his dicta concerning the blessings of poverty were inspired by Roman literature, where the praise of her often took a specifically civic tone. Late Roman admiration for voluntary poverty—in Cicero, Sallust, Virgil, Seneca, Lucan, and Florus—had largely expressed a political romanticism that favored the simple life and was indifferent to material things. These authors viewed such indifference as a personal advantage to Romans of the early *Respublica Romana* and as one of the sources of the dedication and will power that created the Roman Empire. For Boccaccio, recognition of the educative force of poverty, in the Roman sense, led less to the sage's deliberate avoidance of enjoyment and possessions than to a political ideal in which the health of the community was seen to depend on simplicity in civic conduct and to a conception of Roman history in which a national decline from strength to decadence was the result of increasing greed and pleasure seeking.[18] But in order

[17] In the speech praising *paupertas* in Boccaccio's *De Casibus Virorum Illustrium*, I, 15; moreover, cf. III, 1, "Paupertatis et Fortunae Certamen," and ch. 17, "In Divitias et Stolidi Vulgi Opinionem." L. B. Hall, in his introduction to the reproduction (Gainesville, 1962) of the 1520 edition of *De Casibus Virorum*, describes *paupertas* as the chief virtue praised in this work (pp. x–xi).

[18] Cf. the collection of source passages from Roman literature in W. Meyer, "Laudes inopiae" (diss., Göttingen, 1915), 44ff.

to see how the political side of the classical praise of poverty
became familiar to Trecento writers, we must go back beyond
the Humanism of Boccaccio's generation to the beginning of
the century, and we must do so in some detail.

II

Among Dominican friars living on the threshold of the fourteenth century—in Florence and in other Tuscan city-states—
we find a kind of prelude to certain later reactions of the Florentine humanists, a prelude entirely medieval in tone.[19] The
leading intellect among these Tuscan Dominicans—more
original and a better writer than Remigio de' Girolami—was
Ptolemy (Bartolomeo) of Lucca, a descendent of the Lucchese
Fiadoni family. One of Aquinas' last intimate disciples, he was
responsible for the completion and publication of Thomas'
unfinished major treatise on politics, *De Regimine Principum*.
Only the beginning of this treatise (up to the fourth chapter of
the second book) was written by Aquinas himself. As in all
the writings of Aquinas' school, Aristotelian philosophy and
political scholarship are the basic elements of the two and a
half books Ptolemy added. But at the same time, Ptolemy's
work shows a feature without counterpart in the school of
Aquinas: a systematic use of the history of ancient Rome as a
background for political discussion. Because of his historical
interest, Ptolemy became more fully aware than any preceding medieval writer of the role of Roman patriotism and the
virtutes Romanae in the rise of the *Respublica Romana*.

An unusual interest in Rome and in the literary memory of
Rome's greatness did not, however, turn Ptolemy into a pro-
tohumanist. Like other members of the Dominican school of
Aquinas, he refrained from any systematic study of the ancient Latin authors. His admiration for Rome's republican
form of government—led by senators of equal status, who had

---

[19] Some aspects of this prelude were already observed in Essay Five, where
we traced the gradual rediscovery of Cicero as the representative of Roman
civic spirit. See page 114 above.

to seek the approval of the Roman people, rather than by a crowned head wearing the insignia of unapproachable majesty—was based on occasional comments in the Second Book of Maccabees, not on authentic Roman sources. He sought another legacy of Antiquity in Stoic wisdom and in so doing gave credence to some erroneous interpretations of ancient authors. This shows him far from having even the rudiments of humanistic historical knowledge. To him Socrates was the leader of the Stoic school (*princeps Stoicorum*) and the creator of the ideal of the sage who has conquered all passion.[20] He believed that the Stoics and Cynics—especially Seneca, "the perfect Stoic"—had already anticipated "the humility and contempt for this world" taught by Christ.[21]

But though the intellectual storehouse of Humanism was still closed to Ptolemy, his contribution to the *De Regimine Principum* proves that his view of Roman republicanism and the *virtutes Romanae* was influenced by the psychological and ethical ideas of the friars. The result was limited by the anachronistic conception of Antiquity that persisted throughout the Middle Ages. Thus, from the viewpoint of medieval chivalry, the Romans had seemed like medieval knights; and when a Dominican like Ptolemy, who spent many of his best years in the surroundings of the Tuscan city-states, endeavored to grasp the nature of the *virtutes Romanae*, he tended to make them conform to the standards of the mendicant friars. It was through the prism of the active, socially minded friars that Ptolemy came to appreciate the Roman public spirit. Roman patriotism and devotion to the state seemed to him to embody love for one's neighbor, ultimately kindred to Christian *caritas*. And since *caritas* was one of the highest virtues, according to the friars, Ptolemy found it easy to approve the Roman insistence that nothing should be allowed to interfere when the survival of the commonwealth was at stake. We have observed that the Tuscan Dominicans were the first to try to rehabilitate

[20] *De Regimine Principum*, Lib. IV, ch. 4.
[21] Ibid., Lib. III, chs. 15–16.

Cicero's ethic of dedication to the state;[22] and it was in the same spirit that Ptolemy, in the *De Regimine Principum*, revived—with greater admiration than had ever been shown during the medieval centuries—the *exempla* of Roman self-sacrifice: Marcus Curtius' leap on horseback into the abyss that opened in the forum and closed after his sacrificial act; and Marcus Regulus' advice to the Roman senate, following his defeat in the war with Carthage, not to conclude a premature peace but to send him back to the enemy to a certain and cruel death.

Ptolemy found these Roman *exempla* easily accessible in the works of St. Augustine and Valerius Maximus. And when he read the related legendary and historical material offered there, he also found the other major virtue of the friars: voluntary poverty and disdain for wealth. In this connection he relates the story of the former commander Manlius Curius Dentatus, who received Samnite ambassadors while enjoying his frugal meal from a wooden vessel after a day of toil on his small estate. The ambassadors saw in this image of poverty a welcome opportunity to bribe an enemy, but were told coldly to "tell your people that Manlius Curius prefers ruling over rich men to being rich himself." We find the same spirit, says Ptolemy, in C. Fabricius, who after winning tremendous victories in the Samnite wars and over King Pyrrhus, remained *pauperrimus* and ridiculed all attempts to bribe him; he felt himself to be "very rich without money," because wealth does not mean that you "possess much" but that you "desire little."[23] The same emphasis on the *paupertas* of early Roman leaders appears elsewhere in Ptolemy's work: Codrus, who sacrificed himself in battle for his *patria*, did so "in effigie pauperis"; and quite a few leading citizens were left so poor after performing great deeds that friends, or the state itself, eventually had to provide them dignified burials. On the other hand, he offers the evidence given in Cato Uticensis' speech

[22] See Essay Five, p. 114.
[23] *De Regimine Principum*, Lib. III, ch. 4.

before the senate (transmitted by Sallust) that by the end of the republic "luxuria atque avaritia" and private wealth, in contrast to the growing *egestas* of the community, had undermined the health of Rome.[24]

The historical appraisal underlying this republican interpretation of Roman history is entirely in the medieval mold. Since the time of the Church Fathers, the historical conception of the *Respublica Romana* was that the early Roman conquest of the world had made possible the emergence of a universal imperial monarchy, which in turn was the precondition for the spread of Christianity. It was generally believed that this universal monarchy was the last of the four divinely ordained world monarchies and that it would not entirely fade away until the Second Coming of Christ on the Day of Judgment. In Guelph Italy, where Ptolemy spent most of his life, there arose for the first time an anti-imperial counterthesis to this imperial theology of history: the contention that Christ, not a worldly emperor, was the true monarch of the world; in other words, that when Christ was born a "fifth monarchy" replaced the rule of the Roman emperors. To be sure, Augustus was allowed to act as Christ's deputy in accordance with the divine plan, but with the Constantinian Donation that temporary concession came to an end, and the Lord himself, or rather his earthly representative, the pope, became the true monarch of the world.

When he adopted this Guelph idea in *De Regimine Principum*, Ptolemy integrated it with his own speculations on the historical role of *paupertas*. Such a view of the past, he remarked, naturally "makes one wonder why Christ, our king and leader, lived in humility and poverty although he was lord of the world."[25] Ptolemy's answer was that if Christ had directly taken over the *principatus* of the world, he would have resembled those other holders of earthly power and could not

[24] Ibid., chs. 14 and 20.
[25] "Admiratione enim dignum est quia humilis et pauper, at tamen Dominus mundi."

then have given the princes of the world the example of *humilitas et paupertas* which alone would satisfy his subjects. Thus Christ "chose a humble life, and yet he was the true Lord and Monarch; . . . on humbleness and poverty, therefore, he founded his dominion." This is why, as the Second Book of Maccabees relates, "the *Respublica* of the Romans was built not by the pomp and splendor of arrogant men"—not (as is repeatedly emphasized in *De Regimine Principum*) by princes wearing precious diadems and royal vestments—but by the senate and the Roman people meeting in their duly constituted councils and assemblies, by people living in *paupertas* and free from presumption.

The longing of Trecento friars for humility, simplicity, and poverty, and the republican instincts of Italian city-state citizens seem to have come together here. Republicanism, based on political experience, has a definite place in Ptolemy's Tuscan environment. For in his own sections of the *De Regimine Principum* (that is, the entire text following Book II, chapter 4) we have the first political treatise of the Middle Ages in which the *regimen politicum* (the constitutional government of laws) and the *regimen regale* (the personal government of kings) are placed on an equal footing.[26] With the help of the newly acquired knowledge of the city-state republics of Antiquity, which had become available through the Latin translation of Aristotle's *Politics* in Aquinas' Parisian days, this became the first attempt to systematically analyze republican government on a comparative basis. The *Respublica Romana* was thought to have been victorious over other ancient city-states and nations, however—or to have been made victorious by divine providence—because the conduct of her citizens closely followed the values of the Tuscan friars: Roman public spirit was akin to Christian *caritas, humilitas*, and *paupertas*.

For Ptolemy the implications of these ideas were truly significant: he was aware that his reflections could lead him to a

---

[26] This fact was first pointed out by C. H. McIlwain in his *The Growth of Political Thought in the West* (New York, 1932), esp. 332f., 335–38, 359.

clash between the convictions of the friars and the realism of Aristotle. When he discussed Aristotle's critique of the constitution of Sparta in his survey of the ancient city-state republics,[27] he had to come to terms with this discrepancy. In Aristotle's judgment, the fact that the office of the Ephors often went to impecunious men was a weakness of the Spartan republic, because poor citizens are prone to corruption. Ptolemy tries to resolve the apparent disagreement about the effects of poverty in the usual Scholastic fashion. We arrive at contradictory conclusions, he argues, because we neglect to distinguish between two kinds of *paupertas*. When each is given its due place in the scale of values, the views can be reconciled. On the one hand, he admits, Aristotle's point of view is supported by the fact that he is not the only one to believe that poverty makes bad citizens. After all, Scipio Africanus must have been of the same opinion when he gave as his reason for indicting two high Roman officials in Spain for corruption that one of them had previously shown great avarice and the other was "too poor" (*nimis pauper*) to be expected to withstand financial temptation. On the other hand, poverty surely did not prove to be an obstacle to good citizenship for Fabricius, who could not be bribed although he was *pauperrimus*, or for the many outstanding early Roman leaders who had to be buried at public expense because they were so poor. "Consequently, one has to distinguish between two kinds of indigence: one voluntary and the other involuntary." Even though it may increase man's shrewdness and energy, the latter will lead to almost irresistible temptation when bribes are offered. But the former increases virtue and honesty; it is, in fact, an indispensable part of good government. Not only Romans of Fabricius' stamp lived in this state of voluntary poverty, Christ and the Apostles also praised and followed it. By means of this Scholastic argument, Ptolemy was able to reconcile to his own satisfaction two lines of thought as widely diverse as the mendicant concept of dignified *paupertas volun-*

---

[27] *De Regimine Principum*, Lib. IV, ch. 20.

taria and Aristotle's judgment in the case of the Spartan Ephors.

But how far should a state go in trying to exclude the poor from active citizenship? They could, after all, be a source of danger for a republic. Ptolemy finally is forced to make up his mind when he deals with the constitution of Carthage, described by Aristotle as a plutocracy in which private wealth was mandatory for admission to high office. One must acknowledge, Ptolemy now says, that a person who has to worry about his material needs cannot be a good statesman. Accordingly, his final judgment, rather illogically, is: "As long as a person lives in conformity with *virtus*, he ought to be accepted in a well-ordered republic whether he is poor or rich. But a rich citizen, who has resources at his disposal with which he can administer his office honestly, is less of a threat—provided, of course, that no injustice is done to subordinates."[28]

III

A full discussion of politically motivated poverty had thus already taken place two generations before the final success of the Franciscan movement propelled the ideal of voluntary poverty into the center of early humanistic thought, and we must make use of the precursory argument if we wish to trace the roots of Boccaccio's humanistic ideas. The thinking of the Tuscan Dominican friars had been guided by the standard of voluntary religious poverty, but at the same time it had been concerned about the effect of poverty on a healthy political life. It is evident, therefore, that one can evaluate the effect of *paupertas* on nascent Humanism in the Florentine republic only if the friars are considered in the broader context of the

---

[28] "Sive pauper, sive dives, dummodo vivat secundum virtutem, assumendus est in vera politia. Sed minus periculum est de divite; quia instrumenta sibi adsunt humanae vitae, per quae honeste suum potest officium exequi, salva tamen justitia subditorum" (ibid.).

Trecento idea of a politically oriented *paupertas*. With this in mind, we return to Boccaccio.

An admiring friend of Petrarch's, Boccaccio seems to have been the first Florentine writer under humanistic influence to depict Roman history in the light of the full Trecento meaning of *paupertas*. Not long after 1360,[29] a socially and politically prominent friend of Boccaccio's, Pino de' Rossi, was exiled by the Florentine government. As was often the case, banishment reduced this Florentine patrician from great wealth to modest circumstances, and Boccaccio comforted him with a letter in which *paupertas*, abhorred by Pino, is no longer recommended as a fortunate escape from the burdens of wealth into rustic but carefree solitude. Boccaccio knew that Pino de' Rossi would be more consoled by a frank admission of the surpassing importance of status and dignity (*onore*) in the life of a citizen and by the recognition that these are threatened by the indigence that results from exile. But so far as civic values are concerned, he tells his friend, this is not the only consideration. For it is also true that it is more difficult for genuine political *virtus* to stand out against a background of affluence than against one of poverty. Excellence tested under indigent conditions will ultimately bring a citizen greater renown than the usual *onore* won during an affluent life.

Here, the letter says, the lesson of Roman history can stand us in good stead because it teaches us that little is needed to satisfy human wants, even in military life. The Roman soldiers who endured inhuman hardships in their conquest of the world carried no provisions other than a ration of flour and lard, trusting that they would find the necessary water—just as acorns and river water were sufficient for mankind in the "golden age," the beginning of all history. And along with the simplicity that marked the life of the Roman armies, we have the integrity, born of poverty, of the political leaders of early Rome. While he still derives his *exempla* principally from Valerius Maximus' *De Factis et Dictis Memorabilibus* (as Ptolemy

---

[29] N. Sapegno, *Il Trecento* (Milan, 1934), 287.

of Lucca had done), Boccaccio recalls how the poverty of Scipio Africanus the Elder's little house on the Mediterranean coast at Linternum had enhanced the "majesty" of his name and virtue, and how the modesty that made Cato the Censor take only three servants with him when he went to Spain to serve in high office increased his stature because the humbleness of his resources made the value of his attainments appear even more impressive. Boccaccio also adopts Valerius Maximus' description of how Cincinnatus was working with his own hands on his tiny farm when the messengers called him from his plowing to take command of the Roman army. The letter further praises the rural simplicity of the life of Manlius Curius Dentatus, which was revealed when the ambassadors of King Pyrrhus came to bribe him—like the messengers of the Samnites, Boccaccio says, who tried to bribe Fabricius Luscinus. All these episodes illustrate that the empire could grow and defend itself as long as Rome's citizens retained poverty as part of their way of life. But "as soon as riches with their weakening effect began to shape private lives, the empire lost ground; and as covetousness increased, the empire declined more and more and finally fell into that state of decay in which it is today, when it exists in name only and not as a political reality." Boccaccio concludes: "Thus no one should be so arrogant as to feel ashamed of being poor, inasmuch as the *Imperium Romanum* was founded on *paupertas*."[30]

How seriously should we take this historical argument? Since the writing in question is a letter of consolation, one cannot dismiss the suspicion that Boccaccio may have tried

---

[30] "E, così come le ricchezze colle loro morbidezze per le private case incominciarono ad entrare, a diminuire cominciò; e, come l'avarizia venne crescendo, così quello di male in peggio vegnendo, nella ruina venne nella quale al presente il veggiamo; che è in nome alcuna cosa, e in esistenza niuna." "E chi sarà colui sì trascurato che d'essere povero si vergogni, riguardando il romano imperio avere la povertà avuta per fondamento" (Boccaccio, in his letter to Pino de' Rossi; see *Boccaccio, Opere in Versi, . . . Prose Latine, Epistole*, ed. P. G. Ricci, La Letteratura Italiana: Storia e Testi, vol. 9 [Milan, 1965], 1125 and 1124).

strong medicine in order to reconcile his friend to his fate and did not really consider the change from poverty to wealth to be the key to the decay of ancient Rome. It is a fact, however, that Boccaccio indicated his belief in the decisive role of political *paupertas* in at least one other context. In his major historical work, *De Casibus Virorum Illustrium*, a personified Paupertas is made to claim that she was "the nurse of the *Imperium Romanum*."[31] Moreover, if we read the letter to Pino carefully, we find that the function of *paupertas* in the Roman past is traced from the standpoint of an involved Florentine citizen: Whereas the political poverty of Rome set an example that later nations could follow, he says, avarice and greed have, alas, been proverbial among the Florentines. He knows of only a single Florentine counterpart to all the cited Roman examples: the "volontaria povertà" of Aldobrandino d'Ottobuono. After a defeat, the Pisans had offered this citizen a considerable sum of money if he would work for Pisa in the Florentine government. He refused despite personal indigence, and later he received a monumental tomb at the expense of a grateful republic.[32]

But though we can be certain that Boccaccio's sketch of early Roman *paupertas* is not merely a rhetorical device, we may still wonder to what extent it is original. At this point Ptolemy of Lucca provides the standard for determining what was new and humanistic in Boccaccio's view. Comparison shows that Boccaccio added or changed little. Petrarch's friend and disciple, of course, read more classical authors and studied them with greater care. But he still presents his evidence in the form of *exempla* and anecdotes taken from Valerius Maximus. No new beginning has yet been made in the development of a truly historical picture of early Rome. This occurred later, when Renaissance humanists applied philological and historical criteria to the exposition of available

---

[31] "Ego Romani Imperii nutrix fui" (*De Casibus Virorum Illustrium*, Lib. III, ch. I, "Paupertatis et Fortunae Certamen").

[32] *Boccaccio, Opere*, 1124.

sources. Boccaccio was nevertheless able to offer a sharply defined historical judgment, just as the prehumanistic friar Ptolemy had been able to form a coherent idea of the role of *pau pertas* in ancient Rome. Both writers could do this simply by repeating the nostalgic eulogies of poverty and honesty encountered in the work of some of the widely read Roman authors—especially in Sallust, whose view of Rome's development from early simplicity and unswerving honesty to unbridled ambition and greed had often been quoted in the Middle Ages. By the same token, Boccaccio did nothing more than reproduce a dictum of Seneca's when he climaxed his eulogy of political poverty with the verdict that "the *Imperium Romanum* was founded on *paupertas*."[33]

As the comparison with Ptolemy's prehumanistic performance shows, one should not overrate this accomplishment of Trecento Humanism. During the fourteenth century a writer did not have to be a fledgling Renaissance philologist to quote or plagiarize well-known Roman authors and carve some similarly oriented anecdotes from narrators like Valerius Maximus. Nor was it a step toward the Renaissance when a medieval or Trecento writer echoed Roman interpretations of the history of Rome because these seemed to him to support mendicant ideas on voluntary poverty. The only Trecento writer who reinterpreted Roman history in a fresh, independent way was Petrarch, when he applied medical conceptions of health and sickness to the growth and decay of the *virtus Romana*. Petrarch's contemporary Trecento disciples, however, were not open to this new approach. Rather, it was the Florentines of the Quattrocento and, eventually, Machiavelli who enlarged upon his ideas.[34]

The significance of Boccaccio's view of Rome must therefore be sought elsewhere. The assimilation of the Tuscan Dominican philosophy of Roman *paupertas* into the work of Flor-

---

[33] Cf. ". . . ut populus Romanus paupertatem, fundamentum et causam imperii sui, requirat ac laudet, divitias autem suas timeat . . ." (Seneca *Ep. Mor. ad Lucilium* LXXXVII.41).

[34] See Essay Two, pp. 25f. and 38.

entine humanists like Boccaccio shows that this view of Rome was in accord not only with mendicant attitudes but also with those of lay citizens. This is borne out by the fact that whereas the view of early Rome encountered in Ptolemy and Boccaccio does not appear to have been echoed anywhere outside of Tuscany during the Trecento, it was adapted and expanded in a work by the Florentine chancellor Coluccio Salutati.

In 1381, about twenty years after Boccaccio's letter was written, Salutati took up the theme of *paupertas* in the early *Respublica Romana*. As in the case of Boccaccio, the writing in question, *De Seculo et Religione* (*On Secular and Religious Life*), is not a work of historiography. Rather, it is a treatise dedicated to a friend who had entered the Camaldulensian Order and was intended as a vade mecum, with chapters devoted to each of the monastic vows, including *de voto paupertatis*. In Salutati's discussion of the value and function of voluntary poverty, the viewpoint has shifted from religious and Stoic *paupertas* to political *paupertas*. Only a lay citizen would have discussed the role of the latter in the history of Rome. The psychological assumptions that are offered as a prelude include the two profound convictions of the century: that the rich are the true *pauperes* because the human thirst for riches is insatiable; and that the wealthier a man becomes, the more impossible it is for him to fulfill his desires. As soon as he tries to rise above the level of poverty, he will toil, lie, deceive, and murder in order to amass riches; "once these are his, the fear that he may lose them will torment him; if they are in fact lost, he will be in the greatest misery."[35]

From this psychological introduction Salutati turns to Roman examples, and in his hands what was formerly a collection of didactic anecdotes starts to become a genuine historical conception based on the critical use of an enlarged body of source material. The way Salutati uses the Roman anecdotes takes his work unquestionably beyond Boccaccio's rhetorically styled encouragement to a friend. His basic thesis—that

---

[35] *De Seculo et Religione*, ed. Ullman, 121–24.

the Romans were strikingly poor during the time they conquered the world—is documented with new information. We
know that "Romulus was poor" (*Romulus pauper fuit*), Salutati's historical reconstruction begins, because in their descriptions of a fire in Rome, later authors mention that poor shep-
herd dwellings from the time of Romulus were consumed by
flames. Moreover, it is said that when King Numa Pompilius
established Rome's religious cult, he was unable to have precious vases made for dedication to the gods, "but yielding to
necessity, he consecrated earthen vessels, a proof of extreme
poverty" (*quod maxim[a]e paupertatis argumentum est*). And
when the last two kings erected their public buildings, magnificent for their time, the effort, we are told, quickly ex-
hausted the treasure stored up by several generations. So one
may infer, says Salutati, that when, soon afterwards, the Romans waged war against wealthy cities, they did so in order to
refill their coffers. He found other signs of great poverty in
early republican Rome, especially in tales about early Roman
leaders who had so little means after performing glorious
deeds for the republic that they had to be buried at public expense. When the state gave dowries to the daughters of these
men, the sums reported down to the time of Scipio Africanus
the Elder were astonishingly small. The traditional accounts
of early Roman *exempla* of poverty are consistent with this
picture, Salutati continues. Thus we are told of the great victor Cincinnatus, who was "compelled by *paupertas*" to use
primitive implements to till his fields. The state, then already
a flourishing republic, nevertheless called him to the solemn
office of dictator while he was in the midst of ploughing and
sowing, "without any sense of shame," and after his tenure of
six months had ended, he returned to his humble work in the
fields.

Salutati judges the Roman *exempla* accordingly. "How worthy Cincinnatus would have been to live at the time of Christ!"
he exclaims, "for he was not only ready to suffer poverty, but
even loved and cultivated *paupertas*." One need not repeat this
for all the other early Romans and their age, he adds. "These

I. AN ANATOMY

impoverished men founded the great empire that their rich successors later ruined," as Sallust so aptly described it. It was the wealthy men from Sulla to Caesar, Salutati concludes, who essentially destroyed (*funditus destruxerunt*) "the Roman commonwealth which a poor Romulus had founded and even poorer leaders had raised to such greatness. . . . Thus mankind can see in the memory of these deeds, as in a mirror, that in the foundation, development, and conservation of this *civitas terrena* of mortal men, the poor have done better than the rich."[36]

In this work of humanistic philology and historical reinterpretation, Salutati, a spokesman for the Florentine civic milieu, made his contribution to the Trecento ideology of *paupertas* by presenting the rudiments of a new critical scholarship within a surviving medieval frame.[37] Medieval, in particular, is his clinging to the old Augustinian concept of the two, related *civitates*: the *civitas terrena*, usually identified with the *Imperium Romanum*, and the *civitas Dei*, usually identified with the Church. Both universal institutions (*utraque civitas*), he ultimately judges, "were built by the poor and undermined and corrupted by the rich."[38]

With respect to the growth of the *civitas Dei* on earth, Salutati had learned from history that the Apostles and their disciples, as well as all the martyrs from the time of Nero to that of Diocletian, either lived in "abjecta paupertas" or sold what they possessed and made the proceeds common property. They chose "paupertas voluntaria" while creating the Catholic Church. But after the latter had been accepted by Constantine

[36] ". . . rem enim publicam Romanorum, quam pauper fundavit Romulus et pauperrimi principes ad tantam magnitudinem erexerunt. . . . Ut in hac rerum gestarum memoria quasi quodam in speculo videri possit mortalium genus ad hanc terrenam civitatem instituendam, augendam, atque conservandam pauperes divitibus prestitisse" (ibid., 124–28).

[37] He did the same—contributed historical discoveries without upsetting traditional assumptions—in his conclusions regarding the Roman foundation of Florence, as has been shown in *Crisis*, 2d ed., 63–64, 99–100, and 159.

[38] *De Secolo et Religione*, ed. Ullman, 124f.

and had received his gift, "there arose among the leaders of
the Church first an inordinate desire for money and then the
greed for power, just as there had among the leaders of the
civitas terrena." The churchmen began "to bedeck themselves
with gold and silver and to don magnificently colored vestments," and finally "illam civitatem gloriosam abominabilem
reddiderunt." Gradually, the eastern part of the Church drew
away from the papacy, and at the end (three years before Salutati wrote) the unity of the Church was destroyed. Here, too,
the result was obvious: "Just as the leaders and founders of the
two *civitates* not only laid lasting foundations but splendidly
enlarged them by their labor and sweat as long as they loved
poverty, so later the rich, when money had corrupted them in
mind and conduct, destroyed almost everything with their
greed and ostentatious wealth."[39]

But why, twenty years after Boccaccio had applied it exclusively to the secular history of Rome, did Salutati find the concept of a fatal decline from wholesome poverty to corruptive
wealth applicable to the history of the Church? It has been
suggested that we should consider the fact that during the two
decades separating their works (the 1360s and 1370s)—a period of growing disagreement and eventually war with the papacy in Avignon—Florence had tolerated the sect of the Fraticelli. During the 1370s, especially, the city was full of its
adherents, whose call for absolute religious *paupertas* led to the
rejection of the wealthy modern Church in the name of pristine Christian poverty. Salutati's reasoning in his chapter on
paupertas in *De Seculo et Religione* could thus be said to have
been written under the influence of sectarian thought.[40]

This theory is reasonable, provided that it is not used to
maintain that Salutati's discussion betrays personal sympathy
for the Fraticelli and provided that the view of ecclesiastical
wealth as an open sore on the body of the modern Church is

[39] Ibid., 129–30.
[40] This was suggested by Martin Becker, "Florentine Politics and the Dif-
fusion of Heresy in the Trecento: A Socio-Economic Inquiry," *Speculum* 30
(1959): 74f.

not considered necessarily to have been adopted from the Fraticelli. Such inferences would overlook the complexity of the controversy over *paupertas* that raged in Florence. By 1381 the excitement of the war with the papacy was a matter of the past, and a strong reaction had set in against the extremism of the leniently treated Fraticelli sect. It is quite improbable that Salutati, the chancellor and friend of many a leading citizen, could still have been impressed at that time by the view of the Fraticelli. Moreover, the distinction made between the "poor Church" of early Christian times and the "rich Church" of later centuries was by no means the exclusive intellectual property of the Fraticelli, and Salutati could have picked up the idea practically anywhere in the Florence of the 1370s. Even that sharp critic of the Fraticelli, Giovanni dalle Celle (whom we will presently use as a guide), felt obliged to concede that in the eyes of God there must have existed in the course of history not one church but two successive churches: "the one poor, such as the Church was in the beginning; the other rich, such as the Church has become in the declining centuries of the world."[41]

All things considered, the most important contribution of the Fraticelli to the history of Trecento *paupertas* may well have been their lack of success. The humiliation of so widespread a sect based on the love of poverty was a lasting blow to the belief in *paupertas* itself. From the early 1380s on, everything seemed to cooperate in undermining the acceptance of the *paupertas* claim. During the 1370s, Petrarch's inflammatory letters and poems against "avaricious Avignon" and her insatiable greed had been reread and welcomed in Florence like all the Franciscan warnings against riches and avarice, and the government had been reluctant to keep out the preachers of the Fraticelli, who came from various parts of the peninsula to find refuge in the city. But the end of the 1370s made in-

---

[41] ". . . l'una povera sí come ella fu nel principio, l'altra richa sí come è diventata nella fine del mondo" (in Giovanni's letter "Ai Fraticelli," written between 1378 and 1383, ed. F. Tocco, 127; see also note 50, below).

creasingly clear the heretical consequences of the Fraticelli claim that where there was no absolute poverty there could be no true church and no acceptable priests. Moreover, during the civil strife that culminated in the revolt of the Ciompi in 1378, spiritual faith in poverty was sometimes transformed into a social outcry against the rich. The ascendency of *paupertas* in civic circles came, therefore, to an abrupt halt. Out of the struggle against the Fraticelli emerged the first fundamental critique of the ideal of *paupertas*. Proof that such was, indeed, the course of events is provided by the writings of Giovanni dalle Celle, the earliest influential controversialist against the Fraticelli in Florence, who belonged to an offshoot of the Benedictine Order, the Camaldolese hermits.[42]

IV

Giovanni dalle Celle was a churchman in whom spiritual motivation and loyalty to Florence seemed indissolubly fused. He was a descendent of an old noble family in the Florentine territory and kept up friendships and correspondence with mem-

[42] The statement that there was a vital change in the "fascination with *paupertas*" and in the significance of the Fraticelli in the period of Giovanni dalle Celle remains valid even though research in the last few decades has brought to light a greater underground presence of Fraticelli in Quattrocento Florence than had been expected. John N. Stephens, who has carefully collected evidence on the Florentine survival of Fraticelli beyond 1400 ("Heresy in Medieval and Renaissance Florence," *Past and Present* 54 [1972]: esp. 42ff.), nonetheless characterizes their life in the Quattrocento as follows: unlike the Fraticelli of the Trecento, they were "only indulging their sectarian appetites in the privacy of the night and of their own houses, and their friars escaped identification by wearing ordinary clothes. This public conformity may have satisfied the conscience of the ecclesiastical hierarchy and dissuaded them from repression" (p. 45).

For Giovanni dalle Celle, see Decima L. Douie, *The Nature and the Effect of the Heresy of the Fraticelli* (Manchester, England, 1932), 232ff., and Pia Cividali, "Il beato Giovanni dalle Celle: Memoria," *Atti dell' Accademia dei Lincei, Memorie, Classe di Scienze Morali* (1906), 354–477. Cividali's "Memoria" includes a survey of Giovanni's correspondence (see p. 403) and publishes some of it for the first time.

bers of the Florentine patriciate even after he withdrew in the 1350s from his position as abbot of S. Trinità in Florence and retired to a hermit cell high in the Apeninnes. During the 1370s, when Florence was at war with the Church and was punished by papal interdict, he reacted very differently from the great saint of his generation, Catherine of Siena, who could see only sin and crime in armed resistance to a pope. Catherine implored Giovanni to make his spiritual disciples oppose Florence's antipapal policy, or at least leave the territory of the sinful city. Like his Florentine contemporary, the Augustinian friar Luigi Marsigli, Giovanni did the opposite: when Guido del Palagio, twice gonfalonier of the republic, asked for Giovanni's pastoral counsel, he was told that he need have no qualms of conscience. A citizen has to defend his *patria* and help her with his counsel at any time. If he should be given high office at a time when his city is in conflict with the Church, he should be regarded not as someone waging war with the pope but as someone who wishes to protect his *patria* in accordance with his duty. At the time when Giovanni gave this counsel he had long been living in the Apennine forests. There he was prevented from coming in contact with nascent Florentine Humanism, in which some friars and monks who lived in the city were already participating,[43] most of all the Augustinian friar Luigi Marsigli, the respected spiritual friend of Salutati and his circle. But Giovanni kept in touch with the outside world by correspondence, and his letters helped to shape the spiritual life in literate Florentine circles, not only during the last third of the Trecento but, after his death, in the Quattrocento as well, as the astonishingly large number of manuscript copies of his letters in Florentine libraries indicates. Some of them are an incomparable source of information for our understanding of the beginnings of the revolt against the Trecento idea of *paupertas*.

---

[43] It has been proved that Giovanni dalle Celle was not the author of the Volgare translations of Cicero and Seneca that have traditionally been attributed to him. His pre-humanistic frame of mind is recognizable in the warnings in his letters against "libri de' pagani." See Cividali, "Memoria," 419.

Initially, Giovanni dalle Celle had taken a stand influenced by the Spiritual Franciscans and even by the Fraticelli.[44] Undoubtedly, he would not knowingly have participated in anything heretical or destructive to the authority of the Church; yet he did acknowledge in later years that some of the Fraticelli had seemed to him at that early time "Christians who passionately took the cross of Christ and total poverty upon themselves."[45] Before long, however—about the time of Salutati's *De Seculo et Religione*[46]—he learned of defections to the Fraticelli in his own Florentine circle and began to question the justice of the call to *paupertas* if it could so easily result in apostasy. He soon became embroiled in an extended polemic with the Fraticelli, showing himself to be their first consistent critic in Florence and casting skeptical eyes on the use of *paupertas* as a general moral and social standard. To a certain extent, of course, one can view this polemic of a semi-Benedictine monk as a reassertion of the principles of the older monastic orders against the postulate of the Spiritual Franciscans, that is, that it was not enough for the individual monk to rid himself of property if the monastic orders continued to own it corporately. But Giovanni was too deeply rooted in his Florentine environment to think only in monastic terms, without considering the consequences for Christian laymen. Even though he wore the cowl of a Camaldolese hermit, he thought as a member of the civic world of Florence when he

[44] His correspondence from that period shows familiarity with the contemporaneous prophecies of the Spirituales that predict an imminent transformation of the all too worldly Church. One of his letters discusses in detail a prophecy that assigns a special place to Florence during the expected coming of a succession of Angel popes, indicating that Giovanni was inclined to believe that there was at least some element of truth in the current predictions of the Spirituales and Fraticelli. See Douie, *Heresy of the Fraticelli*, 216–17.

[45] He had believed himself to be in communication with "christianis ferventer portantibus crucem Christi et maxim[a]e paupertatis," he said. See Douie, *Heresy of the Fraticelli*, 232, n. 5.

[46] Letters 20 and 22 in Cividali's count, which are those of major interest here, were written between March 1378 and March 1383. See Cividali, "Memoria," 403 and 406.

argued that Franciscan poverty ought not to be the ultimate standard outside the boundaries of the religious orders.

In one of Giovanni's polemical letters against the Fraticelli, the Franciscan concept of *paupertas* and that of its critics are both traced back to the Scriptures. There Jesus himself is shown to have two distinct approaches to *paupertas*. He and his Apostles go into the fields at meal time to gather what wheat they can find. This type of poverty, exemplified by the simile of the birds that neither sow nor store anything, is the source of the idea of poverty followed by Sts. Francis and Dominic. On other occasions, however, when nature fails to supply their needs, Jesus and his disciples take money from a common purse, and this is the type of personal poverty that became the model for Sts. Benedict, Basil, and Martin, "who had possessions in common and stored the yield in barns. . . . These two forms of religious poverty are in themselves of equal value and perfection, but to an outside observer one seems more perfect than the other; namely, the one that represents a life similar to the birds', provided that it springs from a desire to become perfect and not from mental frailty."[47] But this is not Giovanni's final word on the matter. "To me, it is more perfect to live a life of great poverty in the midst of riches owned in common and to remain [mentally] the master of these riches than to throw them away because one does not have the virtue [needed to be master over them]. Moreover, it appears to me more in keeping with a virile mind to engage in battle with the enemy and to conquer him than to run away from him for fear of dying in battle."[48] He adds that there is another alternative pointed out by Christ, "the saintly way of life for good, rich laymen" (*la via santa a buoni secolari ricchi*).

[47] "Queste due sante povertadi dentro sono d'igual merito e perfezione, ma di fuori l'una pare più perfetta che l'altra, cioè quella che vive come gli uccelli, s'ella procede da amore di perfezione e non da fragilità di mente" (ibid., 466).
[48] ". . . più perfetta cosa pare vivere nelle ricchezze in comune poverissimo e tenelle sotto i piedi, che gittarle per non avere questa virtù. Ancora mi pare di più anima virile combattere col nimico suo e vincerlo che per paura di non morire in battaglia, fuggirlo" (ibid.).

For Jesus chose to seek rest in the house of his rich disciple Zacchaeus, one of those who do not put their hearts into their treasure but use it to help the indigent. The truth is, therefore, that there are three distinct ways, for each of which precedents can be found in Jesus' life and teaching. If the "perfetta povertà" were a total lack of material belongings, "many poor people would surpass St. Francis [in merit]. One must conclude, therefore, that [true] poverty is a matter of the heart rather than something physical. . . . For this reason I believe that many of the poor are wealthy, insofar as their real desires are concerned, and that there are many rich who in their attitude are like the truly poor."[49]

Giovanni dalle Celle thus gave both Franciscan and Benedictine *paupertas* their due, but in doing so he mainly gave comfort and help to his many Florentine lay readers. This may have been even more the case when his contemporaries read another of his letters, written expressly to refute the claim of the Fraticelli that an affluent church cannot be Christ's true church. This claim turns the teachings of Christ upside down, Giovanni insists, because Christ really said that "riches are good for those who know how to administer them well in accordance with the will of God." In fact, by saying that giving is more blessed than receiving, Christ gave greater credit to the rich. "If this is true, as indeed it is, then the rich man who gives has greater merit than the poor man who receives. You [Fraticelli] idolize poverty! . . . Christ, our Lord, had not only poor disciples but also some who were very rich."[50] Again Giovanni singles out "the rich Zacchaeus"; Christ stopped at his house "in order to show that He did not disap-

---

[49] "Onde io penso che molti poveri sieno ricchi per volontà e molti ricchi sieno poverissimi" (ibid.).

[50] "Et se questo è vero, ch'è pur vero, più merita il riccho che dà che 'l povero che riceve. Voi fate un vostro idolo di questa povertà! . . . Cristo nostro non solamente ebbe disciepoli poveri, ma egli ebbe de' ricchissimi" (F. Tocco, "L'Eresia dei Fraticelli e una lettera inedita del Beato Giovanni dalle Celle," *Rendiconti della Accademia dei Lincei*, Classe di Scienze Morali, ser. 5, 15 [1906]: 127).

prove of wealth. . . . And when He heard how much money Zacchaeus dispensed in the proper manner, He praised him." Why, then, did Christ pick Zacchaeus and a few other wealthy men for so much grace and praise? He did so, Giovanni concludes, because there are very few men who succeed in doing the right thing with their riches. "This is the reason why Christ appeared in the image of a poor man; it was not because He would not have known how to handle wealth in the right manner but because He wished to abstain from it out of love for us. For He saw that riches expose people to danger and that only a few are good riders of a horse so difficult to manage."[51]

Basically, this was a return to the attitude of the early thirteenth century, although Giovanni offered a much more refined exegesis of the Scriptures for his view of biblical ideas of wealth.[52] Even if it was only advanced as part of a theological controversy with the Fraticelli, this reasoning was a striking argument against everything said in favor of voluntary religious poverty during the Trecento by the mendicants in general and the Spiritual Franciscans in particular; it was an argument against the very postulate that *paupertas voluntaria* ought to be regarded as the supreme standard in Christian life, not only inside the cloister but also outside in the world of the layman. The doctrine of Christian poverty was being disputed from the vantage point of a changed vision of man's conduct: A person should have the courage to make use of the worldly goods given him by God, trusting to reason and will power to

[51] "E perciò Cristo prese forma di povertà, non perch' egli non avesse saputo bene dispensare le richeze, ma astenettesene per nostro amore; perchè vedeva ch' elle pericolavano la gente, et che pochi erano buoni chavalchatori di così malagevole chavallo" (Tocco, 127–28). If the letter discovered by Tocco is not an authentic work of Giovanni's (as J. Moorman, *A History of the Franciscan Order . . . to 1517* [Oxford, 1968], p. 335, considers possible), Giovanni's intellectual profile would, of course, be somewhat less sharp, but we would then have evidence that his line of thought on poverty was actively shared by at least one contemporary in Florence.

[52] Cf. what was observed about Albertano da Brescia in Essay Seven, p. 161.

put them to good use; he should not shun the resources of this world for fear of being incapable of overcoming his own weakness and sin.[53]

Among those spokesmen of the Trecento whom we have consulted, only Petrarch had arrived at the conclusion that there is an element of insecurity and lack of self-confidence in the rejection of wealth because it is a potential source of danger. Even in Petrarch it led only to occasional remarks and did not evolve into a new, positive view of human nature and man's destination: the view that man should not allow his divine endowment to go unused; that he should not avoid the struggle against sin by withdrawing; and finally, that this is the right and necessary view of life, because man is made for moral action. It is highly improbable that Giovanni was acquainted with the few relevant epistolary remarks made by Petrarch; he left no evidence of any interest in humanistic letters or writings, though this is not absolutely excludable in view of the fact that, in his later years, Petrarch exchanged letters with the other urban theologian of Giovanni's generation, Luigi Marsili. In any event, the crucial point remains that even Petrarch's genius fell short of the boldness and dynamism of Giovanni's view of the relevance of the active life.

We should certainly not overestimate Giovanni's stature, forgetting that he was merely the author of a number of impressive religious letters which cannot, after all, have had any decisive theological impact, even though they were frequently read by his Florentine countrymen during the next few generations. This does not make his voice insignificant, however. It merely suggests that his place in the history of the late Trecento is determined by the independence of mind with which he managed to articulate the experiences and needs of Florentine lay society. For us he is an indispensable witness to the

[53] In other contexts, of course, the belief that it is more courageous not to protect oneself by running from temptation was not unknown in the medieval centuries. For parallels in northern European countries, see Giles Constable, "Twelfth-Century Spirituality and the Late Middle Ages," in *Medieval and Renaissance Studies*, ed. O. B. Hardison, Jr. (Chapel Hill, N.C., 1971), 41f.

changes that were taking place during the last decades of the Trecento in the spiritual climate of Florence and, probably, of other Tuscan cities as well.[54]

Moreover, Giovanni's criticism of the Trecento ideal of poverty anticipated the attitude that Franciscans of the Quattrocento were to have toward poverty. For after heresy had made headway during the 1370s in the name of *paupertas*, a new religious branch was formed within the Franciscan Order, one which was intent on strict Franciscan poverty but remained loyal to the Church: the "Franciscan Observants," whose first settlement in Tuscany was founded in 1390. By the early decades of the fifteenth century, dozens of reformed houses had joined this new observance, and by the 1420s and 1430s their leaders and charismatic preachers—Bernardino da Siena in particular—had become a great moral force in the religious culture of the Quattrocento, thanks to the strictness of their lives, as well as a major weapon in the Church's resistance against heresy.

"Franciscan poverty," in other words, was far from dead during the Quattrocento, but its social as well as its cultural function had changed. The sermons of the great Franciscan preachers of the early fifteenth century brought whole city populations to a pitch of pious agitation and contrition. They mediated apparently impossible reconciliations between hostile families and thus stilled civil strife, at least temporarily. More than ever, the houses of the Franciscans became centers of social work and relief for the poor. But the Quattrocento Observants no longer regarded Franciscan poverty as the sole

---

[54] There can be no doubt that Giovanni dalle Celle's letters were read and copied by the civic humanists. For an example, see the Florentine manuscript from the Archivio Cerchi (in the Archivio di Stato Fiorentino) described in vol. 1 of Kristeller's *Iter Italicum* (London, 1963), 64–65. It incorporates Giovanni's religious letters within a collection of works which together form a true mirror of nascent civic Humanism: Boccaccio's *epistola* to Pino de' Rossi (see notes 16 and 30, above) along with other letters by Boccaccio and Petrarch; works by Luigi Marsigli; Bruni's *vite* of Dante and Petrarch; Boccaccio's *Vita di Dante*; Bruni's *Difesa del popolo di Firenze* and his address to Niccolò da Tolentino (see Essay Six, note 24); and Stefano Porcari's orations.

standard in the lay world or even in the Church. Rather, it was a special way of life practiced in the houses of the mendicant friars. San Bernardino's point of view can here be taken as typical of the Observants as a whole: "When God sees that a soul can be saved better through riches than through poverty, He bestows riches. . . . God calls each of us to the estate that best befits us. The rich are necessary to the state and the poor to the rich." The same reversal of the Duecento and Trecento attitude caused an older contemporary of Bernardino, the Dominican friar and later cardinal Giovanni Dominici of Florence, to point out that wealth may well have been decreed by God for certain men; riches are not to be condemned as such, and one should encourage saving for one's own needs as well as for those of the Church and the poor.[55]

It is not necessary to demonstrate in greater detail how these teachings of some of the most respected and influential friars of the early Quattrocento reveal the cast of mind encountered in the letters of Giovanni dalle Celle. But it is important to remember that in the time of Dominici and Bernardino, more than a generation had passed since Giovanni dalle Celle's changed evaluation of wealth and poverty had emerged from the reaction of Florentine civic sentiment against the Fraticelli.

Before that reaction had set in about 1389, there had been only one exception to the general predominance of Franciscan spirituality; namely, the opinion of the great Guelph jurists of the Trecento. The Guelph school of law had evolved basically untouched by the Franciscan controversy and the Stoic philos-

---

[55] For San Bernardino, see I. Origo, *The World of San Bernardino* (New York, 1962), 109–10. Marvin B. Becker quotes St. Bernardino ("Aspects of Lay Piety in Early Renaissance Florence," in *The Pursuit of Holiness in Late Medieval and Renaissance Religion*, ed. C. Trinkaus and H. A. Oberman [Leiden, 1974], 187): "while man may be destined to lead a contemplative life in his true fatherland in heaven, it is his calling in this world to act and to love." Similar ideas are found in R. de Roover, *San Bernardino of Siena and Sant'Antonino of Florence* (Boston, 1967). For Giovanni Dominici, see Y. Renouard, *Les hommes d'affaires italiens* (Paris, 1949), 193, and John F. McGovern, "The Rise of New Economic Attitudes—Economic Humanism, Economic Nationalism . . . A.D. 1200–1550," *Traditio* 26 (1970): 231.

ophy of *paupertas*. Thus, some of the ideas that were to characterize the civic point of view in the Quattrocento could be utilized by lawyers long before they were adopted by humanists. Baldo de Ubaldis, whose interest in the new social and economic problems of the age made him the most famous of these jurists and who was made an honorary citizen of Florence seven years after he began lecturing there in 1358, praised trade and commerce as the source of political power and advised cities to encourage wealth and produce a large merchant class. Bartolo of Sassoferrato, long a leader of this group of jurists, wrote a protest against Dante's Stoic exclusion of riches from the Aristotelian definition of nobility and his insistence on the supremacy of personal virtue. *Politica et civilis nobilitas* must be distinguished both from *naturalis nobilitas* and from what theologians call *nobilitas*, Bartolo argued. In the case of civic nobility he agreed with everything Aristotle and St. Thomas Aquinas had taught concerning the role played by wealth in human *felicitas* and in such virtues as liberality.[56] When the Florentine citizen and jurist Lapo da Castiglionchio the Elder formulated rules for the patrician life about 1377, he characteristically adopted this favorable view of riches from Bartolo, despite Dante's high reputation among Florentines.[57]

But jurisprudence, like medicine, was a professional branch of intellectual life and in the fourteenth century did not have the power over minds exerted by theological doctrine and the spiritual ideas of the mendicant friars. Even the notary Salutati—who in his official correspondence as chancellor was often compelled to express ideas about the importance of wealth and trade for the republic that were similar to those of

[56] Cf. C. Witte, *De Bartolo a Saxoferrato, Dantis Alighierii studioso, commentatiuncula* (1861); reprinted in Witte's *Dante-Forschungen* (Halle, 1869), 461ff. The whole Bartolus passage (from *Comm. on Codex, Tres Libri*, c. XII 1.1) is printed there on p. 464. For Dante's critique of the inclusion of riches, see Essay Seven, pp. 163f.

[57] Lapo da Castiglionchio, *Epistola a Bernardo suo figlio*, ed. L. Mehus (Bologna, 1753), 13. See Essay Five, note 38. Lapo has taken over, confirmed, and translated the whole Bartolus passage into the vernacular.

the lawyers—was influenced by the ideology of *paupertas*. In 1381, indeed, he showed himself to be under the influence of both these forces. In a letter of that year addressed to the city of Perugia, the merchants of Florence are described as "the sort of men who are indispensable to human society and without whom, in fact, we cannot live."[58] Yet in the same year he also wrote the admiring chapter on *paupertas* found in his treatise *De Seculo et Religione*. Trecento Franciscan poverty, one might say, exerted so strong a pressure that the burden of religion and theology had to be lifted before civic thought could come into its own. The changes indicated here in the spiritual attitude toward *paupertas*—from the view expressed in the humble work of Giovanni dalle Celle to that of the Observants who replaced the *Spirituales*—represent an indispensable preparatory phase of the intellectual revolution that took place about 1400 and ushered in the transformation of Humanism in the Quattrocento.

[58] E. Garin, *La Cultura filosofica del rinascimento italiano* (Florence, 1961), 14.

NINE

Civic Wealth and the New Values of the Renaissance: The Spirit of the Quattrocento*

I

IT IS easy to understand why city-state citizens could not fully articulate their point of view in the *paupertas* controversy until the fourteenth-century tradition had been significantly weakened. Only then did it become possible for humanists to look at life not with the eyes of the "sage" but with the eyes of citizens proudly acknowledging work and self-acquired possessions as the foundation of morality and the greatness of their city. Viewed somewhat differently, the increasing participation of citizens in the creation of humanistic literature may help to explain the change that took place at the beginning of the Quattrocento. From the first decades of the century on, the demand for *paupertas* was replaced, both in Florence and in Venice, by the voices of citizens who felt at home in the active life and with worldly goods.

We have seen that as late as 1408, the philologist Guarino da Verona was still attempting to convince the rich Venetian nobleman Francesco Barbaro of the rightness of the Stoic rule that a truly moral life requires poverty.[1] The little book *De Re Uxoria* (*Concerning Marriage*), which Barbaro wrote in 1415 on the occasion of the wedding of his Florentine friend Lorenzo de' Medici, the brother of Cosimo, was something like a response to that attempt—the first, it would seem, to justify marriage in humanistic terms after so many medieval paraphrases of the dictum that it is impossible to serve both studies

---

* See the preliminary note to Essay Seven. The present essay is the Quattrocento portion of the paper of 1937–1938, changed in style and formulation.
[1] See Essay Eight, p. 195.

and a wife. In defining the qualifications for the bride of a patrician, Barbaro insists on the much higher value of gifts of character and physical beauty, but he takes up the matter of her dowry in detail. Charitable sentiments, the joy of giving, and the best intentions of our heart will earn us little praise, he observes, "if we are unable to prove our feelings by deeds." Such deeds require possessions, and these are therefore "exceedingly useful," if not for ourselves then to help our friends or others and thus to awaken gratitude that might benefit our descendants. Most important of all, riches enable us to give our children the best education. Thus we should cherish our wealth so that later generations will not look upon us as self-gratifying egoists who have failed to increase our riches for the advantage of those under our care.[2]

Barbaro's justification of *divitiae* is limited in one basic respect. Although it is the first humanistic writing to reveal civic instincts with frankness, it does not yet attempt to set forth a systematic defense of the desire for wealth. It merely asserts pragmatically that liberal donations and a patrician education require affluence. In fact, it is characteristic of Venetian Humanism in general that the decisive steps toward a reasoned response to the new values were not taken until the latter half of the century. For the early phases we have to turn to the Florentine republic.

Even in Florence, the fourteenth-century ideals continued at the beginning of the new century to be so firmly anchored that men of the older school still felt the rising spirit of the younger generation to be alien and offensive. Not long after 1400, Cino Rinuccini, good citizen and patriot that he was, gave vent to his indignation because, as he said, younger men were ascribing to Cicero the opinion that human happiness is not independent of the possession of worldly goods and hon-

---

[2] *De Re Uxoria*, ed. Gnesotto, in *Atti e Memorie della R. Accad. di scienze, lettere ed arti in Padova*, n.s., 32 (1916): 48ff. Barbaro's little work accorded with the taste of the new period. It remained popular until the late seventeenth century and was printed six times between 1513 and 1639, and translated into German (1534), Italian (1548), and French (1548 and 1667).

ors.[3] We know that this ascription—already anticipated by Petrarch in his later years[4]—was closer to Cicero's intent than was the usual Trecento reading of his philosophy as an unqualified warning to the wise man to reject all wealth and participation in public life. In the end, Cino's uncritical protest achieved nothing.

Shortly after the Venetian Barbaro wrote his book on marriage, the new attitude gave rise to a more incisive apology for *divitiae*. Its author, as in so many other aspects of Florentine Humanism, was Leonardo Bruni. Owing to the fact that he had spent many years in the international milieu of the Curia and had become a citizen of Florence by choice, he was able to view the Florentine world with sympathy but also with a certain distance. He showed in his defense of wealth, as elsewhere, an earlier and keener perception of rising self-awareness than did the civic writers who had grown up in Florence. Bruni's thrift and striving for property distinguished him (some of his contemporaries thought) from the type of literati usually found in humanistic circles. In his obituary of Bruni, Poggio Bracciolini did not refrain, despite his respect for his older friend, from uttering the reproach that "pedantry and thrift" (*morositas parcitasque*) were stronger in him than was appropriate for a literary man.[5] But most of Bruni's fellow Flor-

---

[3] "Di filosofia morale dicono [i.e., the younger men whose views are contested here] O quanto è bello prociesso di Tullio Cicerone nel libro De Ofizis; nè sanno però che si sia felicità umana e ch'ella non è nelle richeze nè negli onori nè ne' diletti corporali, ma è nell'operazioni della virtù perfetta, nella vita perfetta nella quale, modificate le passioni, attende poi alle contemplazioni, che è contenta di se medesima . . ." (Cino Rinuccini, *Invettiva contro a certi calunniatori di Dante . . . Petrarca . . . Boccaci*, in A. Wesselofsky, *Il paradiso degli Alberti* [Bologna, 1867], vol. I, pt. 2, app. 17, p. 314). The treatise cannot have been written after 1406, as is rightly stated by V. Rossi, *Scritti di critica letteraria*, vol. I (Florence, 1930), 296, since Salutari is presumed still to be alive.

[4] See Essay Seven, p. 181.

[5] Poggio in his "Oratio funebris" on Bruni, ed. Mehus, in vol. I of Bruni's *Epistolae* (Florence, 1741), p. cxxii. In 1429 Poggio had feared that his dialogue *De Avaritia* might be looked upon by Bruni as an allusion "propter avaritiae suspicionem" (Poggio in a letter to Niccoli, in Poggio's letters, ed. Tonelli, vol. I [Florence, 1832], 274).

entine citizens praised this quality, because it enabled him to bequeath a considerable fortune to his son although he himself had been born in modest circumstances.[6]

It was not by chance, therefore, that Bruni was the one to pierce the defenses of the philosophy of *paupertas*. The first to reveal the kinship between Aristotelian ethics and the political conduct of a citizen in a city-state, he also became the first to rediscover the other "civic" mark of Aristotelian ethics, the acknowledgment of material goods as a necessary tool for active *virtus*. Studying the *Economics* (mistakenly attributed to Aristotle, but in any case Aristotelian in conception),[7] Bruni sensed a kindred spirit. In 1420–1421 he dedicated his Latin translation of this Greek work to Cosimo de' Medici and wrote a commentary on it.[8] In the preface, addressed to Cosimo, he states that, according to Aristotelian teaching, the *divitiae* not only help and adorn their owners but "give them the capacity to exercise their virtue." Like Barbaro, he did not forget to add that inherited wealth can make life easier and thereby improve chances to rise "ad honores dignitatesque" in the republic. He discovered an analogous opinion in the poems of Juvenal, the same Roman poet who had provided Brunetto Latini, two centuries before, with the image of the man of property who lives in abject fear of losing his possessions. Juvenal had written that "men whose virtue is limited by the meagerness of their domestic resources do not rise eas-

[6] Manetti, "Oratio funebris" on Bruni, ed. Mehus, in Bruni's *Epistolae*, vol. I, pp. xcvif. Cf. the "Laudatio Leonardi Historici et Oratoris" of an anonymous citizen in Cod. Laur. lat. plut. 90 sup. cod. 5 (in Emilio Santini, "L. Bruni Aretino e i suoi Hist. Flor. Pop. libri XII," *Annali della R. Scuola normale di Pisa* 22 [1910]: 149–55).

[7] No longer ascribed to Aristotle; the first book is the work of an early Peripatetic, possibly Theophrastus. Cf. Wilhelm von Christ, *Geschichte der griechischen Literatur*, 6th ed., rev. by W. Schmid (Munich, 1912), vol. I, p. 754; Friedrich Ueberweg, *Grundriss der Geschichte der Philosophie*, vol. I, *Das Altertum*, ed. Karl Praechter, 12th ed. (Berlin, 1926), 372.

[8] Cf. H. Baron, ed., *Leonardo Bruni Aretino, Humanistisch-philosophische Schriften* (Leipzig, 1928), 164f. For the date, see *Crisis*, 2d ed., 568.

ily."[9] In the commentary accompanying his translation, Bruni reiterates the old warning that when one amasses more *divitiae* than are necessary to meet the needs of one's family, the craving for wealth may become limitless ("nullus est terminus divitiarum"). Nevertheless, he continues, "it is the opinion of wise men that such enhancement of fortune is not blameworthy if it does not harm anyone. For riches can serve as an aid to such virtues as magnanimity and liberality, and they are useful to the republic" since "money . . . is necessary to maintain the state and safeguard our social existence."[10]

The discovery that Aristotle was an ally of civic attitudes was rendered even more important by the unusual publicity given to Bruni's annotated translation of the *Economics*. Throughout the fifteenth century, first in Florence and later throughout Italy and even beyond the Alps, this work, in which the old ideal of poverty was implicitly opposed, was one of the most widely circulated pieces of humanistic literature.[11] In the conflict which began to rage at the time, Bruni

[9] In the *Praefatio in Libros Oeconomicorum [Pseudo-] Aristotelis ad Cosmam Medicem* (*Bruni, Humanistisch-philosophische Schriften*, 120f.). Cf. Juvenal *Satir.* III.164f.: "quorum virtutibus obstat res angusta domi, haud facile emergunt."

[10] Bruni's commentary on the *Economics* (at the beginning of the commentary on the second book): When more "divitiae" are collected than are necessary for the satisfaction of the family's needs, "nullus est terminus divitiarum. . . . Placet tamen sapientibus hanc patrimonii amplificationem, si nemini noceat, non esse vituperandam. Nam et ad magnificentiam et ad liberalitatem opes prosunt et rei publicae conducunt" (wording according to Cod. Laur. lat. plut. 79, cod. 19, and Cod. Vat. lat. 3347, written in Florence in 1419 and 1425). "Nummus . . . res necessaria ad civitatem continendam tuendamque vitae societatem" (as quoted in E. Garin, *La cultura filosofica del Rinascimento italiano* [Florence, 1961], 65). An indispensable access to Bruni's commentary is now afforded by Hermann Goldbrunner's "Leonardo Brunis Kommentar zu seiner Übersetzung der Pseudo-Aristotelischen Ökonomik," in *Der Kommentar in der Renaissance*, ed. August Buck and Otto Herding (Bonn–Bad Godesberg, 1975). It includes "Brunis Beurteilung des Reichtums."

[11] See J. Soudek, "Leonardo Bruni and His Public: A Statistical and Interpretive Study of His Annotated Latin Version of the (Pseudo-)Aristotelian Economics," *Studies in Medieval and Renaissance History* 5 (1968). Cf. also Essay Ten, note 35.

found himself compelled to justify his acceptance of the Aristotelian view of wealth. To an old friend who could not accept the scorn Bruni had shown in his preface for the Stoic postulate that only *virtus* and intellect should be counted among the true *bona* of human life, Bruni wrote the following comment in a letter: Epicurus indeed sided with the Stoics when he demanded that the philosopher should in no sense consider *divitiae* as *bona*. But how could the followers of Epicurus count against those of Plato and Aristotle? Plato also regarded possessions as *bona*, and Aristotle's teachings on wealth were perpetuated by the entire Peripatetic school—by Theophrastus, Cratippus, "and countless other philosophers."[12]

In his declaration of adherence to Aristotle in the same letter, Bruni emphasized that from Aristotle on, the Peripatetics had built upon the harmony of human nature; that is to say, the harmony of body and soul. "As the soul, although it is much more valuable, needs the body in order for a human being to exist, so the goods of the soul may be more valuable by far and still need material as well as corporeal goods to produce happiness." This is the basic principle which Bruni, in his epistolary polemics, takes from Aristotle. In his hands it becomes a weapon against any doctrine teaching the self-sufficiency of *virtus*. The Stoic rule, Bruni maintains, cannot be practiced by "human beings" but only by "soulless blocks" that have cast aside their "humanity"; Aristotle's doctrine considers what makes human beings human.[13] In keeping with the thinking of the new century, Bruni quotes the *Nicomachean Ethics*: man needs material prosperity "because he is a human being"; and as a citizen he emphasizes that *virtus* needs the help of material goods in the *civilis et negotiosa vita* and cannot dispense with them even in the *vita contemplativa*, because there are many resources, like good health and food, that all human beings need. "In hac civili vita in qua versamur," says Bruni,

[12] Bruni, *Epistolae*, vol. 2, pp. 9f., *Ep.* v 2 (1420/28), to Tommaso Cambiatore. See *Bruni, Humanistisch-philosophische Schriften*, 208.

[13] Bruni, *Epistolae*, vol. 2, pp. 12ff., *Ep.* v 2.

the precondition for liberality is money; for justice, possessions; for courage, strength. "All in all, we need many material goods in order to accomplish deeds, and the greater and
more excellent our acts of virtue, the more we depend upon
those means."[14] "Of course," he adds, "if I were to claim that
wealth ought to be aspired to for its own sake, I could be
rightly criticized. . . . But what I maintain is that wealth
should be striven after for the sake of *virtus*, as an instrument,
so to speak [*tamquam instrumentum quoddam*], for bringing *virtus* into action." Let Stoic opponents say that this Aristotelian
combination of virtue with material things makes the heart
petty and narrow. In truth, their own rigid maxims lead to
pettiness. "If goods are instruments of virtue, and great and
outstanding affairs have need of them because they cannot
succeed without their help, whose heart is it that is narrow and
petty? . . . Which of us keeps the more noble goal in view: I,
who intend to attempt great things and to acquire the instruments I need for that attempt, or you, whose thoughts are not
directed toward anything great and noble?"[15]

With Bruni the way had been cleared for the free expression
of civic attitudes and, indirectly, of many other related Quattrocento ideals. Thus Boccaccio, who in the Florence of the
fourteenth century had been the strongest advocate of *paupertas*, now came under scrutiny in a biography written by Bruni's younger friend Gianozzo Manetti. Manetti suggested that
in Boccaccio's own life poverty had been not a goad but a se-

---

[14] According to *Eth. ad Nic.* x.8.9–10 (ed. Bekker, edition of the Berlin
Acad., ch. 9), x.8.4–5 (ed. Bekker, ch. 8). Bruni translates: "Denique ad res
agendas multis est opus, et quanto maiores et praeclariores sint, tanto magis."
This is then repeated a little differently: "Vide igitur in hac civili vita, in qua
versamur, multum nos externis indigere bonis, et quanto maiora et praeclariora virtutis opera, tanto magis."

[15] "Ad parvos, inquis, et angustos faciendum animos haec tua commenda-
tio pertinet. Vide, ne tu potius hoc agas. Si enim haec sunt virtutis instrumenta et celsae praeclaraeque res illa desiderant, cum sine his fieri non possint;
quis parvos et angustos facit animos? . . . Utri nostrum praestantius animi
propositum est? mihine, qui celsa aggredi cogito ac iam instrumenta ad hoc
paro? an tibi, qui nihil grande celsumque meditaris?" (Bruni, *Epistolae*, vol. 2,
pp. 14f., *Ep.* v 2).

rious hindrance to virtue; it had forced the poor poet to support his studies by the bothersome process of copying classical
texts at night and to confess to himself the truth of Juvenal's
verses claiming that it is difficult for a man to rise if he has
meager resources.[16] Even Boccaccio's idealization of the Roman soldiers who were satisfied with a little flour, lard, and
whatever fresh water they could find now met with opposition. Stefano Porcari, the young Roman who in 1427, in his
capacity as Florentine *capitano del popolo*, expressed the moods
and convictions of Florentine citizens so well that his public
speeches were soon circulated widely in Florence, boldly declared that such wretched frugality could have existed among
the soldiers of Caesar and the emperors only after the best of
Rome's citizens had been destroyed by tyranny and the *respublica* was no longer healthy.[17] This daring opinion was aired
on the Florentine piazza in a speech culminating in a veritable
hymn of praise for the blessings of wealth. "Let us contemplate the requirements of private life," Porcari began:
"Whence come our houses and palaces . . . ? From riches!
Whence come our clothes . . . ? Whence the meals for us and
our children? From riches! Whence the means to educate our
children and make them virtuous . . . ? From riches. . . .
These consecrated churches with their decorations, your
[Florentine] walls, towers, defenses, . . . Your palaces and
dwellings, your most noble buildings, bridges, and streets:
with what have you built them, and where do you obtain the
means of preserving them, if not from riches?"[18]

Funeral orations of that time breathe the same spirit. They

---

[16] *Vita Boccaccii*, ed. A. Solerti, in *Le vite di Dante, Petrarca e Boccaccio scritte
fino al sec. XVI., raccolte* in the series Storia Letteraria d'Italia (Milan, 1904),
689.

[17] "Quivi dir contra si potrebbe, che alla vita umana non sieno necessarie
tante cose, chè nel tempo di Cesare, di Affranio e di Petrejo sarebbe bastato
alla assetata ossisa milizia avere avuto pure dell'acqua. Ma non era in quel
luogo Republica dalla quale parliamo; anzi tradotto il pubblico vigore, ed in
gran parte conferito nelle potenze particolari degl'Imperadori, non avvertenti
del bene universale" (Porcari, *Orazioni*, in *Prose del giov. Buonaccorso da Montemagno* [Bologna, 1874], wrongly ascribed to Buonaccorso, pp. 40f.).

[18] Ibid., 39f.

no longer praise the deceased for his reputed renunciation of vain, worldly goods but for his acquisition of wealth through labor and industry and for the praiseworthy use he had made of his possessions. We have already seen how Bruni was commended after his death for having left a fortune to his son despite his own early indigence. When Matteo Palmieri, the citizen closest to Bruni in thought and feeling, died in 1474, the image drawn of him by Alamanno Rinuccini provided a measure of the extent to which belief in the blessings of *paupertas* had lost ground. Rinuccini tells us that Palmieri, who was obliged to work his way up from poverty, "realized how much riches contribute to a dignified civic life." He therefore so increased his small inheritance by lifelong industry that it sufficed not only for his needs "but for a brilliant life, for fame, ever-increasing honor, . . . magnificent buildings in the city and in the country, . . . as well as for foundations honoring God"—even though he "otherwise made frugality and civic modesty his goal."[19]

Palmieri was the Florentine who brought Bruni's train of thought on *divitiae* to a climax. This could only have been done by a citizen whose life was spent in both mercantile pursuits and the administration of public affairs. When in the 1430s Palmieri undertook the adaptation of Cicero's *De Officiis* in his *Vita Civile*, he went far beyond Cicero's recognition of wealth.[20] For although in his *De Finibus* Cicero had leaned toward the Aristotelian doctrine of worldly possessions, in *De Officiis* he had not departed from the Stoic teaching that only the "virtuous" life is "useful" and that philosophers could

[19] Since Palmieri had not inherited a big fortune, "intelligeret autem quam multum ad vitam civilem cum dignitate peragendam divitiae conferrent, sua diligentia et honestis artibus ita rem auxit familiarem, ut non modo sumptibus necessariis abunde sufficeret, sed ad decus, ad gloriam, ad dignitatem augendam suppeditaret: quod in privatum usum magnificae in urbe et in agris extructiones et rerum immortalis Dei cultui dicatarum amplitudo testatur, cum in reliqua vita frugalitatem et civilem modestiam sectaretur" (*Alamanno Rinuccini, Oratio in funere Matthaei Palmerii*, in F. Fossi, *Monumenta ad Alamanni Rinuccini vitam contexendam* [Florence, 1791], 123).

[20] For the date of Palmieri's *Vita Civile*, see Essay Six, note 13.

therefore not give material goods a proper place in moral philosophy.[21] As a true citizen of Quattrocento Florence, Palmieri instead appended to his presentation of the civic philosophy of morals—in clear opposition to abstract philosophy[22]—a special book concerning "the Useful," in which he presented in large scale a picture of all the public and private values that gave life in Renaissance Florence its strength and splendor. His description dealt not only with marriage, friendship, and health but also with the importance of individual economic acquisition; it emphasized the blessings to the community not only of a favorable geographic site and a citizenry proficient in arms but also of honorable riches possessed by citizens and the splendor of public buildings. All this was displayed with the same naive delight and self-confidence we have observed in Porcari's speeches.

A citizen who is aware that he has received these treasures to use them, Palmieri wrote, should realize that human beings "ought not to scorn usefulness and their own advantage," that "it is blameworthy to despise useful things one can acquire lawfully and that such contempt is not at all in conformity with the nature of a virtuous man." Like Bruni, Palmieri referred to Juvenal's dictum that no one who is hampered by poverty at home can easily attain virtue; like Bruni, he adopted the Aristotelian maxim that the true commendation of all virtue is to be found in action. For capable men ("valenti huomini"), riches and abundance are instruments for the exercise of virtue, the *Vita Civile* says, and there are many virtues that need such help; without it they remain "weak and fragmentary [*deboli et manche*] and never attain to perfection." The charitable man and the patron of the arts must have money to spend; the temperate man must prove himself in the face of temptation; "he who passes his life in solitude and is neither experienced nor skilled in important matters, in public

---

[21] *De Off.* II 3.9; III 3.11.
[22] *Vita Civile* (autograph), fol. 26v and 74v–75r (in the edizione critica of 1982, pp. 63 and 151).

office, and in the business of the community will never become just and courageous." The concept of the virtuous citizen is developed here with complete clarity: man is destined for active deeds, and everything that increases his field of action may be looked upon as good.[23]

After the revitalization of Aristotelian civic ethics by Bruni and his group had thus begun to affect the values accepted by Florentine humanists, it became evident that Aristotle was not the only classical writer who could be cited in support of the rehabilitation of worldly goods and economic activity. Leon Battista Alberti, the scion of an old Florentine family who had grown up in exile and was accustomed to privation, was unwilling to share the proud belief of the wealthy merchants on the Arno that great possessions are a condition for the full development of moral life. When he temporarily returned to the city of his ancestors in his thirties, he did not follow the civic Aristotelianism of many of his Florentine compatriots. Instead, he found encouragement in those Stoic treatises of Seneca's which have often lent assistance in misfortune to strong, self-sufficient natures. But even as a Stoic—indeed, because he was one—Alberti did not disavow the far-reaching transformation of values that had been achieved by Florentine citizens. The Stoic independence of fortune striven for by this fifteenth-century Florentine was no longer combined with contempt for the world and its goods. Rather, it harked back to the true Seneca, who did not forbid riches in the house of the wise man, but only demanded that they not be taken into his heart. When Alberti judged in his *Libri della famiglia* (in the mid-1430s) that riches bring not servitude but inner freedom and cheer to a noble mind, he was reawakening the true spirit of Seneca rather than superficially imitating him. Virtue needs material possessions in order to appear dignified and beauti-

[23] "Justo nè forte non sarà mai chi in solitudine viverà, non experimentato nè exercitato in cose che importino, et in governi et facti apartenenti a più. La virtù non è mai perfecta dove ella non è richiesta. Non si conosce la fede in chi nulla è conmesso, ma in chi sono credute le cose grandi" (*Vita Civile* [autograph], fol. 76r; in the edizione critica of 1982, pp. 153f.).

ful, he argued; wealth is a source of fame and reputation, because it renders possible the creation of great and noble things. "We should not despise riches, therefore, but [should] remain lord over our desires when we live with ample possessions or in superfluity." Together with Aristotle's beliefs, Seneca's faith in the power of the wise man to bear both fortune and misfortune without succumbing to the temptations of wealth thus triumphed in some Florentine Quattrocento minds over the tendency to fear worldly temptations.

A counterpart to this revival of the true, pre-medieval Seneca was the rediscovery of Xenophon's *Oeconomicus*, of all classical works probably the most kindly disposed toward economic acquisition and the closest to the capitalistic spirit. Its influence, too, began with Alberti. It had not been known in Italy until Aurispa brought the Greek original from Byzantium in 1427.[24] About the middle of the century the book was translated into Latin by Biraghi, a Milanese, and dedicated to Pope Nicholas V.[25] From then on, Xenophon's work furthered the positive attitude of the Renaissance toward material goods and industrious acquisition in the same way that the pseudo-Aristotelian *Economics*, newly revealed to his contemporaries by Bruni, had begun to influence thought in the previous decades.[26]

[24] R. Sabbadini, in the journal *Historia* 1, pt. 2 (1927): 77ff. In 1427 Aurispa brought all of Xenophon's works, "omnia quicquid scripsit," back with him from Byzantium.

[25] Cod. Laur. Strozz. LI (cf. A. M. Bandini, *Catal. Codd. latt.*, suppl. 2, p. 388), probably the dedicatory copy of the translation for Pope Nicholas V; this must therefore be attributed to the period of his pontificate (1447–1455).

[26] Cf. W. Sombart, *Der Bourgeois* (Berlin and Leipzig, 1913), 289. But Sombart does not mention that Xenophon's *Oeconomicus* could not have had an influence until after 1427, i.e., a whole decade after the way had been prepared by Bruni's translation of, and commentary on, the pseudo-Aristotelian *Economics*. Concerning Alberti's use of Xenophon's *Oeconomicus*, cf. G. S. Scipioni, *L. B. Alberti e Agnolo Pandolfini* (Ancona, 1882), 38ff. Max Weber's reply to Sombart that Alberti did not know Xenophon's book is therefore erroneous (*Gesammelte Aufsätze zur Religionssoziologie* [Tübingen, 1920], vol. 1, p. 39; English trans. by Talcott Parsons [London, 1930], 196).

II

Familiarity with these Florentine developments in the early fifteenth century provides a platform from which we can observe the progress of the new values throughout the peninsula.

In Florence itself the Aristotelianism founded by Bruni was now so firmly entrenched that its basic civic conceptions continued in the age of Florentine Neoplatonism, if not in the thought of Ficino, the leading philosopher, then in the civic groups that propagated his Platonism. The second book of the *Camaldulensian Disputations* by Cristoforo Landino is an example of this, and the forgotten treatise by Giovanni Nesi, *De Moribus* (*Concerning Morals*), dedicated to Pietro di Lorenzo de' Medici in 1483, proves convincingly that the victory of religious Platonism did not mean that Aristotle was a forgotten ally of the citizen against the Stoic demand for poverty. Though it may be true—says Nesi, upholding the convictions of the early fifteenth century—that indigence, illness, and wretchedness cannot crush a true philosopher's mind, he who infers from this that virtue alone creates happiness is indeed caught up in the "chains" of Stoic dogma. "Anyone whose life is spent in administering the state and in civic pursuits" must prefer to follow Aristotle, knowing that civic happiness remains "incomplete and fragmentary" (*imminuta et manca*) without the possession of material goods and public honors. He must admit that the "virtuous acts on which felicity depends are hindered by a lack of such goods." "Civilis felicitas," does not arise from poverty, Nesi maintains, but as a "cumulata complexio omnium bonorum."[27]

---

[27] "Verum licet sola virtus beatam pariat vitam, ea tamen minime contentus est qui in rei publicae administratione civiumque societate versatur, nisi his, quae vel a Peripateticis *bona* vel a Stoicis *praecipua* sive *producta* [emphases added] dicuntur, satis abundet. . . . Licet Stoici severi hi quidem, sed suae disciplinae vinculis astricti, eum qui virtute praeditus sit beatum velint, . . . nobis civilem praesertim vitam degentibus in clementiori Peripateticorum schola deambulandum est potius, quam in porticu Stoicorum more considendum. . . . Adesse igitur oportet corporis externaque bona, . . . ne actiones virtutis, in quibus felicitas collocatur, illorum indigentia impediantur. Ex quo

These Florentine conceptions played the leading role in the development of thought throughout Italy. After civic Aristotelianism had emerged in Florence, the new attitude gradually spread to other centers of Humanism, though nowhere was it as pure and fresh as in the Florence of Bruni's, Palmieri's, and Porcari's day. Among the humanists of the princely courts and chanceries, the Florentine spirit lost some of its saliency and was forced to share its dominion with other influences, which was equally true of Florentine influence in architecture and in the plastic and pictorial arts in the rest of Italy. In particular, the pride of acquisition through one's own efforts, which was the background for the civic championship of the good things of life, was lacking in the case of courtiers and humanistic literati. Thus, the bent of the century often fostered in them nothing but that unashamed will to unscrupulous enjoyment of life so strongly emphasized in many modern descriptions of the Italian Quattrocento. Lorenzo Valla's dialogue *De Voluptate* is an example of this tendency. Nevertheless, Epicureanism did not become predominant in the Renaissance. The persistent influence of the Italian citizenry alone would have prevented this. Not Epicurus but Aristotle, in the new interpretation of the fifteenth century, determined the intellectual climate of the mature Renaissance.[28]

The attitude of courtier humanists toward the outlook of

---

colligitur, ut civilis felicitas sit omnium bonorum cumulata complexio" (Giovanni Nesi, *De Moribus Dialogi Quattuor*, in Cod. Laur. lat. plut. 77, cod. 24, dedicatory copy, fol. 17–18). Between and after these utterances there are certainly impressive warnings against exaggerating the value of *bona*, with references to a Platonic doctrine that should be understood in a religious sense; but cf. again fol. 25vff.: sickness, poverty, and wretchedness do not defeat the wise man, but for "nobis ipsis qui ad civilem felicitatem aspirare oportere diximus" complete "felicitas" is not possible without the gifts of fortune.

[28] A perusal of the two best appreciations of early-Renaissance Epicureanism—Giuseppe Saitta's "La rivendicazione d'Epicuro nell'Umanesimo," in his *Filosofia italiana e umanesimo* (Venice, 1928), and Eugenio Garin's "Ricerche sull'Epicureismo del Quattrocento," in his *La cultura filosofica del Rinascimento italiano* (Florence, 1961)—will suffice to remind the reader of Epicurus' comparatively limited influence on the Italian Quattrocento.

civic Aristotelians can be studied at an early stage in Milan. Here Pier Candido Decembrio, the most eminent Milanese humanist of the early fifteenth century, protested as vehemently as did the Florentines against the view of life held in Petrarch's day. As the child of a new epoch, Decembrio could no longer understand how the Stoic ideal of the sage's independence and indifference to material wants had ever moved the hearts of men, since it was not possible for any philosophy to argue away the real human need for goods and possessions. Many things can be said against the consolation offered by Petrarch in his *De Remediis Utriusque Fortunae*, Decembrio laments in a confidential letter. "Poverty cannot be removed by words," anymore than can other sufferings and evils; words are "futile." "The stomach, as Annaeus [Seneca] says, does not listen to words, even when they have the appearance of truth; the stomach orders and commands and must be obeyed. Do you think you can feed your children with words and endow your daughters for marriage with castles in the air? Possessions are powerful. Examples from books do not always console us. The body needs money day and night (as the satirist tells us), and not high-sounding, weighty phrases."[29] Whereas the itinerant teachers and secretaries of the fourteenth century had become resigned to the fate that largely excluded them from the good things of life by making poverty their "gentle guest" in accordance with Stoic doctrine, the fifteenth-century humanist Decembrio betrays nothing but scorn for such self-deception. In a special treatise, he opposed Lombardo della Seta's maxim of the indifference of the wise man to ma-

---

[29] "O quam multa adversum [i.e., Petrarch's *De Remediis*] dici poterant. Non levatur verbis egestas, dolor, exilium, infamia et plurima que in dies patiuntur homines. He nuge sunt, et quamquam veritatis specimen pre se ferant, venter tamen, ut Anneus inquit, verba non audit, poscit, appellat, dandum est. Tu filios verbis pascere, tu filias delinimentis nubere existimas? Multum fortuna potest. Non exemplis et litteris semper consolamur. Nummis nocte dieque corpus eget, ut Satyricus inquit, non sonantibus seriisque sententiis" (*P. Candidus* [*Decembrius*] *Bartholomeo Facino*, in Cod. Ambros. I, 235 inf., fol. 126r).

terial goods with the new realization that there is no happiness in life without possessions. Yet unlike the Florentine citizen-humanists, the Milanese author by no means esteemed material goods acquired through man's activity in industry and commerce. This secretary-humanist, who found a livelihood in the service of the Visconti, despised all professional and social ties to the civic sphere. It is true that undisturbed happiness is bound up with material prosperity, he argued against Lombardo; but Decembrio did not know how to achieve his goal. He thus resigned himself to giving the title *De Vitae Ignorantia* to the treatise in which he acknowledged the chasm between his own longing for affluence and the inevitable indigence of someone who despises acquisition and social ties. He could only visualize a rich marriage as the last resort.[30]

In general, particularly in the second half of the century, a humanist living in a Quattrocento principality could expect to obtain the help he needed from princely patronage. The new Aristotelianism did the humanist the service of justifying his claim to such help. Thus, a dedication to the Marquis Ercole d'Este by Pandolfo Collenuccio (who offered his services in the second part of the century to many Italian princes) contains the statement that gold no less than wisdom is an indispensable "instrument" of happiness and that, as man must necessarily yield to this coercion, it is only "equitable that those who are endowed with power should aid virtue when it has been deserted by good fortune."[31]

At the same time as Collenuccio, the Neapolitan courtier Gioviano Pontano wrote the important works that played a prominent role in preserving the Aristotelianism of the fifteenth century for later times. In some of the writings of this courtier-humanist, carefully thought-out formulas have replaced the Florentine citizens' ardent partisanship of the active

[30] Pier Candido Decembrio, *De Vitae Ignorantia*, ed. E. Ditt, in *Memorie del R. Istituto Lombardo di Scienze e Lettere* 24 (1931): 99–106. Cf. Ditt's analysis, pp. 36ff.

[31] *Misopenes*, dedicated to Ercole d'Este, in vol. 2 of Pandolfo Collenuccio's *Opere*, Scrittori d'Italia, vol. 116 (Bari, 1929).

political life. In others, the contemplative existence of the scholar again comes into its own. A life dedicated to "rerum naturae causis cognoscendis divinisque contemplandis" will not be greatly furthered by riches, Pontano observes. But he acknowledges the value of affluence for public life. In agreement with the Florentines, he feels that the Stoic philosophy of poverty distorts the true picture. Anyone who praises the alleged "poverty" of Fabricius and Valerius Publicola, he warns, is closing his eyes to the fact that these early Romans were scions of noble families, who received their education in the greatest city of the world, temporarily held high office, and thus led a life indirectly dependent on the richest possible endowment with worldly goods, in spite of their personal renunciation of riches.[32] But even Pontano does not share the citizen's belief in the dignity of economic acquisition. The counselor at princely courts—who through political ambition has raised himself above those who amass goods by trade, and who prefers to gain more from the munificence of a prince than from common commercial strivings—remains Pontano's standard. The Neapolitan courtier and scholar warns his prince not to allow himself to be defiled by the low commercial spirit of citizens.[33]

Half a century after Pontano, the philosopher Agostino Nifo, who enjoyed a high reputation in Italy in the early sixteenth century, carried this view to its logical conclusion. Having become an Aristotelian in the university atmosphere of Padua, Nifo (like Pontano before him) found his proper

[32] "Ita quidem sentiendum est, civilem felicitatem sine bonis externis nequaquam posse perfici. Nam si Fabritius, si Publicola Valerius, si alii non pauci rem familiarem vel admodum exilem habuere, adeoque angustam, ut neque liberalitate neque magnificentia illustrare eam possent, tamen et nobiles nati sunt et in urbe clarissima educati et summis etiam functi magistratibus, quae quidem inter externa numerantur bona suntque fortunae ipsi subiecta . . ." (Gioviano Pontano, *De Fortuna*, Lib. I, in *Opera* [Venice, 1518], vol. I, fol. 284v–285r).

[33] Ibid., *De Liberalitate*, fol. 116f. Cf. Fr. Engel-Jánosi, *Soziale Probleme der Renaissance* (Stuttgart, 1924), 108f., and A. v. Martin, *Soziologie der Renaissance* (Stuttgart, 1932), 104f.

element in the world of the south Italian courts—with the Prince of Salerno and, for a time, as a teacher at the University of Naples. In a treatise on riches, published in 1531 and entitled *De Divitiis*, he combines the attributes of the courtier and the scholar when he declares that, though the *vita civilis* has need of material goods, the only inoffensive wealth is that which is not infected by the sweat of work for profit. The nobility of intellectual work is destroyed, Nifo says, as soon as art and ability are abused for the purpose of acquiring money. Anyone who does not possess inherited riches, or who loses them and is obliged to make his fortune anew, is debarred from nobility and forced to stain his life with debasing things. When wealth is inherited, its origin is forgotten; the long survival of riches is usually a sign that their source cannot have been corrupt, since ill-gotten goods do not prosper for long. It is permissible to take as a standard Aristotle's saying (from his *Rhetoric*) that the newly rich are more debased as a rule than the possessors of old wealth.[34] This adaptation of Aristotle's recognition of ancestry and riches as the foundation of nobility continued to influence the courtly society of the late Renaissance, after the citizens of the fifteenth century had discovered a vindication of economic acquisition in the Aristotelian argument used to rebut Stoic as well as ascetic conceptions of life.

The papal Curia in Rome played a unique role in the long process of convergence between the civic spirit and the outlook of humanistic literati in monarchic states. At the Curia, where so many Florentines were employed as secretaries or in other posts, Florentine ideas had a better field for propagation than anywhere else. On the other hand, the Roman atmosphere was not without influence on the issuing ideas. In Rome there was a powerful historical tradition, the memory of both

---

[34] "Qui pro laboribus mercedem accipit, mercenarius est et sordidus et vilis et servilis." ". . . sordities, sine qua nemo quaestus est consecuturus." "[Divitiae] diu servatae nihil sordidi habent; novae . . . semper nonnihil mercenarii atque sordidi habere censentur" (*De Divitiis*, in Nifo's *Opuscula Moralia et Politica* [Paris, 1645], vol. 1, pp. 92f., 100).

a religious and a classical past, which was strong enough to cause even the Florentine secretaries to develop a different view of the world than that afforded by their own Arno. To this must be added the internationalism of the Curia; in this one spot, nearly all the Italian currents of thought collected and mingled with those of other European nations. Many a Florentine thus found himself surrounded by broader views and learned to look beyond the narrower limits of his own world. What the Florentine mind lost in strength and uniformity on Roman ground, it regained by contact with the forces alive in the Church and in humanistic movements outside Florence.

The very atmosphere of the Curia can explain the unique attempt made by Lapo da Castiglionchio the Younger to strike, with the help of tools forged in Florence, at the old Franciscan opposition to the growing tendency toward worldliness in the pontificate. Lapo, a descendant of one of the oldest Florentine patrician families and a member of the groups that formed around Bruni and Manetti,[35] eventually took service with a number of cardinals at the Curia, and in 1438 (at the Council of Ferrara) he was inspired to describe in a dialogue the advantages that life at the Curia, with its thousand opportunities for enjoyment and profit, could offer to the humanist. The book justifies this life with arguments purportedly revealing, though perhaps with tongue in cheek, the fallacy of the religious claim to poverty in past ages; it states that the pope and the Curia are not only justified in possessing wealth but are obligated to do so.[36] The first obstacle to his

[35] Vespasiano da Bisticci, *Vite di uomini illustri*, ed. Frati (Bologna, 1892), vol. 2, p. 229, says concerning Lapo's youth in Florence: Lapo "fu assai noto a messer Lionardo d'Arezzo e a messer Gianozzo Manetti." We now have a thorough survey of Lapo Castiglionchio's difficult life (in Florence after Cosimo de' Medici's ascendancy as well as at the Curia) and of his scarce humanistic works (largely translations from the Greek) by Riccardo Fubini in vol. 21 of the *Dizionario Biografico degli Italiani* (1979).

[36] Lapo da Castiglionchio, *De Curiae Romanae Commodis*, ed. R. Scholz (1913–1914), according to Cod. Vat. lat. 939 (the only manuscript known to Scholz), in *Quellen und Forschungen aus italienischen Archiven und Bibliotheken*

argument that Lapo endeavors to remove is the traditional
Stoic psychology of covetousness: he refutes it by describing
the criminal driven to crime by want. The consequences of
riches, should they fall into unworthy hands, are merely idleness, luxury, or corruption, his argument runs; but poverty
and deprivation easily lead men to commit theft, robbery,
treason, and murder, thus resulting in far more serious sins.
This proves that one of our most important duties is to strive
for sufficient wealth.[37] Lapo's next problem was the Franciscan demand for poverty. In essence this had been a call to return to the evangelical poverty of apostolic times. Lapo's answer to this is that there are historical differences between
early Christian times and the contemporary epoch. At the
outset of Christianity, he says, the world was supersaturated
with riches. Many philosophers reacted by despising worldly
things and many prophets preached frugality. Had Christ not
taken up the cause of poverty, he would not have won the people over to his religion. Had he not set an example of strict
poverty by his own conduct, he would have been accused of
being in the pay of the rich and mighty. But since then, times
have changed. If today the pope were to follow the example
of Christ and walk on foot or ride on an ass, he would appear
ridiculous to his contemporaries. Once Christianity had become unshakably fixed in human hearts, it was bound to sur-
round itself with outward splendor in order to please the eye.
Christianity should be no less attractive (by the royal magnif-
icence of its priests and churches) than the religions of the Per-
sians, Egyptians, Assyrians, and even the Hebrews were in
former times. Not apostolic poverty but the ancient custom
of decorating idols with costly gold must be the model. Al-

---

16. A good analysis of the treatise by Scholz is found in *Archiv für Kulturgeschichte* 10 (1913): 399ff. I am using the autograph in Cod. Magb. XXIII, 126;
it differs from Scholz's version at unimportant points only. The existence of
another copy in Cod. Paris 1616 (cf. *Catalogus codd. MSS. Bibliothecae Regiae*
[Paris, 1744], III, 159) shows that the treatise did not remain entirely unnoticed.

37 Fol. 87r-v; in Scholz's text, pp. 145–46.

though Christ's words seem to demand papal poverty, it is possible to interpret them as a call for freedom from covetousness (the vice of wealth) and as a wish that the popes would rejoice in doing good and spending freely, in being true representatives of *liberalitas*.[38]

It was only the contact of the Florentine spirit with the world of the Curia that could have brought such thoughts into being. This young and audacious humanist, bred in Bruni's sphere of influence, had learned in the papal service to contemplate the great problem of his time from the standpoint of the Roman Curia—but with the straightforward energy of a Florentine. His bold, youthful challenge, however, had no effect on the development of Humanism at the Curia. The opposite view, the old ideal of poverty, was generally so strong in this clerical world that Florentine ideas could not simply override it but were forced to seek an accommodation. Stoicism had survived wherever humanist scholars and authors lived their own lives without making close intellectual contact with the civic or courtly society of the Renaissance. To such writers the international world of the Curia offered favorable conditions similar to those of a modern metropolis, and for this reason several of the greatest humanists were happy to live in Rome. In the atmosphere of the Curia, more directly than elsewhere, the civic philosophy of life was thus brought face to face with the Stoic ideal of the independent sage. And once again it was a Florentine, Poggio Bracciolini, who in these Roman surroundings brought out the contrast most clearly; he couched the dispute between the *vita civilis* and Stoic *paupertas* in the literary form in which it was preserved for future readers.

Although he perhaps played a greater part in the spread of Quattrocento Humanism among the educated of Europe than any other humanist, Poggio did not have one of the most original intellects. His importance lay in his having understood how to combine—often disjointedly and inconsistently but al-

[38] Fol. 88r–91v; Scholz, pp. 147–51.

ways with frankness and power—the inheritance of his native Tuscany with the suggestions emanating from the Curia. This made him an inspired journalist of Humanism, so to speak, a brilliant reporter on the ideas and movements of his environment. As a humanistic writer he called himself Poggius *Florentinus*, and he defended the view of Florentine citizens in a number of literary feuds; it was his talented pen that often set the most effective literary seal to these contests. But although he praised Petrarch, the hermit of the Vaucluse, for his "high-minded" disdain of civic striving for possessions and political honors,[39] he also called the Roman Curia his "civilis patria," which for everyday living he greatly preferred to Florence, his "naturalis patria," because of the libertinism found there. When the office of Florentine chancellor devolved upon him after Bruni's death, he found himself unable to endure for long either this burden or the compulsion exerted by a life in civic circles.

This joyful child of the Quattrocento, who found inspiration for his lascivious *Facetiae* in the "chamber of lies," as he called the parlor of the papal secretaries, at first sought at the Curia only the freedom to enjoy life. He did not wish to lead the strict life of a Stoic sage, he said, for he was not a "block of wood"; he had grown up intellectually at the Roman Curia, where people knew how to appreciate *voluptas* with the Epicureans and worldly goods with the Peripatetics.[40] At times he himself designated Peripatetic *mediocritas* in the enjoyment of wealth as the true mean between Epicurean frivolity and Stoic bitterness.[41] But as a writer he was Florentine enough not to mistake this semi-Epicurean Aristotelianism for the moral rehabilitation (desired by Florentine citizens) of worldly goods as an indispensable aid to the virtues of political and

---

[39] Poggio, *Epistolae*, ed. Tonelli, vol. 3, pp. 219f. and 255ff.; vol. 1, pp. 129–35.

[40] Ibid., vol. 3, pp. 270f.

[41] "Epicurei dissoluti sunt nimis: Stoici severiores: mediocritatem Peripatetici servant, admittunt divitias, dignitates non aspernantur: hos censeo amplectandos" (ibid., vol. 2, p. 124).

active life; he was Florentine enough to perceive that the real threat to the model of the wise man's poverty and independence (which he revered in Petrarch) was not Epicurean levity but the civic view of life. It was the civic ideal with which the Stoic teachings had to cross swords. This occurred in the dialogue *De Nobilitate* of 1440, in which Poggio revived the old humanistic question concerning the part *divitiae* play in true *nobilitas*—the question introduced into the intellectual life of the Renaissance by Dante.[42]

Poggio's starting point is the observation that all nations, and even the diverse populations scattered throughout Italy, have conflicting opinions in regard to nobility. Does not this disparity support the Stoic claim that nobility should not be dependent on changing customs and usage, that true *nobilitas* is nothing but true virtue? The dialogue then contests the Aristotelian formula—as Dante had contested the definition ascribed to Frederic II—that true *nobilitas* is the result of a combination of virtue and old inherited wealth.[43] Moreover, the disputation sets forth as evidence (as did Dante) the pride of the self-sufficient individual: would not a nobility that is tied to possessions and worldly goods become dependent on the deceptive moods of an inconsistent Fortuna? Would not the capacity to bequeath nobility to one's progeny depend on the uncertain chance that one can pass on worldly treasures? And would not wealth, which Aristotle considers a condition for nobility, teach noblemen to be arrogant and to lust for enjoyment, thus depriving nobility of its second condition, virtue? But the civic side of Poggio's reasoning counters these Stoic challenges: Aristotle is nevertheless right when he upholds the "necessity of external goods" (*necessarias esse fortunas*), because he is thinking of the virtues "in quibus civilis vita versatur." In

---

[42] The text of *De Nobilitate* in Poggio's *Opera omnia* (Basel: Henricpetri, 1538)—the *Opera* was republished in a facsimile edition by Riccardo Fubini in Turin in 1964—contains numerous errors, as I ascertained by a comparison with Cod. Laur. lat. plut. 47 cod. 19 (designated "Liber Poggi Secretarii Apost.") and Cod. Vat. Urbin. lat. 224.

[43] *De Nobilitate* (Basel, 1538), 74.

this civic world, the gifts of fortune have the power to become "a necessary instrument" for the moral man, leading him, as it were, to a "battlefield . . . on which virtues can distinguish themselves" (*velut in aciem educere, in qua elucescere virtutes queant*). Here affluence can be of service to a man who wishes to assist his friends; it can aid liberality and the defense of one's country. If men are deprived of the help given by possessions, all the virtues of the *civilis vita* would remain "fragmentary and weak" (*mancae et deboles*)—Bruni and Palmieri had formulated it in almost the same terms—and could not fulfill their task of leading men to action. "After all, what help to me in sustaining my daily life is the gift offered by the Stoics; that is, one tied to one's frame of mind and not to one's work?"[44]

These arguments are given in the dialogue by the citizen Lorenzo de' Medici, the brother of Cosimo. His Stoic opponent can only reply with even greater firmness that *virtus* and *nobilitas*, as he perceives them, should abandon an active life that is inseparable from the transitory gifts of fortune. As Plato, the Stoics, Cicero, and Seneca agree, only wise men—philosophers—are truly noble ("solos sapientes nobiles esse"). Cleanthes, who watered his own garden, and the Cynic Demetrius, who slept on straw, were "more noble" than Pericles and Themistocles, "who were ennobled by the splendor and dominion of their native city rather than by their own virtue"; for these statesmen were obliged to allow companions, soldiers, and good fortune to help make their *virtus* visible, whereas the philosopher is only dependent on his own strength. Thus the gap is widened between the civic world and the independence and self-sufficiency of the Stoic sage.[45] *Virtus*, rejoins Lorenzo de' Medici, is certainly also possessed

[44] "Quid enim mihi ad vitae communis sustentaculum praesidii prodest Stoicorum liberalitas, in ipso animi affectu, non opere collocata?" (ibid., 77–78). According to the quoted manuscripts, "prodest" and "collocata" should replace "affert" and "locantur" in the edition of 1538.

[45] Pericles and Themistocles "magis patriae decus et imperium quam sua virtus nobilitavit . . ." (ibid., 78–80; in the 1538 ed. "claritas" instead of "decus").

by the philosopher who passes his life "contentedly in his library" or lives temperately, piously, and wisely, "hidden in a little country house," his name unknown to his fellow men. But this "Stoic virtue" of the wise man who lives only for himself remains "naked" and "partial" (*nuda* and *egens*); "it does not permeate the civic community but appears deserted and hermit-like." Even a virtue that does not admit the superiority of civic life, however, needs protection and help, possessions and a native country, and many other things "ruled by Fortuna." If you wish to take all this away, says Lorenzo, "your virtue will truly be cold, lonely, and indigent, and will not emerge into human society or be useful to the community."[46]

The Stoic opposes this civic insistence on public deeds and worldly goods with the justifiable objection that the creative work of a philosopher in his peaceful study can be as useful, or more useful, to mankind than the activities of a statesman or warrior.[47] But the citizen's experiences are not set aside by these arguments, even though Poggio's Stoic has the last word and ends impressively by lauding as supreme that virtue which is dependent only on itself and needs no help from the outside world. The conclusion nevertheless remains—as Poggio himself wishes it to—that life has become richer and that *two* forms of genuine *nobilitas* must actually be recognized.[48] Though Poggio may personally place the *nobilissima* virtue of the philosopher, which is sufficient unto itself, above the *nobilis* virtue of the citizen,[49] Stoic poverty and self-sufficiency are no longer the sole component in the philosophy of Hu-

[46] "Quibus si privata erit vita mortalium, algebit profecto virtus vestra velut sola atque egens, neque in hominum coetum et communem usum prodibit" (ibid., 81–82; in the 1538 ed. the word "et" is erroneously added between "profecto" and "virtus").

[47] Ibid., 82.

[48] He did not wish to deny "civem egregium in sua civitate honoribus et dignitate praeditum, si idem fuerit servator honesti, nobilem esse," it is expressly said; but "illum adiungam qui procul a rei publicae negotiis virtuti deditus sibi vacat et bonae menti" (ibid., 82).

[49] Ibid.

manism. As Poggio expresses it at the end of his work, "only the more discerning can judge whose opinion is most valid. Everyone is free to think as he likes."[50]

The great humanist scholars of the mature Renaissance were not to give up this legacy, although they sometimes felt compelled to defend the contemplative life at a time when the scope of philosophy was again expanding. For them the problem no longer lay in the possible moral value of the active life and its attendant goods, but in discovering what enabled the contemplative existence of the philosopher to be of equal value with the active life, although the former included no riches and therefore offered little opportunity for great deeds. Pontano, who as we found was among the most widely read authors on morals and the conduct of life in later Humanism, already regarded the retired contemplative life as no more than a special path followed by those who devote their lives to learning and the investigation of *res naturae*; and even among the Florentine devotees of Plato, the Aristotelian doctrine of the value of great possessions for the activities of men in civic life never died out. The attitude that characterized the early sixteenth century in Italy is best exemplified by Agostino Nifo, to whose treatise *De Divitiis* we have referred. Aristotle's warning that anyone attempting to live without the help of the human community must be more than a mere mortal and must lead his life in pure contemplation "like a god," now serves in the great expansion of natural philosophy as a justification for the self-sufficient existence of the "divine man" who probes the meaning of all things. This divine man

---

[50] "Liberum est omnibus sentire quod velint." That this phrase advocating freedom to have an opinion of one's own is not merely rhetorical becomes evident when this ending is compared to that of the dialogue *De Avaritia*, in which Poggio, far from exhibiting a similar tolerance, shows that he knows how to convey the intention of taking sides—in this case by condemning *avaritia* despite the fact, as he says, that it is defended by some. On Poggio's goal when he wrote the ending of *De Avaritia*, see H. M. Goldbrunner, "Poggio's Dialog über die Habsucht," *Quellen und Forschungen aus italienischen Archiven und Bibliotheken* 59 (1979): esp. 448f.

makes possible the impossible (as Nifo depicts him), can be liberal without wealth, temperate without acts of renunciation, munificent without display, and brave without weapons. In this case, *divina dispositio* and the wisdom of contemplation permit setting aside the Aristotelian rule (otherwise emphatically upheld by Nifo against the Stoics) that insofar as virtue demands action, it needs the cooperation of material goods. Only the very few who devote their lives to study and contemplation, that is, only those who lead a philosopher's life, can bring virtue to fruition within themselves without the help afforded to the rest of mankind by participation in the active life.[51] Thus, at the height of the Renaissance, philosophy upheld the result achieved during the fifteenth century by the civic champions of the active life; the accomplishments of Quattrocento Humanism were kept alive on the threshold of an age in which philosophy was destined once more to reign supreme and to culminate in Giordano Bruno's faith in the divine man's "eroici furori."

III

We need the insight we have won into the long development leading from Petrarch and Boccaccio to the Renaissance of the sixteenth century, we need the survey of the whole segment of history which we have traversed, in order to recognize the true Renaissance features in the structure of humanistic thought. We cannot expect, of course, that in and after the fifteenth century no humanist was capable of personal attachment to the ideas that intellectually dominated former generations. In no age is intellectual life as uniform as that and least of all in a pioneering period like the Quattrocento. But the important gain is that we are now equipped to distinguish the old from the new, to recognize what was preserved from the past and what was developing from the new outlook of the nascent Italian Renaissance.

For instance, in the same Rome that harbored so many het-

---

[51] Agostino Nifo, *De Divitiis*, 99, 101f.

erogeneous influences, the decades following Poggio's well-balanced work witnessed a recrudescence of the Stoic spirit in the "Roman Academy" that formed around Bartolomeo Platina, the humanistic historian of the popes; characteristically, Platina retained the fourteenth-century ideal of *paupertas*. Naturally, this late Stoicism was in many respects different in character from the semi-medieval Stoicism of the Trecento nourished on Franciscan soil; like every movement of the time, the Roman Academy was in part influenced by Quattrocento thought. Platina himself did not remain untouched by the civic philosophy of the Florentines. On the occasion of a visit to Florence, he had learned to admire the civic belief in the preeminence of the active political life.[52] Partly owing to these Florentine impressions, partly to Roman memories in Roman surroundings, his ideal of poverty acquired a strongly political tone. A reader who is acquainted with Poggio's work and compares it with Platina's dialogue on true *nobilitas* (written in the 1470s)[53] might, therefore, think that with respect to political *paupertas* the biographer of the popes had something

[52] This is stated by Platina himself in the preface to his treatise *De Optimo Cive*, dedicated in 1474 to Lorenzo de' Medici (preserved in Cod. Vat. lat. 2045, fol. 65, and printed in Venice in 1504 and several times afterward).

[53] *Dialogus De Vera Nobilitate*, in Platina, *Opera* (Paris, 1530), fol. LIʳff. The *terminus ante quem* is established by the death of the Archbishop of Trani, Giovanni Orsini, to whom the dialogue is dedicated: at the latest the spring of 1477, possibly in 1476. The date of Orsini's death can be inferred from a bull of Pope Sixtus IV for Cardinal Latino Orsini, Archbishop of Tarentum, of 25 May 1477, in which the Benedictine Abbey of Santa Maria de Farfa is transferred to the latter after the death of Giovanni Orsini, Archbishop of Trani, who had owned it until then; cf. the regestum in De Cupis, "Regesto degli Orsini," *Bulletino della R. Deputazione Abbruzzese di Stor. patr.*, ser. 3.a, 11–13 (1921/27): 374f. The statements by F. Ughelli, in vol. 7 of his *Italia sacra*, 2d ed. (Venice, 1721), 910, according to which Giovanni Orsini had already died in 1469, and in Gams, *Series episcoporum*, p. 934, where 1479 is stated to be the year of Giov. Orsini's death, are thus both disproved. The successor to the archbishopric of Trani was, according to Eubel, *Hierarchia catholica* II, 278, appointed on 1 April 1478, according to Ughelli and Gams, on 1 April 1479. A *term. post quem* may be inferred from the final sentences of the dialogue, in which Sixtus IV (elected on the tenth of August 1471, consecrated on the twenty-fifth) is already mentioned as Pope.

new to say, because he introduced the conception that the greatness and power of the ancient Roman Imperium was due to the poverty that ruled early Rome.[54] But having studied the development of thought in fourteenth-century Florence, we recognize that this aspect of Platina's work is a mere repetition of the view of the rise of Rome that had formed in Florence a hundred years before. In actual fact, Platina's picture of the poverty of early Roman times adds no substantial feature to what had already been set forth by Boccaccio and Salutati; the classical sources—Seneca in the forefront—are the same. Even this ripest form of Stoicism in fifteenth-century Italy outside Florence led to no new paths so far as the old ideal of *paupertas* and its application to history is concerned.

Conversely, the productive interplay between Aristotelianism and the spirit of a new age becomes wholly evident when we look beyond the boundaries of Italy. True, in countries in which the decisive sociological element of the Italian Renaissance, the city-state, was either lacking or underwent a less far-reaching development, we do not find the simplicity and uniformity of evolution which gives to Florentine Humanism its typical and permanent importance. But generally speaking the pattern of intellectual growth was the same when the transition from medievalism to the Renaissance took place. For England it is certainly possible to show a similar course of events,[55] leading from Peckham's *Tractatus Pauperis*, with

---

[54] ". . . Romani illi veteres, qui non minus laudis ex paupertate consecuti sunt quam ex imperio et rebus praeclare gestis." There follow the usual examples of Menenius Agrippa, Valerius Publicola, Cincinnatus, Attilius Serranus, Scipio, "qui ex paupertate tantum nominis consecutus est, quantum nullus antea ex divitiis. Fuit olim res publica romana apud omnes gentes et nationes magno in pretio, dum Romani cives paupertate gloriabantur." Until "posthabita gloriosa paupertate" general covetousness (*avaritia*) took possession of the citizens, civil wars arose, "cum opes orbis terrarum in unam urbem congestae victorum praemia essent" (*Opera* [Paris, 1530], fol. LXIIIr–v; the wording in Cod. Vat. lat. 2045 does not differ from this edition).

[55] For what follows, cf. the important observations of A. Bertolino, in "Appunti sugli albori del pensiero economico inglese," *Studi Senesi* 44 (1930)

which the Franciscan spirit descended upon the island in the thirteenth century, to Francis Bacon's *Of Riches* in the sixteenth. The figure of Reginald Peacock here marked the moment of transition from the earlier to the later epoch. In Italy the movement of the Franciscan *Spirituales* had in some respects eased the way into the future and yet at the same time had consummated the medieval struggle for religious poverty; in England the same double role was played, a hundred years later, by the Lollards. It was in reaction to the Lollard ideals of poverty—in obvious parallel to earlier events in Italy—that Peacock rediscovered the way to the Peripatetic point of view. In his *Repressor* (about 1455) he called "richessis" the "instrumentis of vertu" in Aristotelian fashion, and—like the Italians of the early Quattrocento—gave it as his opinion that poverty is sometimes more dangerous than riches.[56]

When in the sixteenth century *divitiae* were finally vindicated in European thought, the period of Florentine civic history that had been the primary condition for the emergence of the new valuation of the active life had long since come to an end. Toward the close of the Quattrocento, the Florentine Dominican friar Savonarola, in his struggle against the worldliness of the century, had compared wealth to a "bitter medicine" both loved and hated by man. Wealth, Savonarola had said, may be a tonic for man's physical existence, an indispensable help in his life, but it is detrimental for his soul and spirit, for these are endangered whenever love of riches transcends physical needs.[57] When Florentine civic liberty was collapsing in the early sixteenth century, the stern critic Machiavelli considered one of the most serious causes of Florence's decline to be the optimistic belief that the wealth of individual citizens

---

and 46 (1932, esp. 310ff., 348f.); and in "[Francis] Bacone e l'Economia," ibid. 43 (1929).

[56] *The Repressor*, ed. Ch. Babington, in vol. 2 of *Rerum Britannicarum Med. Aevi Scriptores* (1860), 303ff.; the reference to Aristotle is on p. 308.

[57] Savonarola, *Della semplicità della vita cristiana*, Lib. IV. The passage is quoted in A. Fanfani, *Le origini dello spirito capitalistico in Italia* (Milan, 1933), 120.

could promote virtue. "Properly constituted states," Machiavelli declares in his *Discorsi*, "must keep the community rich
but the citizens poor"; not *ricchezza* but *povertà*, which forces
the depraved nature of mankind to develop a communal spirit
and compels men by dire need to preserve *virtù*, has been the
foundation of all greatness in civic life.[58]

Thus, when the Renaissance reached its climax in the sixteenth century, the naive confidence of the early Quattrocento
in the all-powerful blessings of riches was no longer unshaken.
The humanistic ideas, which a century before had fought their
way to the top in Florentine civic circles and which at that time
had apparently broken down all barriers, were indeed not lost
but had now taken their proper place in a wider experience of
life. Once again we can draw an obvious parallel here to the
development from early Quattrocento Florentine art to that
of the mature Renaissance in the Cinquecento. Erasmus is an
early sixteenth-century witness of this later age. About 1519
he attacked the rigidity of Stoicism with the old humanistic
argument that anyone who affirms that indigence, sickness,
and a lack of freedom are not evils will fail to touch the hearts
of men. You may forbid the greed for material goods, he
wrote, but if you want to amend the lives of those who possess wealth and are in high positions, you must teach them not
to despise wealth but to make of it an "organ" of virtue. The
fact that every excess in life brings its own punishment does
not reverse the truth that a virtuous man becomes "still better
qualified for the exercise of virtue" if he has sufficient means
at his disposal. "More people perhaps are corrupted by poverty than by moderate wealth"—thus even Erasmus repeats
the Quattrocento formula, while relieving it of its original
rigor.[59]

The saying with which Francis Bacon opens his essay *Of
Riches*—wealth in relation to virtue is in truth what "the bag-

---

[58] Machiavelli, *Discorsi* I 37; III 16; III 25.

[59] See *Opus Epistolarum Des. Erasmi Roterodami*, ed. P. S. Allen, vol. 3 (Oxford, 1913), letters 957–59. Erasmus' dictum "et fortassis plures corrumpit
paupertas quam opulentia moderata" is on p. 571.

gage is to an army. . . . It cannot be spared nor left behind, but it hindreth the march, yea, and the care of it sometimes loseth or disturbeth the victory"—may be looked upon as a symbol of the later Renaissance. It teaches that the optimistic spirit of Florentine citizens in the early Quattrocento could not remain the sole standard forever, but that this civic spirit marks the beginning of the path on which Humanism parted from the late Franciscan Middle Ages and crossed over into the new epoch.

TEN

Leon Battista Alberti as an Heir
and Critic of Florentine
Civic Humanism*

I

I
T WAS the habit of linking the *vita activa* with the *vita poli-tica*, rather than the mere acceptance of a need for the *vita activa*, that set apart Florentine—and sometimes Tuscan—thought from that of the rest of Italy in the early Quattrocento. Even when those Florentine writers whose ideas we have traced argue in defense of "riches," they incline to view wealth not simply as a basis for family life and commercial enterprise but in connection with the ideal of the political citizen, the public man. Behind this tendency is a conception of city-state life in which the worth of a full member depended on his ability to serve in elective office and to contribute large sums in times of war and fiscal emergency. In such a civic atmosphere, the old problem of material goods tended to be seen not only within the Franciscan and Stoic framework of a comparison between the lives of the rich and the poor but also in the light of the ability of prosperity and wealth to stimulate those virtues underlying the ideal of citizen participation in the government of the republic.

This concatenation of *bona externa*, political engagement, and active virtues had already been the thrust of Aristotelian moral philosophy as it developed within the Greek polis. In like manner, the widespread acceptance of Aristotle's reasoning in the Florentine city-state of the early Quattrocento was inseparable from the political reality of citizens serving their *patria* in the offices and assemblies of the city. Acceptance of the Aristotelian evaluation of *divitiae* in Quattrocento Florence

* A product of the 1970s, revised in 1984. Unpublished.

thus did not simply mean adherence to one of the competing philosophical schools (the others being Platonism, Stoicism, and Epicurism); it also involved a political attitude. By the same token, when, two generations later, Florentine Aristotelianism had to compete with a revived Neoplatonism, the result was not merely a change within the framework of philosophy but also a movement of Florentine society and institutions away from republican traditions.

The participation of full-fledged citizens in government was thus a vital element in the rise and long survival of humanistic Aristotelianism in Florence. The thorough political education received in public office was not, however, available to everyone in the upper ranks of the citizenry. In virtually every Italian city-state, important families and individuals could be found who were temporarily or permanently deprived of the practical exercise of the privilege of holding office. Within the city and the territory of Florence, the disqualified were, of course, in the minority, and the impact of the many who did serve in office was strong enough to make participation in government, in the Aristotelian sense, a generally recognized virtue in the early Quattrocento. But a second Florence existed abroad: it comprised the many young men who would return home after a period of mercantile apprenticeship in order to take advantage of the full rights of citizenship, as well as those merchants and their agents who spent most of their lives abroad and mingled with exiled members of formerly powerful families, and sometimes with entire banished clans. These elements formed large colonies, which remained consciously and typically Florentine despite their separation from the processes of the *vita politica* in their *patria*, and they made their own contribution to the world of Florentine ideas. In the mid-Quattrocento, the exile group included probably the greatest Florentine writer of the generation after Bruni, Leon Battista Alberti.

In more than one respect, Alberti is the most interesting contributor to our understanding of Florentine civic Humanism in its later phases. He was born in 1404—more than a generation after Bruni—into one of the eminent Florentine patrician families of the late Trecento. Beginning in 1387, the Alberti, as luckless opponents of the Albizzi, were sent one by one into exile in northern Italy, a banishment that was not revoked until 1428 and did not actually end until Cosimo de' Medici's return from exile in 1434. In that year the then thirty-year-old Leon Battista (unlike Petrarch, who was permanently separated from the city of his ancestors) came to live in Florence for a time. Now, after a youth filled with hardship—due partly to the fact that he was illegitimate and that both of his parents had died prematurely—he was to come into daily contact with Florentine architects and artists, writers and humanists. At thirty he was too old to become a permanent resident of the city; he had already entered upon a chancery career in the households of high prelates, eventually at the papal Curia, living (as Petrarch had done) on ecclesiastical benefices and taking the lower orders. He could not, therefore, found a family of his own and never became an active citizen, despite his membership in one of the old patrician clans. If seven of his next ten years were spent mostly in Florence, it was because the Curia happened to be there instead of in Rome. Yet despite the limitations of his Florentine sojourn, Alberti's contact with his *patria* at the very time when he was composing his first major literary works, served to increase the "Florentine" quality already stamped on his ideas by his proud awareness of descent from an outstanding Florentine family. At various times in the course of our discussions, we observed the vital significance that Petrarch's *vita solitaria* in the Vaucluse and at tyrant courts had for him and for his humanism. The effects of Alberti's relatively long symbiotic relationship with the world on the Arno were of comparable importance.

We do not know whether the *Libri della Famiglia*, Alberti's literary magnum opus of those transitional years, was substantially influenced by his encounter with his *patria*. As his autobiography tells us,[1] the first three books of *Della Famiglia*

---

[1] That it is Alberti's autobiography and not the work of a contemporary

were drafted in ninety days, just before he left Rome in 1434, but they were not put into satisfactory form in the Volgare until he moved to Florence. The necessary rewriting can only have been done there; this applies especially to the third book, the proem of which was written in 1435. But we may never know to what extent the linguistic and stylistic rewriting incorporated Alberti's Florentine experiences.

In recent times, some well-known inquiries into the Florentine origins of modern "bourgeois" and "capitalistic" attitudes have drawn attention to Book III of *Della Famiglia*. Whereas the first two books are concerned with individual aspects of family life—such as the choice of a mate, the mutual duties of the young and their elders during the years of child-rearing and education, and certain issues of property and wealth—the conversation of the third (entitled *Oeconomicus* like its classical Greek model, Xenophon's dialogue of the same name) deals directly with the fundamentals of economic and civic instruction. Giannozzo degli Alberti, the patriarchal head of the Alberti clan in exile (the scene is set in the year 1421), is made to define some precepts, formed during his long life as a merchant, in which Werner Sombart in particular[2] saw a major Florentine Renaissance contribution to the development of modern economic behavior: that business and the management of patrician households should be pursued with absolute rationality; that one's time should be used methodically; that idleness was the source of all sin; that thrift (*masserizia*) was the root of all "economic virtues," even in a patrician home; and last but not least, that merchants should

---

has finally been proven by Renée Neu Watkins, "The Authorship of the Vita Anonyma of Leon Battista Alberti," *Studies in the Renaissance* 4 (1957), and by Riccardo Fubini (together with Anna Menci Gallorini), "L'autobiografia di Leon Battista Alberti," *Rinascimento* 22 (1972). For the biographical, bibliographical, and chronological facts on Alberti established up to the 1950s we have an excellent critical overview in Cecil Grayson's "Alberti, Leon Battista," in vol. I of the *Dizionario Biografico degli Italiani* (Rome, 1960).

[2] W. Sombart, *Der Bourgeois* (Munich, 1913), and A. Fanfani, *Le origini dello spirito capitalistico in Italia* (Milan, 1933).

devote themselves entirely to business and shun political involvement as an activity irreconcilable with the mercantile
way of life.

The elaboration of these precepts into a system of thought
makes the beginning of the third book of *Della Famiglia* an
important document, not only for the history of economic
thinking but also for the vicissitudes of civic Humanism in the
generation after Bruni. This does not mean that we should
regard the tenets of the exiled merchant-patrician Giannozzo
Alberti as the credo of Leon Battista, the humanist, man of
letters, and architect. We should remember that Leon Battista's youth was difficult because the exiled Alberti merchants
who decided about his education felt strongly that the orphan
should prepare himself for a mercantile career and not for art
and letters. Leon Battista later complained in both his *De
Commodis Litterarum atque Incommodis* and his *Della Famiglia*
that in his ancestral Tuscany "everyone seems bred to the cul-
tivation of profit. Every discussion seems to concern economic wisdom, every thought turns upon acquisition, and
every art is expended to obtain great riches."[3] Indeed, one en-
counters no period in his life or page in his relevant writings
outside *Della Famiglia* that shows the least conformity with
the way of life recommended in Giannozzo's speech. In his
autobiography Leon Battista characterizes himself as a "de-
spiser of all pecuniary matters and of money-making." In
open conflict with Giannozzo's worldly advice not to lend
friends large sums of money, the *Vita* states that Leon Battista
"was used to lending friends money and other possessions in
good faith and giving them the profit of their use."[4]

[3] *De Commodis*, ed. Farris (see note 15, below), 125–27, 131–35; *I Libri della
Famiglia*, ed. Cecil Grayson, in Leon Battista Alberti, *Opere Volgari*, vol. 1,
Scrittori d'Italia, vol. 218 (Bari, 1960), 41. For the English rendition of quotations from *Della Famiglia*, here and in what follows, I have used the translation, with some changes, of Renée Neu Watkins, in *The Family in Renaissance Florence: I Libri della Famiglia by Leon Battista Alberti* (Columbia, S.C.,
1969). For the above quotation, see Watkins, 56–57.

[4] "Itaque verum, quae ad ingenium artesque pertinerent, scrutator fuit as-

How, then, should we assess the first part of the third book? Giannozzo degli Alberti, as he states there, had kept clear of political activity even before his banishment. In exile he became so exclusively a merchant, so avoided politics—although he did not deny his cruel *patria* financial help in emergencies—that during the 1420s he was the first of the Alberti to be readmitted to the Florentine territory.[5] Why Leon Battista, who had suffered so much from commercially minded members of the Alberti clan, was so deeply sympathetic to this old merchant who had little formal education, emerges at various points. Although Giannozzo could not read Latin and Greek, he seemed the very model of the Stoic so often depicted in Seneca's writings: a brave man who would not admit defeat despite the lashes of Fortuna, who was never idle and valued nothing more than his time, even though he believed in using it for acquisitive pursuits and not, as Seneca did, for studies. Moreover, when Leon Battista became acquainted with Xenophon's *Oeconomicus*, he discovered that the unschooled merchant Giannozzo had often held views in his *vita economica* that essentially harmonized with those of the ancient author. Besides, Giannozzo's example seemed to bear out Leon Battista's growing conviction that experience was superior to bookish erudition.[6] Yet Leon Battista also saw clearly the limitations of Giannozzo's world. The literary structure of Book III is meant to bring this out. For when Giannozzo has laid down his general principles for the *vita economica*—thrift amidst riches and the need to value one's time and fight idleness—and is asked to defend his scorn for the *vita politica*, he finds himself opposed by a different set of ideals—those of a city-state

---

siduus; pecuniarum et quaestus idem fuit omnino spretor. Pecunias bonaque sua amicis custodienda et usu fruenda dabat" (Fubini and Gallorini, "L'auto-biografia di Leon Battista Alberti," 72).

[5] A helpful survey of the actual behavior of the various Alberti in exile is found in the introduction to *I primi tre libri della famiglia: Testo e commento di F. C. Pellegrini, riveduti da R. Spongano con una nuova introduzione* (Florence, 1946).

[6] Cf. esp. *Della Famiglia* III, trans. Watkins, 161, 163, 177.

citizen—and defended by a younger member of the Alberti family.

To understand the thrust of the reasoning in the third book, one must pay special attention to the occasion that kindles the controversy. Dissension comes to the surface when Giannozzo suggests that there are four essential benefits a good and capable man can obtain even away from his native city: family, wealth, friendship, and honor (*onore*). To Florentine ears, the word *onore* sounded very much like *onori*, the term used for high administrative offices in the city-state. As a result, a member of the Alberti clan questions whether one can really speak of preserving a citizen's *onore* so long as exile robs him of the capacity to fill the *onori* essential for full-fledged citizenship. Thus the scene is set for Giannozzo to explain why *onore* in exile is not a real problem from the viewpoint of his merchant ethic. The life the Alberti have been forced to lead, he says, has merely strengthened the disdain he has always had for a life built on political *onori*.

Giannozzo's conception of the good life involves a nearly total alienation from the political ideals of the city-state: "I have always thought any other way of life to be preferable to that of these public men [*statuali*—those who possess and exert full citizen rights in the city-state], as we might call them, . . . a life of worries, anxieties, and burdens, a life of servitude." Like "public servants," these *statuali* are "obligated to ignore [their] own concerns in order to untangle the follies of other people." This makes you a servant, Giannozzo insists, because in office "you must now organize taxes, now expenditures, now provide for wars, now clarify and revise laws" (the very versatility so often seen as the major benefit of city-state life). Their life is "an evil, . . . not generally detested . . . , I suppose, only because this form of servitude is thought to bestow a kind of glory." But the real result is that you have to "forgo domestic tranquillity and true peace of mind." The holding of office is tantamount to gaining an opportunity to "steal and use violence with some degree of impunity." It is a life fit for those who cannot live without wielding great power, oppressing weaker people, and misusing their role in the state "to make private what is public." Admittedly, says Giannozzo, holding office is more acceptable if "your country calls on you . . . after you have displayed great excellence [in private life]." But the normal procedure when establishing a public career in Florence—first rendering service to a senior politician, then making up the tail of his procession, and finally becoming a master of others—is fundamentally evil.[7] "A man wants to live for himself, not for the community. True, he should be willing to help his friends if they ask for it, so long as he does not neglect his own concerns and incur serious losses."[8] But a citizen who aims to make a political career for himself acts very differently, Giannozzo maintains, and his final advice to his listeners is: "Do not abandon your private concerns to guide public affairs. . . . For if a man finds he has less than he needs at home, he will find even less outside; nor will the public power he holds requite his private needs. Public honors will not feed the family."[9] "My children, let us . . . [try] only to be good and just householders [massai]. Let us delight in our excellent family. Let us delight in those goods which fortune bestows on us. . . . A man attains high enough honor when he lives untainted by vice and untouched by shame."[10]

If this were the only point of view offered in Della Famiglia, the work would deal a blow to Bruni's and Palmieri's teachings. But the basic tenets of Giannozzo degli Alberti's merchant wisdom are opposed, as already mentioned, by another member of the clan, Lionardo degli Alberti, who is presented as a great reader of books and a man of learning. It has been rightly remarked[11] that continued opposition to the funda-

[7] Della Famiglia, trans. Watkins, 175–77; ed. Grayson, 179–82.

[8] "E' si vuole vivere a sé, non al comune, essere sollicito per gli amici, vero, ove tu non interlasci e' fatti tuoi, e ove a te non risulti danno troppo grande" (ibid., trans. Watkins, 177; ed. Grayson, 182).

[9] Ibid., trans. Watkins, 179–80; ed. Grayson, 185.

[10] Ibid., trans. Watkins, 177; ed. Grayson, 182.

[11] See C. Grayson, "The Humanism of Alberti," Italian Studies 12 (1957): 47, and F. Tateo, Tradizione e realtà nell'umanesimo italiano (1967), 300f.

mental theses of the major speaker is unusual in Leon Battista's dialogues, which as a rule elaborate a theme until all those present are in agreement. Not that Lionardo degli Alberti is presented in *Della Famiglia* III as the victor in the debate. He and Giannozzo offer opposing views of the *vita civile* which are impossible to reconcile. One must add to this observation that Lionardo's outlook on life is clearly that of the civic humanists, but in a perfected form; his arguments are sharpened because they are intended to answer the objections raised from the standpoint of the *vita economica*.

Giannozzo's eulogy of a private existence devoted to mercantile pursuits is followed by one of the most eloquent pages written in the spirit of political humanism. "Like you," Lionardo replies to Giannozzo's speech, "I would say that a good citizen loves tranquillity, but not so much his own tranquillity as that of all good men. He rejoices in his private leisure but does not care less about that of his fellow citizens than he does about his own. He desires the unity, calm, peace, and tranquillity of his own house, but much more those of the country and the republic. These goods, moreover, cannot be preserved if wealthy, wise, or noble citizens seek more power than those who are equally free but less fortunate. Yet neither can republics be preserved if all good men are content with their private leisure. Wise men say that good citizens should undertake to care for the republic and should labor for their country. . . . So you see, Giannozzo, that the admirable resolve to make private *onestà* one's sole rule in life, though noble and generous in itself, may not be the proper guide for spirits eager to seek glory. Fame is born not in the midst of private peace but in public action. Glory is gained in public squares; reputation is nourished by the combined voices and judgments of many honorable people and in the midst of the multitude. Fame avoids the solitary and private place and dwells gladly in the arena where crowds gather and celebrity is found; there the name of one who has sweated and toiled assiduously for noble ends and has raised himself out of silence and darkness, ignorance and vice, is bright and luminous." Service in public office and the endeavors of young citizens at the beginning of their public careers "to gain the favor of an honorable and well-established citizen" must be viewed in this light. "I would not call it servitude to do my duty; but it has without doubt always been the duty of young men to respect their elders and to eagerly seek out among them that same fame and dignity for which the elders themselves are loved and revered. Nor would I call it lust for power if a man shows great care and interest in doing hard and generous things, for these are the way to honor and glory." Looking forward to the hoped-for return of the Alberti to Florence, Lionardo thus concludes: "This is my own longing, Giannozzo, so much so that if I could earn fame, favor, and reputation, and be honored, loved, and adorned with dignity and the respect of my fellow citizens in my own country, I would not shun it or be afraid of the enmity I might incur from some citizen who was baneful and wicked."[12]

To regard this public-spirited and clear-sighted attack on Giannozzo's unpolitical sentiments as a reflection of Leon Battista's personal opinion would be as wrong as to identify his convictions with Giannozzo's belief in a private and commercially oriented life. The real intention of *Della Famiglia* III is to confront the two outlooks, the two opposing ways of life, both of which impressed Leon Battista. His impressions may have been formed in the Florentine environment or earlier in the ambiance of the exiled Alberti clan; in either case the origin of his thought is more complicated than that. In Giannozzo's discourse at least, it is clear that some aspects of his approach to economic values—set down in certain episodes of his narrative with a deceptively personal ring—are actually borrowed from Xenophon's *Oeconomicus*.[13] It was thus from Xenophon that Leon Battista took his conceptual tools for the analysis of a patrician household. On the other hand, this

[12] *Della Famiglia*, trans. Watkins, 178–79; ed. Grayson, 183–85.

[13] This is true of the introduction of the young wife to the household by means of the common prayer uttered by husband and wife, which impressed Burckhardt so strongly.

Greek source could not have made him aware of the basic antagonism between a purely mercantile, private way of life and the political, communal ethics of a city-state citizen. Despite his literary borrowing, Leon Battista was ultimately building on ideas inspired by his environment. This is obvious with regard to the influence exerted on him by merchants during the long years of his exile. The persona of Lionardo degli Alberti, with his philosophy of the active political life, presents the antithesis to this influence. Only if we include in our picture both the line of thought developed by Giannozzo in exile and its clash with civic Humanism as it had developed on the Arno, will we be able to grasp the rich variety of these Florentine ideas.

II

In Bruni's generation, Florentine humanists had ventured the first complete rejection of Franciscan Stoic *paupertas* as a standard for laymen and citizens; and this rejection had been based on the vindication of *divitiae*, not only as an instrument of active individual virtue but also as one of the necessities for the flowering of the community. In the mid-1430s, all these elements were still strong in Palmieri's *Vita Civile*. Is anything of this outlook present in Alberti's early works?

There are indications that during his years in exile Alberti had not fully abandoned the *paupertas* model typical of late Trecento humanists. Belonging as he did to a younger generation, he would not, of course, have called *paupertas* his "nurse" and "gentle guest," as Vergerio had done,[14] but in his first work, *De Commodis Litterarum*, he had agreed that those who want to be literati and men of virtue and wisdom must despise "riches, honors, and greatness" and resign themselves to the fact that poverty will be their lifelong companion.[15]

---

[14] See Essay Eight, p. 196.

[15] *De Commodis Litterarum atque Incommodis*, ed. Giovanni Farris (Milan, 1971), 149–51.

Some portions of recently found writings by Alberti make it certain that this resignation ended at the time when he came in contact with Florentine life. We know today that there was a third major literary work of Alberti's—in addition to his *Della Famiglia* and *De Pictura*—which bears upon his state of mind about 1434: eleven books of table talk (*Intercoenales*), his most mature work in Latin. There has never been any doubt that some parts of this work go back to the end of Alberti's university years and that it was finished toward the end of the 1430s; that is, during Alberti's Florentine sojourn. Not all of the *Intercoenales* have survived, but in the late nineteenth century one of the dialogues, entitled "Paupertas," came to light.[16] A proem to this piece has recently been discovered: it was addressed to Bruni at the moment when Alberti first tried to make contact with him (Bruni is asked to show a sympathetic interest in the studies of his younger fellow humanist), but it cannot have been written later than early 1435.[17] It was certainly not by chance that Alberti asked Bruni to give his authoritative judgment on the portion of the *Intercoenales* that is critical of the *paupertas* ideal; for in the early 1430s Bruni's circle was still the only one in Italy to defend *divitiae* without

[16] Published in *Leonis Baptistae Alberti Opera inedita*, ed. H. Mancini (Florence, 1890).

[17] The date derives from the fact that Bruni is celebrated in the proem as "hac etate litterarum princeps" and as the leader in this kind of studies, whereas his assumption that Latin and the Volgare coexisted in ancient Rome soon alienated Alberti, who bitterly contested it because of its practical implications for the valuation of the Volgare. By the middle of 1435, Bruni's theory was being widely discussed in Florence, with Alberti participating (cf. for background Bruni's *Ep.* VI 10 [May 1435]). It made Alberti quite contemptuous of Bruni, as we know from the preface to the third book of *Della Famiglia*, where Alberti exclaims passionately that the theory of two languages in ancient Rome could be devised only by an ignoramus. The proem to the table talk "Paupertas," with its homage to Bruni, must therefore have preceded the second half of 1435, and the table talk itself probably also falls into the years 1434–1435. Alberti's proem addressed to Bruni was first published by Eugenio Garin in *Rinascimento* (1964), 127f., and reprinted in Garin's edition of Alberti's *Intercenalia inedite*, Quaderni di Rinascimento (Florence, 1965), 11–12.

any restraining trace of the high regard of Trecento humanists for *paupertas*. And it was precisely to the changed attitude toward *paupertas* that Alberti wished to contribute.

His table talk on *paupertas* discusses what should be done by a wealthy man whose friends, though generally full of praise for his conduct, suspect him of *avaritia* because he has occasionally seemed parsimonious (*parcus*). The rich man defends himself by arguing that nothing is more foreign to him than avarice, since he has spent beyond his means for friends. His only mistake may have been in not telling them clearly that they were overestimating his wealth. Yet what would have been the consequence of his so informing them? The answer reveals much about the attitudes of a wealthy Quattrocento citizen as compared to one of the Trecento. The latter would not have found it difficult to admit that he was less affluent than he appeared, because it would have been of the utmost importance to him not to be stamped as avaricious; for avarice was one of the cardinal sins and the feared result of wealth. Alberti's wealthy man thinks differently. He wishes to avoid the psychological consequences not of being rich but of being poor, or even of being less affluent than expected. He describes the social consequences of insufficient means as follows: Everyone will suspect a less-than-rich man of having been frivolous during his lifetime, or guilty of stupidity or some dishonorable act. If a theft occurs, suspicion will fall on a poor man, because it is known that he has unrequited desires. No one will give credence to his assertions. He will be increasingly alienated from his fellow citizens, and, worst of all, this experience will affect his character and conduct. For however great his virtue may be, "it will not bring him even a minimum of authority and dignity." Careworn, suspect, derided, he will eventually lose all sense of security. He will submit to any act of insolence, will begin "to respect all rich people as if they were his lords, and will no longer follow the dictates of his own will but laugh, speak, keep quiet, or shed tears according to the judgment or whim of others."[18] The

[18] *Opera inedita*, 169.

lesson to be learned is that however much one abhors the vice of avarice, "it is clearly better to be thought avaricious than poor." Let those who are not parsimonious criticize those who are; their scorn for a parsimonious man will be less than it would be for a poor man. Few able men have agreed with Plato and other philosophers who praised poverty. Alberti's wealthy man ultimately decides, therefore, that his supreme consideration must be "that the opinion of my wealth formed by the crowd will not be lowered." He adds that "after careful consideration of every aspect I have arrived at the following conclusion, which nobody will turn me from; namely, that I prefer to be thought an avaricious man than one who steals, procures, or betrays—crimes and ignominies that are all believed to be . . . the consequence of poverty. . . . I am convinced, therefore, that a wise man should not allow himself to give even the slightest suspicion of being poor."[19]

Before Alberti, in Bruni's generation, Florentine humanists had not yet arrived at this blunt rejection of the consequences of one of the fundamental Trecento views. On the other hand, the same fear that lack of affluence might endanger social esteem and human dignity is encountered in one of the most characteristic expressions of Florentine civic thought during the High Renaissance, Francesco Guicciardini's *Ricordi*. Like Alberti, Guicciardini contended that to desire great wealth only for material enjoyment is "the sign of a base and deformed mind. . . . But since a reputation nowadays can scarcely be made or maintained without riches, men of virtue should seek them—not immoderately but as much as is needed to gain or preserve respect and authority." Or as another of the *Ricordi* puts it: "With wealth, those very virtues shine forth and are esteemed which in a poor man are little respected or even unnoticed."[20]

[19] Ibid., 169–72.
[20] From two kindred *Ricordi*, B 18 and B 141, the first of 1512, the second of 1528. Cf. R. Spongano, edizione critica of the *Ricordi* (Florence, 1951), 239, 247. The English translation basically follows that of M. Domandi (New York, 1965).

Thus the old conviction that *avaritia* was most dangerous had lost much ground. It was the religious connotation of *avaritia*—one of those sinister vices which according to medieval theology were bound to produce whole families of related sins—that had inspired Petrarch's morbid fear of this sin and led to the belief of nearly all Trecento writers that new appetites would proliferate if the striving for *divitiae* was not drastically repressed. Yet avarice—greed and stinginess—could be regarded psychologically as one of the "perturbations" or "emotions" of the spirit which the Stoic sage was taught to conquer and which the disciple of Aristotle tried to put to good moral use; and the more avarice was placed on a level with other human passions and vices, the more its theological implications waned.[21] In a previous essay we traced a different phase of the same historical process, the change in late Trecento and early Quattrocento Humanism from the critique of *ira* (anger)—another of the dreaded Seven Deadly Sins—to the Aristotelian acknowledgment that anger and wrath are among the indispensable incentives to moral action.[22] In the question of *avaritia*, Alberti's interpretations similarly brought about the moment when discussions of humanistic conduct would no longer inevitably take the theological background into consideration.

With the fear of *avaritia* attenuated and, conversely, a new anxiety over the consequences of a life of indigence in the ascendancy, pride of *paupertas* was put on the defensive. A striking passage in the fourth book of *Della Famiglia*, written during Alberti's Florentine sojourn, reads as follows: "I will not say [that poverty] wholly hinders a man, but it keeps his virtue . . . hidden away in obscure squalor. . . . It is thus necessary that virtue should be supplemented by the goods of fortune.

---

[21] Namely, in *Della Famiglia*; this is evident in the principal defense of wealth in the second book (ed. Grayson, 146, 148f.; trans. Watkins, 146–48), where *avaritia* appears as one of the regular and conquerable emotions. The same is true of the discussion of wealth in the third book (see Grayson, 160f., 163f., and Watkins, 158, 161).

[22] Essay Six, pp. 148ff.

Virtue ought to be dressed in those seemly ornaments which it is hard to acquire without affluence and without an abundance of the things that some men call transient and illusory and others call practical and useful."[23] Alberti here comes very close to Aristotle's position; and elsewhere in *Della Famiglia* he specifically scorns *paupertas* as the indication of a lazy or insufficiently ambitious mind. He has Giannozzo's opponent argue that "if riches come through profits, and these through labor, diligence, and hard work, then poverty, which is the reverse of profit, will follow from the reverse of these virtues; namely, from neglect, laziness, and sloth. These are the fault neither of fortune nor of others but of oneself."[24]

III

Alberti's preference for Stoicism over Aristotelianism, then, did not make him less attuned to Quattrocento ideas—a conclusion that would doubtlessly be drawn by anyone who takes sufficient account of the quality (not merely the name and terminology) of his "Stoic" philosophy. An activism and a yearning for fame and glory not in keeping with Trecento Humanism determine the character of nearly everything he wrote. His reevaluation of wealth in the second book of *Della Famiglia* is part of a discussion of creative and productive competition as the basis of happiness. Every youth, says Alberti, must first discover the activities, whether exalted or lowly, for which nature has suited him. He must then conduct his life as if it were a race. For lesser achievers "remain unknown; no one speaks of them." One has "to fight wholeheartedly for a place among the first, if not for first place. One must surpass entirely that obscure and forgotten crowd in back. One must struggle with all the force . . . at one's disposal for a certain measure of fame and glory. . . ." One can gain "honor and

---

[23] ". . . quali altri chiamano fragili e caduchi, altri gli appella commodi e utili a virtù" (*Della Famiglia*, ed. Grayson, 268; trans. Watkins, 250).

[24] Ibid., trans. Watkins, 144; ed. Grayson, 144.

fame . . . from any work or achievement. . . . In every craft the most skillful master . . . obtains the most riches and has the best position and the greatest stature among his companions. Think how even in so humble a profession as shoemaking men search out the best among the cobblers."[25] Quattrocento individualism has here left its mark on the *divitiae* debate; a new activism has transformed the old Stoic maxims. Though wisdom and felicity remain dependent on "virtue" in the Stoic fashion, virtue is now identified with incessant hard work and thus excludes all those qualities which Trecento humanists had associated with contemplation and withdrawal from the world. *Della Famiglia* is full of examples illustrating this view of virtue, and pertinent dicta appear in almost every writing of Alberti's later years: men, like ships, are not built "to rot in port but to ply the seas on long voyages"; idle people (*uomini oziosi*) are "like sleepers, neither wholly alive nor totally dead. . . . But if we strive continuously there will be life in us"; "man is born to be useful to himself, and no less to others. . . . No mercenary occupation is so low as not to be preferable for a youth to a lazy and inert life."[26]

It is essential for our understanding of Alberti's Stoicism to view it in the context of developing humanistic thought. Even

[25] Ibid., trans. Watkins, 139–40; ed. Grayson, 138–39.

[26] Cf. the second volume of Alberti's *Opere Volgari*, ed. Grayson (see note 38, below), 132, 239, 198. This vital aspect of Alberti's Quattrocento humanism has not always been accounted for in Alberti studies, and some scholars have been inclined—especially since the discovery of a strong Aristotelian trend in early Quattrocento Florence—to interpret Alberti's moral philosophy as "una nuova umanistica 'Weltflucht,' " a "regresso" by Alberti to the "stoicismo che loda la virtù in astratto" in Petrarch's day. This certainly misleading approach is epitomized in M. Petrini's "L'uomo di Alberti," *Belfagor* 6 (1951): esp. 651, 660f., 662f. However, the Quattrocento character of Alberti's Stoicism had already been recognized by G. Saitta, *L'educazione dell'umanesimo in Italia* (Venice, 1928), esp. 214 and 221, and basically repeated in Saitta, *Il pensiero italiano*, 2d ed. (1961), vol. 1. It has recently been reemphasized in J. Gadol, *Leon Battista Alberti: Universal Man of the Early Renaissance* (Chicago, 1969), esp. 225–31, although she ignores the narrowing of Alberti's social horizon in his last work, *De Iciarchia*, to which attention will be drawn a little later.

the strikingly optimistic activism that makes Alberti's work so unusual must not be considered a merely personal trait. A similar transformation of Stoic thinking in Florence during the decade preceding the composition of *Della Famiglia* can be found in the *Disputatio de Nobilitate*, that small literary work written in Bruni's circle, presumably by Buonaccorso da Montemagno the Younger, a jurist and writer who immigrated to Florence from neighboring Pistoia.[27] The hero of this humanistic altercation, which is set in ancient Rome, praises *paupertas* and voices the Stoic sentiment that "though misfortune should rob me of my little farmstead, it cannot rob me of my *virtus*." But just as in Alberti's case, the *virtus* that here defies the whims of Fortuna is no longer the disheartening withdrawal from *divitiae* and the active life advocated by Trecento Stoicism, but promotes the willpower and ability necessary to regain a livelihood. For this Tuscan Stoic of the 1420s, true *virtus* is the energy that allows his hero to exclaim self-confidently, "a thousand approaches to life's opportunities will be open to me if misfortune should strike."[28]

For a proper appraisal of this brand of Stoicism we must recognize that its interpretation of Seneca and other ancient Stoics was by no means due to an arbitrary projection of Quattrocento attitudes into the ancient works. Alberti's understanding of Stoic virtue amounts instead to a Quattrocento rediscovery of certain aspects of ancient thought that had been given little heed during the Middle Ages. In the Trecento, Petrarch had become aware that the value placed by Seneca on man's time and activity was difficult to reconcile with the medieval stress on withdrawal and a more static life, and that

---

[27] We have already had recourse to Buonaccorso in a different context. See Essay Six, pp. 140f.

[28] *Prose e Rime de' due Buonaccorsi da Montemagno* (Florence, 1718), 92. Paul Oskar Kristeller remarks about Buonaccorso's work: "Il trattato di Buonaccorso ebbe larghissima diffusione nei manoscritti, fu tradotto in italiano, spagnolo, francese, inglese e tedesco e dal punto di vista della popolarità va considerato uno degli scritti più importanti del Quattrocento" (in *Lauro Quirini Umanista* [Florence, 1977], 35). See also my *Crisis*, 2d ed., 421–23.

Seneca had not always advised poverty for the sage. It was the Quattrocento Stoic Alberti, for whom Petrarch was a precursor of sorts,[29] who finally developed Seneca's view to its full extent.

But Alberti's historical place may best be defined by measuring its relationship to the civic view of life current in Florence during the first decades of the Quattrocento. In the second book of *Della Famiglia* he asks how the possession of *divitiae* can ultimately be justified, in view of the fact that substantial riches normally come from the profits of trade, an activity which is after all "mercenary" and, as many people feel, not altogether honest. His answer is that wealth can nevertheless be valued highly, because a rich merchant "is very useful to the republic and still more to his own family." Riches often bring friendship, praise, and dignity, and they can be of great use to the *patria*. It is not always possible from public funds alone to pay the wages of those who defend the country's independence. "Nor can republics increase their glory and their might without enormous expenditure." Consequently, they must be able to call on the good will of wealthy citizens. "A great treasury is not one that depends on a great number of people who are forced to pay. It is one that commands the loyalty of those who are not poor. It is a treasury to which all rich citizens faithfully and conscientiously contribute." This, says Lionardo degli Alberti, the Alberti family has always done for Florence. "Of every thirty-two pounds of gold spent in the days of the Alberti by our government, the records show that more than one represented the contribution of our family alone. This means a great sum of money, but still greater was the good will, the love, the readiness to serve which we showed at all times. Thus did we acquire great reputation, fame, and high esteem. . . ." Alberti ends this conversation on civic-mindedness with the assertion that although "one would rather work for one's family than for others, for friends than for strangers, . . . one's country, of

[29] See Essay Five, pp. 118f.

course, has priority over everything."[30] With a clarity rarely found in humanistic writings, Alberti here uses the role played by Florentine wealth in the half-century of the last pre-Medici republic as an apology for the accumulation of great riches.

The fact that he shows little interest in those ancient authors who had nourished the city-state ethos of the earlier Florentine humanists—Aristotle, Cicero, and the author of the pseudo-Aristotelian *Economics*—should not prevent us from stressing the impact of that ethos on his thinking. For the ancient source that Alberti so closely followed, Xenophon's *Oeconomicus*, though more individualistic and "capitalistic" than those other writings, was still within the scope of Greek city-state thinking. There is a scene in Xenophon's work in which the main speaker, before embarking on the subject of the careful management of a private household, is asked by Socrates whether he really wishes to become rich and thereby bring trouble into his life. Xenophon's speaker replies that there are three reasons why he wants to be rich: to be able to honor the gods without counting the cost, to help his friends in time of need, and to be able "to see to it that the city [Athens] will lack no adornment that means can provide." Whereupon Socrates exclaims that "these are noble aspirations, truly worthy of a man of means" and that those who manage to maintain their own estates "and yet have enough left to adorn the city and relieve their friends can indeed be thought great and powerful men."[31] This comes very near the civic spirit of Alberti's discussion in *Della Famiglia* of the significance and justification of great wealth.

At the beginning of our analysis of *Della Famiglia*, it was stressed that Alberti's ideas have to be distinguished from those expressed by individual speakers in his work or adopted from ancient authors. But a common element does exist. The community-oriented defense of *divitiae* appears in virtually every utterance on wealth found in *Della Famiglia*, whether

---

[30] *Della Famiglia*, ed. Grayson, 141–42, 149; trans. Watkins, 142–43, 148.
[31] Xenophon *Oecon.* XI.9–10.

one turns to Giannozzo degli Alberti's views in the third book (his objections to the *vita politica* in the city-state notwithstanding) or to the apology for wealth and the condemnation of *paupertas* in the second and fourth books. Another aspect of *Della Famiglia* also marks the work as an expression of civic Humanism: the republican sentiment that comes to the surface in occasional judgments of life at the princely courts. Thus we find Giannozzo, on the basis of his experiences as a merchant in exile, warning the younger members of the Alberti clan not to trust great lords and princes or, for that matter, form any connection with princely courts. Princes, he says, have no gratitude, are wholly unreliable, are surrounded by flatterers and sycophants, and prefer these to people of austerity and religious piety. All of this is quite natural and to be expected, because "the majority of courtiers live in idleness and waste their time. They have no occupation by which to earn an honest living."[32] That this opinion is not limited to Giannozzo becomes abundantly clear when his city-state-minded adversary and critic, Lionardo, expresses himself elsewhere in the debate in a nearly identical fashion.[33] In this case, too, the crux of the argument is the relationship between Florentine republicanism and respect for rational economic activity. Princes, Giannozzo's opponent agrees, become pleasure-seekers "surrounded . . . by deceivers and flatterers" because they are "unencumbered by any sort of honest work." Though the prince may begin by making friends with those who are rich, before long he will covet their wealth and "search out the friendship of those who will astutely and maliciously encourage him on his ill-chosen path."[34]

IV

We have seen how much one can learn about Florentine civic Humanism from the conversations depicted in *Della Famiglia*

[32] *Della Famiglia*, trans. Watkins, 237; ed. Grayson, 251–52.
[33] In Book IV, composed about 1440.
[34] *Della Famiglia*, ed. Grayson, 251f. and 265f.; trans. Watkins, 237 and 248.

and from other records of Alberti's first encounter with the Florentine world. This is not to say, however, that *Della Famiglia* was an important source of ideas for civic Humanism in its own time. For whereas Bruni's translation of the pseudo-Aristotelian *Economics*, usually accompanied by his commentary and a combative preface-introduction, was one of the most widely copied books of the early Quattrocento (an indication of its great influence),[35] only three complete manuscripts of *Della Famiglia* have come down to us. To these can be added two manuscripts containing Books I–III, two containing Books I–II, five limited to the third book, and one to the fourth. Printed editions go back only to 1843, when Book III alone was printed.[36] This publication record points to a work with a minimal influence in its time and in following centuries.

Now it is true that this judgment does not fully apply to Book III, which contains Giannozzo degli Alberti's guide to the economic virtues, the management of the household, the Florentine merchant ethos, and the weakness as well as the value of the *vita activa politica*. That this one book had somewhat wider influence is suggested by the fact that nearly half of the thirteen preserved Quattrocento manuscripts of all or portions of *Della Famiglia* are separate copies of Book III. Moreover, about two decades after the completion of Leon Battista's work, someone in Florence revised the text of Book III according to the tastes and needs of the second half of the Quattrocento, turning it into an anonymous *Trattato del Governo della Famiglia*. The revision, though closely following Alberti's diction, order, and argument, created virtually a different work insofar as its relationship to the civic Humanism

---

[35] In Florence as well as in the rest of Italy, and eventually all over Europe. More than two hundred manuscripts have been preserved, and between 1469 and 1598 there were nearly seventy printed editions of it. See J. Soudek, "The Genesis and Tradition of Leonardo Bruni's Annotated Latin Version of the (Pseudo-)Aristotelian *Economics*," *Traditio* 12 (1958): 260.

[36] Based on the explorations and survey of the editor of *Della Famiglia*, Cecil Grayson, pp. 367–80 of his edition.

of the first half of the century is concerned. This is not due chiefly to those alterations to which literary critics usually refer: obliteration of most references to the Alberti family; transference of the role of major speaker from Giannozzo degli Alberti to an older contemporary, Agnolo Pandolfini; insertions dealing with taxation and politics in the later Quattrocento; and frequent meddling with Leon Battista's style. It was due more to the dilution of the true character of Book III as a contest between two opposing ways of life. In the revised version, the dramatic struggle between values (represented by Giannozzo on the one hand and Lionardo on the other) is abolished by the device of putting both the praise of the *vita economica privata* and the defense of participation in the *vita politica* in the mouth of one and the same speaker. The original altercation is thus turned into advice to patricians suitable for whatever changes Fortuna may bring: into a combined eulogy of the *vita economica privata*, offering comfort in periods of exclusion from the privileges of the *statuali*, and defense of the Florentine *vita politica*, appropriate for times when a more favorable Fortuna again opens the door to the ruling circle. The *Governo della Famiglia* is already used for such pragmatic purposes in the well-known *Miscellany* of Giovanni Rucellai, written during his debarment from the *stato* of the ruling Medici party (before 1461, when he was readmitted). Similar circumstances may explain the purpose of other Quattrocento manuscripts of the *Governo* found in the libraries of Florentine patrician families.[37]

The most helpful witness to Florentine political conscious-

---

[37] Agnolo Pandolfini's equal commendation of both a "vita libera, lieta, quieta," far removed from politics, and the life of a citizen that participates in the "cose pubbliche," provided that he is not primarily impelled by ambition and personal interest, is found in the paragraphs of the *Governo* published in vol. 5 of Alberti's *Opere Volgari* (Florence, 1849), 143–44. For the date, authorship, and distribution of the *Governo*, see F. C. Pellegrini, in *Giornale Storico della Letteratura Italiana* 8 (1886): esp. 19 and 52. See also vol. 1 of *Giovanni Rucellai ed il suo Zibaldone*, ed. A. Perosa (London, 1960), 3ff., 39ff., 146, and now vol. 2 (1981), 112f.

ness in the second half of the century, however, is Alberti himself. To be sure, we have the works and letters of the Neoplatonists as sources of information on the outlook of Florentine patricians during those decades. But these are useful only up to a point. The mode of thinking they represent does not embrace and further develop the legacy of early Quattrocento Humanism. Rather, it accepts it as a whole while relegating it to a lower level, beneath the level measured by Platonic teachings. We have had a glimpse of this composite and gradational vision in the writings of Landino and Nesi. Moreover, the kind of Platonic superstructure accepted by these late Quattrocento Florentines exhibits little of the political consciousness of city-state citizens; it is a Platonism rooted primarily in art and religion. This is true, for instance, of Ficino's resuscitation of Dante's ideal of a universal monarchy, which is unrelated to the conditions of Florence or Italy during the 1460s and 1470s and consequently throws little light upon the humanistic legacy in the Neoplatonic years.

Alberti, fortunately, fills this lacuna. During the forties, fifties, and sixties, when he was leading the life of a wandering architect in various Italian cities and at princely courts, and when his separation from Florence again allowed some of the Stoic ideals of the sage to reappear in his works, he continued to visit his native city. Under the impact of these visits, about 1469—not many years before his death—he wrote a second major work on the family, *De Iciarchia*, which in some respects reads like a reprise of his first work on the subject. With it the old man seeks to inculcate in a younger generation an attitude toward the *vita politica* worthy of Florentine patricians and discusses their studies, social ambitions, and economic pursuits; but he does so very differently from the way he had done it in *Della Famiglia*. The title *De Iciarchia* clearly indicates Alberti's changed perspective on both the family and the *vita politica*. It is a newly coined Italian term, which tries to render the Greek οἰϰαρχία, a combination of ὸίϰος (house and household) and ἀρχεία (government, "-archy" as in "monarchy" and "oligarchy"), and expresses the idea that rulers over

281

households (families including younger business associates and members of the clan, according to Florentine custom) exercise a "government" no different in essence from that of the "publici magistrati" provided by the state. As Alberti argues, "el governo e moderazione degli altri" can be exerted over many or over only a few. In the former case, a city, an army, or a province will be provided by the state with a "rettore." But even when the group being governed is only a small "number of men united by confederation, social intercourse, kinship, and the like," it will still need a "moderator." "This will indeed be an authority, but not a public one; rather, it will be an agency set in operation by family concern combined with public solicitude."[38] Thus it appears "that the city . . . is almost like a very large family, and, conversely, the family is almost a small city."[39]

In such a vision of society and government, the balance in the valuation of the patrician family and the city-state republic begins to shift. Family and clan are like a *corpo*, of which the individuals are "come innati instrumenti e membra," all firmly bound together by "an indissoluble bond in which the one sustains and is sustained by the other." "Hence . . . one can with good reason assert that one owes more to one's family than . . . to one's city." Moreover, "the principates and lordships in [Italian] cities are frequently acquired through plots, frauds, and . . . risks, . . . and are ruled with violence, . . . dissimulation, . . . and cruelty. The government of which we speak [that is, of family and clan], on the other hand, is acquired with simple and open-hearted kindness. . . . Again, in the *publico principato civile* all strength and steadiness has its roots in things that by nature are fickle and uncertain." By

[38] ". . . numero d'omini couniti per confederazione, conversazione, consanguinità, e simile"; "E questo sarà magistrato sì, non però publico; ma sarà officio composto della cura domestica colla sollecitudine publica." Alberti, *De Iciarchia*, in vol. 2 of his *Opere Volgari*, ed. Cecil Grayson, Scrittori d'Italia, vol. 234 (Bari, 1966), 265.

[39] ". . . che la città . . . sia quasi come una ben grande famiglia; e, contro, la famiglia sia quasi una picciola città" (ibid., 266).

contrast, "ours [the government of family and clan], grounded as it is in the sure generosity of a virile soul who is more eager to be a true leader [*principe*] and a very good *rettore* of his own actions than to appear excellent in the eyes of others, is filled with faith, piety, kindness, and beneficence. . . . Consequently, it will be abler and steadier."[40]

For the aged Leon Battista Alberti, then, the emphasis has shifted from public to private life: protective family groups, which had always been powerful in the Italian city-state aristocracy, have acquired a far greater value than the public offices and institutions of the state. For Giannozzi degli Alberti, as depicted in *Della Famiglia*, it was right for a citizen to forgo political ambition, to strive instead for success in his *vita privata economica*, waiting for the time when his fellow citizens would beseech him to serve in high office. In the third book of *De Iciarchia*, the best training ground for young, politically ambitious patricians, each of whom "desires to be a most excellent man and superior to others,"[41] is considered to be a miniature government for the benefit of the family and clan. Preparation in such a government, Alberti remarks, will not only provide exercise in good leadership but will ensure that the efficient man will prevail in competition for the offices of the state. "Rarely, indeed never, will it happen that you who are born into a noble family which is not without power, not base, who are raised according to the best instruction, . . . will not attain, among your own and in the republic, to a lofty rank, one of the first and most illustrious."[42]

This is a far cry from the communal spirit and political-mindedness of civic Humanism. In Bruni and Palmieri's time, the guiding models had been the Greek *polis* and the Roman *respublica*, with their respective public institutions. But the political vision behind the third book of *De Iciarchia* can only be characterized as a socially and politically reactionary kind of

[40] Ibid., 266–70.
[41] Ibid., 264.
[42] Ibid., 265.

romanticism. In contrast to anything found in the early Quattrocento, *De Iciarchia* insists on the naturalness and humaneness of freely developed social structures like the family, as against the egotism that gives rise to city-state institutions. "It seems to me," Alberti tells the younger men, "that the first step in the formation of the family was love, and hence the primary bond holding its members together is piety and benevolence and a certain duty required by nature toward one's own people." In the relationships of people in a city or state, on the other hand, "it would seem that a certain purpose, more to preserve themselves than to give any benefit to others, brought them together."[43]

By the same token, for the first time since the Trecento a humanist expressly directs his counsel on morals and behavior to a Florentine audience of noblemen. *Giovani nati in famiglia nobile*, or a similar formula, is how the author of *De Iciarchia* addresses his young friends, and he does so because the rules he lays down for them depend on the privileges they may expect to enjoy as "molto fortunati, e nati in nobile famiglia," as "giovani . . . nati a magnificenza e a signorile amplitudine."[44] Elsewhere in Italy it had become usual by the middle of the Quattrocento to designate the descendants of patrician families as *nobili cittadini*;[45] but the term *nobile* was used with great caution in Florence, where many of the most powerful and respected families were considered to belong to the *popolo*, despite the fact that they represented a potent aristocratic and even oligarchic element in the state. We have the word of Savonarola, a foreigner in intimate contact with Florentine society, that even in his time—some twenty-five years after *De*

---

[43] ". . . che alla origine della famiglia il primo accesso fu amore, e indi il primario vincolo a contenerli insieme fu pietà e carità e certo officio richiesto dalla natura verso e' suoi. In questi altri della città pare che certo fine, per più conservare sé stessi che per punto beneficar gli altri, li congregasse" (ibid., 266).

[44] Ibid., 191, 215, 264f.

[45] This has been traced in great detail for the Venetian region in Angelo Ventura's *Nobiltà e popolo nella società Veneta del '400 e '500* (Bari, 1964).

Iciarchia—one did not call oneself *nobile* in Florence. Twenty-five years after that, Machiavelli was to express the opinion that what still distinguished Florence and some other parts of Tuscany from most of Italy was the absence of a nobility empowered with feudal lordship (not identical with but closely related to the patriarchalism of patrician noblemen that serves as a standard in *De Iciarchia*).

The realization that for Savonarola and Machiavelli, many years after *De Iciarchia*, Florentine society was set apart by the absence of a dominating aristocracy such as typified most Italian regions clarifies the historical context of Alberti's testimony of 1469. Although the ascendancy of a full-grown aristocratic oligarchy in Florence was a drawn-out process, interrupted by reversals from the time of Savonarola on, the decades before Savonarola (the 1460s, 1470s, and 1480s) saw the creation by the leading families of Florence, in conjunction with the Medici, of a manner of life nearer to the splendor and luxury of the contemporary Italian nobility than to that of the Florentine patriciate of the early Quattrocento, with its city-state spirit.[46] What effect then, did remembrance of the social interchange in the generations of Bruni and Palmieri have on the patriciate during the second half of the century, when Florentine society was so drastically transformed? The answer found in *De Iciarchia* is twofold: in part positive, but in part also negative, because it shows so clearly that the very spirit of civic Humanism had disappeared.

The positive role was played by the early Quattrocento Florentine legacy of education for politico-historical thought. Once the scramble for office, so much abhorred by Giannozzo degli Alberti, was replaced by a selection among the best known *iciarchi* within exclusive aristocratic groups, an aspiring citizen's familiarity with the Florentine past and with Italian history in general became the decisive credential. Alberti had this in mind when he wrote that "it will rarely happen that

---

[46] This included the completion of their princely palaces (see Essay One, note 1) as well as their political preponderance in the republic.

those devoted to the *buone arti e dottrine* will not ascend in the course of time to the most honored rank among citizens."[47] Elsewhere in *De Iciarchia* the nature of the new intellectual preparation for politics is spelled out in detail. The "knowledge and experience" most worthy of acquisition is that most useful to the *patria*. Along with the knowledge of everything connected with the provision of armed troops on land and sea, for defense or attack, "the things most worthy of a civic-minded man and most useful to one who presumes to be the leader of others" are such things as "knowledge of the deeds and methods of those ancestors who founded and augmented our and the other republics; knowledge of customs, of the public and private governments of our community, and of the princes with whom one might at some time have to ally oneself; knowledge of the desires and behavior of citizens useful and not useful to the public good." "Such things give one who understands them great authority and reputation in the senate and at the sides of the leaders. . . ."[48] Reading on, we are given an analysis of the nature of these new concerns. "Our reflection as citizens," we are told, "is nothing but a discourse with yourself in which you repeat the things [of the past] known to you and compare their similarities with things that are just now present, thus arguing about what can come of them; and this is what is called prudence, almost providence, whence follows caution against harm. . . ."[49]

Here we are clearly on the road leading from Bruni's revival of historical thinking to the ideas and value judgments found in Machiavelli's *Discorsi* and Guicciardini's works. It is interesting to note that as early as 1469, the year Machiavelli was born, Alberti's historical perspective already included some of the ideas that would typify the intellectual atmosphere in mature Renaissance Florence. But in contrast to *Della Famiglia*, how little of the way of life of the civic humanists is preserved

[47] *De Iciarchia*, ed. Grayson, 229 and 256.
[48] Ibid., 217.
[49] Ibid., 224.

in *De Iciarchia*! Since the days of Bruni (in some respects, of
Salutati), the rapid advance and unique influence of civic Humanism in Florence had been inseparable from the fact that
members of patrician families and of the growing humanistic
community were drawn together by new intellectual interests—beginning with the audience in the lecture hall of Manuel Chrysoloras, the nursery of Greek studies. Florentine patricians had begun to break away from the traditional
aristocratic culture of the Middle Ages earlier than any outside
of Florence. But by the late 1460s, whether or not Leon Battista Alberti overstated the changes he encountered on his later
visits to Florence, some Florentine patrician families were
again beginning to instill in their sons, "nati in famiglia nobile," a kind of culture and attitude toward life intended for
the members of a noble elite.

Two things intrigued Alberti, as he indicates, during those
later visits to Florence. One was the ostentatious use of riches,
including the wearing of ever more expensive clothing for
men as well as for women.[50] The other—more important—
was the inclination of his younger patrician friends to consider
a large fortune indispensable to the acquisition of authority
and power. Great wealth, they said, had been a decisive factor
in the rise of the leading families to nobility and fame. When
Della Famiglia was being composed, a vital issue for the Florentine humanists had been the extent to which *divitiae* were a
necessary instrument for those engaged in the *vita activa politica*. What Leon Battista had learned from Giannozzo degli Alberti at the time he wrote *Della Famiglia* was that for someone
not participating in the *vita politica*, constant work at creating
wealth was a prerequisite for independence and happiness. In
De Iciarchia we encounter a note of doubt whether a persistent
striving for wealth was compatible with a successful aristocratic life. The sequence of cause and effect would appear to
have been reversed during the late 1460s and 1470s: if a young
nobleman lacks wealth (we read in *De Iciarchia*), it will come

[50] Ibid., 203.

to him as he gains recognition within aristocratic circles. He needs to be taught that "a man brought up with zeal and good manners [con industria e buona civilità] will not be poor in his old age," because it is rightly expected "that where there is virtù, riches and power will not be lacking."[51] Those known to have acquired the abilities we have described "earn as much money as they desire. They are welcomed by wealthy leaders and rewarded by them."[52] Conversely, since rich people, even in noble clans, may become poor overnight, the old Alberti proposed that in good times clan members should establish family trusts capable of supporting impoverished members.[53]

When the author of Della Famiglia wrote his De Iciarchia—a book so contrary to the values and mode of life of the early Florentine Quattrocento—the period in which Florence taught the rest of Italy a new attitude toward politics, history, and economic work was drawing to a close. Totally aristocratic city republics and certain Italian courts were soon to offer better opportunities than did Florence, where the older civic traditions still partially survived. For although after the age of Lorenzo de' Medici civic Humanism in its original form no longer suited the temper of the times even in Florence, a long line of dissenting figures, from Savonarola to Machiavelli and the last defenders of the republic around 1530, showed themselves in vital respects to be the heirs of the early Florentine Quattrocento.[54]

[51] "Omo allevato con industria e buona civilità non vedo che possa per età esser povero" (ibid., 277). "Dicono che dove abiti la onestà, ivi sta bellezza, e dove sia virtù, ivi non mancano ricchezze e potentato" (ibid., 246).

[52] "E' dotti acquistano a sé pecunia quanta e' vogliono. Sone riceuti da fortunati principi, e riceveno da loro" (ibid., 213).

[53] Ibid., 278f.

[54] We especially owe the ability to perceive these movements and writers as a correlated undercurrent of later Florentine life to Rudolf v. Albertini's Das florentinische Staatsbewusstsein im Übergang von der Republik zum Prinzipat (Bern, 1955).

INDEX OF NAMES

Abélard, 107–8, 112n
Albertano da Brescia, 111, 112, 160–61, 177n, 220n
Alberti, Giannozzo, 261–68, 273, 278–80, 283, 285, 287
Alberti, Leon Battista, 15, 32, 186, 236–37, 258–88; and Bruni, 269; and Florence, 269, 277
—works: *De Commodis*, 262, 268; *De Iciarchia*, 274n, 281–88; *Della Famiglia*, 15, 260–67, 269, 272–79, 281, 283, 286–88; *De Pictura*, 269; *Intercoenales*, 269–71
Alberti, Lionardo, 265–68, 276, 280
Alberti, Piero, 15
Alberti family, 262–64, 267, 276, 278, 280
Albertini, Rudolf von, 288n
Albizzi, Rinaldo degli, 8, 9n, 145
Albizzi family, 9n, 14, 260
Alcuin, 112n
Aldobrandino d'Ottobuono, 208
Alexander the Great, 146, 162, 166, 174, 184
Alfonso of Naples, 154
Alps, 31, 59, 68, 87, 167
Ambrose, Saint, 105–6, 107, 109, 111, 125, 182
Amiclas, 174
Anonymous of 1385–1409, 71n
Anthony, Marc, 40, 131
Antonino, Archbishop of Florence, 162n
Antonio da Romagno, 193–95
Apennines, 57, 216
Aquinas, Saint Thomas, 112–15, 159–60, 160n, 162, 163, 199, 203, 224
Arezzo, 19, 65, 66, 76, 81, 82, 121n
Aristotle, 13, 94, 99, 159, 163, 199,

234–36, 239, 243, 255n, 258, 272; and Alberti, 273, 277; and Bartolo, 224; and Bruni, 19, 130, 146, 151, 229–32; and Cicero, 97, 109, 114, 142; and Dante, 163–64; and Nesi, 238; and Nifo, 243, 250–51; and Palmieri, 27, 151, 155–57; and Patrizi, 153; and Petrarch, 172–73, 179, 183; and Poggio, 248; and Ptolemy of Lucca, 204–5; and Salutati, 148
—works: *Nicomachean Ethics*, 112–14, 155–57, 231; *Politics*, 203; *Rhetoric*, 243
Arquà, 177, 178, 180, 183
Asculum, 51
Atalante, 54–55
Athens, 4, 120, 277
Athens, Duke of ("signore" of Florence), 77–82
Attalus, 55, 178
Attila, 70
Attilius Serranus, 194, 254n
Augustine, Saint, 30, 113, 160, 201, 212
Augustus, Emperor, 181, 202
Aurispa, Giovanni, 237
Avignon, 116, 167, 176, 213, 214

Bacon, Francis, 255, 256
Baldo de Ubaldis, 224
Balearic Islands, 111n
Baluzius, Stephanus, 33n, 59n
Barbaro, Francesco, 124, 195, 226–27, 228, 229
Bartolo of Sassoferrato, 224
Basil, Saint, 218
Belloni, Gino, 27–28n, 139–40n
Benedict, Saint, 218

Benvenuto Rambaldi da Imola. *See* Rambaldi, Benvenuto, da Imola
Bernardino da Siena, 222, 223
Biondo, Flavio, 49, 52
Biraghi of Milan, 237
Bisticci, Vespasiano da, 14–15, 244n
Boccaccio, Giovanni, 18n, 19, 20, 22, 23, 32, 48, 55, 129, 133n, 198, 205–10, 213, 222n, 232–33, 252, 254; and ancient Rome, 198, 206–9; and Dante, 129; and Petrarch, 206, 208; and Pino de' Rossi, 164n, 197n, 206–8, 222n; and Ptolemy of Lucca, 208–9
—works: *Decameron*, 17, 129n, 197; *De Casibus Virorum*, 164n, 197n, 198n, 208; *Del Comento sopra la Commedia*, 55n; *Labirinto d'amore*, 18n; *Vita di Dante*, 17–18, 197, 222n
Boethius, 104–5, 164n
Bolgar, R. R., 112n
Bologna, 11, 136, 196
Botticelli, 38
Bracciolini, Poggio, 150–51, 154, 186, 228, 246–51, 253; and Bruni, 150–51
—works: *De Avaritia*, 228n, 251n; *De Nobilitate*, 248–50; *Epistolae*, 247n; *Facetiae*, 247; *Oratio Funebris* on Bruni, 150–51
Brescia, 161n
Brucker, Gene, 11n
Brunelleschi, Filippo, 4, 5, 13, 29
Bruni, Leonardo, 5n, 6, 7n, 9, 12, 14, 21, 29–30, 33n, 43n, 44n, 71n, 121, 133n, 186, 195, 228–32, 234–38, 244, 249, 260, 265, 271, 279; and ancient Italy, 31, 34–38, 43–46, 48–49, 50–53, 56–61, 64–65, 72–73, 91, 92, 229, 269n; and Aristotle, 151, 230–31, 232n; and Biondo, 49, 52; and Cicero, 21, 31, 121n, 122–23n, 130, 133, 141,

144; and Dante, 18–19, 20n, 22–23, 129, 130, 133; and Francesco de Fiano, 30; and Machiavelli, 38, 41, 42, 48; and Manetti, 22; and modern Italy, 44–46, 49, 51–52, 60–67, 73–74, 83–91, 269; and Palmieri, 7, 33, 125; and Petrarch, 18–19, 52, 61, 121, 130, 247; and Poggio, 150; and Valla, 49; and the Villani, 77–79, 81, 84
—works: *Cicero Novus*, 21n, 121–22, 123n, 141; *Commentarium Rerum Graecarum*, 91; *De Bello Italico Adversus Gothos Gesto*, 62, 90; *Difesa del Popolo Fiorentino*, 222n; trans. of (Pseudo-Aristotelian) *Economics*, 229–31, 237, 279; *Epistolae*, 59n, 91n, 228n, 229n, 231n, 232n; *Historiae Florentini Populi*, 7, 12, 20n, 29–30, 34–38, 43–93; *Isagogicon Moralis Disciplinae*, 149–50; *Laudatio Florentinae Urbis*, 43n, 46: *Oratio Funebris* on Nanni degli Strozzi, 6, 32, 33n, 59, 145–46; *Ragione* on Nicolò da Tolentino, 146n; *Rerum Suo Tempore*, 88, 89–90n; *Vite di Dante e di Petrarca*, 19–20n, 31, 35, 61–62, 130, 222n
Bruno, Giordano, 252
Brutus, 40, 98, 120
Buck, August, 125n
Buonaccorso da Montemagno the Younger, 16n, 140–41, 233n, 275
Buoninsegni, Domenico, 15
Byzantium, 237

Cacciaguida, 164n
Caesar, 20, 40, 45, 116, 121, 142, 146, 174, 212, 233
Caggese, Romolo, 14n
Cambiatori, Tommaso, 231n
Cambrensis, Giraldus, 106n
Camillus, Marcus Furius, 146
Campaldino, 19, 20n, 21, 126, 130

Campano, Giannantonio, 123
Capponi, Gino, 145
Capua, 56
Carolingian Empire, 61
Carrara family, 177
Carthage, 25–26, 47, 91, 201, 205
Cassius, 120
Castiglionchio, Lapo da: the Elder,
    120n, 224; the Younger, 244–46
Catherine of Siena, Saint, 216
Catiline, 27, 72–73, 131, 157
Cato (the Censor and Uticensis), 19,
    26n, 35, 101, 103, 128, 130, 134n,
    171, 201, 207
Cavalcanti, Guido, 129n
Charlemagne, 63, 65, 70
Christ, 111, 169, 182, 200, 202–4,
    211, 217, 218–20, 245–46
Chrysippus, 153
Chrysoloras, Manuel, 287
Cicero, Marcus Tullius, 13, 20–23,
    94–133, 134, 137–49, 163, 164n,
    167, 190, 192n, 198, 199n, 201,
    216n; and Albertano of Brescia,
    111, 112, 160; and Alberti, 277;
    and Saint Ambrose, 105–6; and
    Francesco Barbaro, 124; and Boe-
    thius, 104; and Bruni, 19, 21, 31,
    72, 121–22, 130, 133, 141–42; and
    Saint Jerome, 107; and Landino,
    131–32; and Latini, 162; and Ma-
    crobius, 102–4; and Palmieri, 21–
    22, 125–26, 138, 234; and Pas-
    chasius, 106; and Petrarch, 20,
    116–19, 181, 191; and Poggio,
    249; and Porcari, 126–27; and Re-
    migio de' Girolami, 114; and Ri-
    nuccini, 227–28; and Salutati, 20,
    119–20; and Sicco Polentone,
    123n; and Saint Thomas Aquinas,
    112–13; and Tolomeo of Lucca,
    114; and Vergerio, 20–21, 120–21,
    127–28; and Vincent of Beauvais,
    109–10

—works: Academica Priora, 30n,
    152; De Finibus, 168, 191, 234; De
    Legibus, 96, 97, 100–102; De Na-
    tura Deorum, 96; De Officiis, 95,
    97, 98, 100, 102, 105–12, 114,
    118, 125, 127, 138, 142, 234; De
    Oratore, 95, 97, 101, 102, 128–29,
    130, 133; De Republica, 97–100,
    102, 143; Leges et Decreta, 112;
    Epistolae ad Atticum, 119; Epistolae
    Familiares, 119; Somnium Scipionis,
    21–22, 98, 102–4, 113, 125–26;
    Tusculanae Disputationes, 95, 98,
    142
Cincinnatus, 254n
Ciompi, revolt, 8, 215
Claudianus, 48
Cleanthes, 249
Codrus, 201
Collenuccio, Pandolfo, 241
Compagni, Dino, 129n
Constantine the Great, 182, 202, 212
Conversino (da Ravenna), Giovanni,
    192n
Copernicus, 52
Coriolanus, 15
Crassus, Marcus Licinius, 101, 128,
    130n
Cratippus, 231
Curia, 30, 228, 243–44, 246–47, 260
Curius Dentatus, 21, 126, 201, 207
Curtius, Marcus, 194, 201

Da Correggio: Azzo, 172n; family
    in Parma, 171, 173
Dante, 19–20n, 23, 28, 31, 32, 35,
    38, 48, 53–54, 59, 60, 62, 70, 114,
    129, 133, 162–64, 192n, 224, 248,
    281; and Boccaccio, 55, 129; and
    Bruni, 20n, 31, 129, 130; and Fi-
    lippo Villani, 48; and Landino,
    22–23; and Machiavelli, 38; and
    Manetti, 22; and Palmieri, 21–22,

Dante (cont.)
126; and Petrarch, 17–20; and
Rambaldi, 55
—works: Convivio, 164; De Mo-
narchia, 28n, 38n, 50; Divina Com-
media, 54n, 163–64; Epistolae, 53n
Dardanus, 54–55
Decembrio, Pier Candido, 240–41
Decii, in ancient Rome, 40
Demetrius the Cynic, 249
Democritus, 166, 181
Dicaearchus, 97, 99n
Dilthey, Wilhelm, 24–25
Diocletian, Emperor, 212
Diogenes (Greek Cynic), 162, 166,
174, 181, 184, 197
Dionysius of Halicarnassus, 56
Dominic, Saint, 159, 218
Dominici, Giovanni, 223
Donatello, 4, 13, 21, 29, 38

Egidio Romano, 162n
England, paupertas and riches, 254–
55
Epaminondas, 40
Epicurus, 178, 231, 239n
Erasmus, 256
Este, Ercole d', 241
Etruria, in antiquity, 36, 37, 50–60,
64–66, 86, 96
Euganean Hills, 177
Europe, 69, 85, 86, 91–93, 221n,
246, 255, 279n

Fabius Maximus, 126
Fabricius Luscinus, 126, 166, 194,
201, 204, 207, 242
Faesulae, 50–51, 53
Ferrara, 145, 147, 195, 244
Fiano, Francesco da, 30–31, 41
Ficino, Marsilio, 131, 132, 238, 281
Fiesole, 54–55
Filelfo, Francesco, 19n
Filelfo, Giovan Maria, 20n, 133

Florence: founding, 45, 50, 53–54,
58, 59n, 70, 72, 212n
—buildings: Baptistry, 5; Bar-
gello, 47, 74; Cathedral, 4, 5;
Loggia dei Signori (dei Lanzi), 4;
Medici (Riccardi) Palace, 4; Or
San Michele, 4; Pazzi (Quaratesi)
Palace, 4; Pitti Palace, 4; Rucellai
Palace, 4; S. Trinità, 216; Spedale
degli Innocenti, 5; Strozzi Palace,
4
—guilds, 4–5, 7–8, 11, 12, 33, 70,
75, 79
—Piazza della Signoria, 4, 16,
126, 146
—Signoria (Priori), 4, 43, 75, 80–
81
Florus, Lucius Annaeus, 26n, 198
Fortini, Ser Paolo, 9n
France, 68, 79, 84, 87–89, 116, 167
Francesco, Duke of Ferrara, 147
Francis, Saint, 159, 163, 164n, 182,
186, 194–95, 218, 219
Frederic II of Hohenstaufen, 63, 73–
74, 164, 248

Gadol, F., 274n
Gaeta, 73–74
Garin, Eugenio, 150n
Gaul, 40, 57–58, 110n
Gelli, 32
Gellius, Aulus, 120
Genoa, 25
Germany, 61–64, 68, 73, 84–87, 89
Ghibellines, 63–64, 67, 70, 73, 74
Ghiberti, Lorenzo, 5
Gianfigliazzi, Rinaldo dei, 12
Giotto di Bondone, 33
Giovanni dalle Celle, 214, 215–22,
223, 225
Giustiniani, Leonardo, 124
Goldbrunner, H. M., 230n, 251n
Gonzaga, Francesco, 59
Goths, 90

Grayson, Cecil, 261n, 262n, 265n
Greece, 27, 40, 54, 55, 58, 59, 65,
  76, 85, 91, 96, 97, 99, 104, 121,
  134, 144, 147, 156, 159, 166, 195,
  196, 229, 237, 258, 277, 283, 287
Green, Louis, 71–72n, 93n
Gregory the Great, Saint, 113, 182
Grundmann, Herbert, 158n
Guarino da Verona, 195 96, 226,
  227n
Guelphs, 63–64, 67, 70, 73, 76, 84,
  165, 202, 223
Guicciardini, Francesco, 44, 85, 271,
  286
Guido del Palagio, 216
Guido of Pisa, 110–11
Guittone d'Arezzo, 162–63

Hades, 116, 120
Hadoardus, 110n
Hannibal, 31, 40
Hercules, 62, 151
Hohenstaufen, 47, 62–63, 68, 74, 76
Holy Roman Empire, 28, 35
Homer, 179
Horace, 56, 162
Horatius Cocles, 16, 21, 57

Imperium Romanum. See Rome, ancient
Innocent VII, Pope, 31n
Islam, 69
Italus, 55
Italy, 7, 11, 42, 45, 50, 59, 60, 63–
  64, 68, 69, 73; ancient, 36–38, 42,
  45, 50–53, 56–59, 61, 68, 85, 91–
  92, 142, 146, 165, 166, 181; and
  countries north of the Alps, 68,
  87, 154, 230, 254; modern, 8, 11,
  26, 32, 35, 44–52, 61–63, 68, 73–
  74, 78, 81–93, 110–11, 113–14,
  123, 160–64, 181, 186, 190, 192,
  200, 202, 209, 212, 230, 239, 244,

246, 248, 251, 254, 255, 258, 284,
  285, 288

Jerome, Saint, 99n, 107, 109, 110n,
  118, 136, 179
Job, 160
John of Salisbury, 107
Joseph of Arimathea, 160
Jubilee of 1300, 48
Juvenal, 162, 229, 233, 235

Kristeller, Paul O., 275n

Lactantius, 105n
Ladislaus, King, 82, 83
Laelius, 127n
Landino, Cristoforo, 22, 30, 132,
  133, 148n, 151–52, 281; and Cic-
  ero, 152; and Rome, 40
—works: De Vera Nobilitate, 30n,
  148n, 152n; Disputationes Camal-
  dulenses, 39–40, 131–32, 238
La Penna, Antonio, 7n
Latini, Brunetto, 162, 163, 164, 229
Leonidas, 40
Linternum, 207
Livy, 27, 44, 48, 56, 85–86, 165,
  166n
Lodi, 128
Lombardo della Seta, 177–79, 187,
  193, 240, 241
Lombardy, 11, 114
Louis of Bavaria, 63
Lucan, 196, 198
Lucca, 9, 14, 23, 66, 78, 133, 199
Luna (Etruscan city), 65

Maccabees, Second Book of, 200,
  203
Macedonia, 26
Machiavelli, Niccolò, 24–25, 27, 28,
  38, 41, 42n, 44, 81, 85, 92, 132,
  209, 255–56, 285, 286, 288; and
  Aristotle, 157; and Bruni, 38, 41;

Machiavelli, Niccolò (*cont.*)
  and Palmieri, 27; and Petrarch,
  25; and Rome, 38, 42
  —works: *Arte della Guerra*, 38n;
  Discorsi, 28n, 38n, 41, 48, 256,
  286; *Istorie Fiorentine*, 38
Macrobius, 98, 102–4, 113, 120n,
  138, 148n, 149
Manetti, Antonio, 32
Manetti, Giannozzo, 15, 22, 23,
  133, 229n, 232–33, 244
Manlius Curius Dentatus. *See*
  Curius Dentatus
Manto, 54
Mantua, 54, 56, 59, 60
Map, Walter, 107
Marius, Gaius, 31, 40, 146
Mars, 70
Marsili, Luigi, 216, 221, 222n
Martin, Saint, 218
Martines, Lauro, 10n
Mary and Martha, 111
Masaccio, 29
Mazzei, Lapo, 164n
Medici family, 3, 4, 6, 9, 14n, 22,
  83, 285; Cosimo, 4, 10, 11, 14,
  15, 83, 91, 131, 133, 226, 229,
  244n, 249, 260; Lorenzo, 226,
  249, 250, 253n, 288; Piero, 131;
  Pietro di Lorenzo, 238
Meinecke, Friedrich, 24, 42n
Menenius Agrippa, 254n
Metellus, 26, 126
Milan, 11–15, 49n, 70, 82–89, 145,
  173, 175, 177, 180, 184, 185, 188,
  237, 240, 241
Molho, Anthony, 10n
Mollweide, R., 110n
Monte Morello, 73
Montepulciano, 88
Moralium Dogma Philosophorum, 108,
  109, 162
Moses, 106

Najemy, John, 10–11n
Naples, 15, 82, 154, 165, 166, 170,
  171, 188, 198, 241, 243
Neckham, Alexander, 112n
Nero, 212
Nesi, Giovanni, 238–39, 281
Niccoli, Niccolò, 228n
Niccolò da Tolentino, 222n
Nicholas V, Pope, 237
Nifo, Agostino, 242–43, 251–52
Numa Pompilius (Roman king),
  103, 211

Ocno of Mantua, 54, 60
Octavian, 40
Orsini, Giovanni (archbishop), 253n
Orsini, Latino (Cardinal), 253n

Padua, 15, 87, 88, 177, 178, 188,
  193, 196, 242
Palmieri, Matteo, 7, 9–10, 16, 21–
  22, 27, 30, 33, 138–39, 141, 144,
  149, 150, 151, 154, 156, 234–35,
  239, 249, 265, 283, 285; and Aristotle, 27; and Bruni, 33, 125, 235;
  and Cicero, 21–22, 125–26, 138,
  139, 144, 234–35; and Dante, 21,
  126; and Rinuccini, 234; *Vita Civile*, 7, 9–10, 16, 17n, 21–22, 27,
  30n, 33n, 125–26, 138, 139n,
  140n, 141n, 146, 150n, 155–57,
  234–35, 236n, 268
Panaitius of Rhodes, 97, 142
Pandolfini, Agnolo, 280
Paris University, 112
Parma, 171–72, 173, 188
Patrizi, Francesco, 152–54
Paul, Saint, 148, 163, 169
Pavia, 177
Peacock, Reginald, 255
Peckham's *Tractatus Pauperis*, 254
Pellegrini, Sancto de', 196
Pericles, 249

Perugia, 11, 65, 66, 82, 225
Petrarch, 24–28, 32, 34, 49, 52, 60,
   61–62, 106, 115n, 116, 119, 120,
   121, 147, 148, 151, 209, 222n,
   228, 240, 247, 248, 260, 272, 275–
   76; and ancient Italy, 34, 45, 55,
   60, 118–19, 171; and Bruni, 18,
   31, 35, 45, 61–62, 121, 130; and
   Cicero, 20, 116–18, 119, 147,
   168n, 181, 191; and Filippo Villani, 48; and Lombardo della Seta,
   178–79, 187; and Luigi Marsili,
   221; and Machiavelli, 25, 27, 28;
   and Manetti, 22; and Milan, 180,
   184–85; and modern Italy, 45,
   173, 177, 180, 186, 188, 189; and
   Parma, 171–73; and Rome, 45;
   and Salutati, 119, 135, 148; and
   vita activa and *solitaria*, 17, 20, 22,
   130, 135, 139, 221; and wealth
   and Franciscan poverty, 165, 167–
   70, 173–93, 197, 214
   —works: *Africa*, 28; *De Remediis*,
   178, 185, 240; *De Otio Religioso*,
   26n, 118; *De Vita Solitaria*, 117,
   118, 135, 139, 170, 178; *Epistolae
   Familiares*, 26, 117n, 148n, 167–
   68n, 170n, 172, 173n, 175n, 176n,
   184n, 185n; *Epistolae Metricae*,
   169n, 171, 172n; *Epistolae Seniles*,
   118n, 147n, 176–78, 180n, 181–
   83n, 184n; *Epistolae Sine Nomine*,
   28n, 188; *Epistolae Variae*, 174n;
   Letter to Posterity, 183; *Rerum Memorandarum*, 117, 118n
Piccolomini, Enea Silvio (Pope Pius
   II), 123
Piccolpassi, F. (archbishop of
   Milan), 49n
Pisa, 11, 47, 65, 66, 76, 86, 91, 110,
   111n, 208
Pistoia, 66, 81, 140, 275
Piur, Paul, 165n

Pius II. *See* Piccolomini, Enea Silvio
Platina, Bartolomeo, 253–54
Plato, 22, 23, 94, 97, 138, 146, 151,
   152, 179, 231, 238, 249, 251, 271
Pliny the Younger, 56
Plotinus, 102, 103, 139n
Plutarch, 56, 121
Poggio. *See* Bracciolini
Polenton, Sicco, 122–23n
Poliziano, 131
Pompey (Pompeius Magnus), 31,
   40
Pontano, Gioviano, 154, 188, 241–
   42, 251
Populonia (Etruscan city), 65
Porcari, Stefano, 16, 17n, 126, 127n,
   222n, 233n, 235, 239
Porsenna of Clusium, 57
Posidonius, 142, 148, 149
Procopius, 62. *See also* Bruni, *De
   Bello Italico*
Ptolemy (Greek geographer), 70
Ptolemy of Lucca, 114, 115n, 199–
   210
Pyrrhus (king of Epirus), 201, 207

Radbertus, Paschasius, 106
Rambaldi, Benvenuto, da Imola,
   55–56
Regulus, Marcus Atilius, 201
Remigio de' Girolami, 114, 115n,
   199
Respublica Romana. See Rome, an-
   cient, and Italy, ancient
Ricci, Giovanni, 83
Rienzo, Cola di, 45
Rinuccini, Alamanno, 234
Rinuccini, Cino, 70, 71–72n, 125n,
   137–38, 227–28
Robbia, Luca della, 5
Robert (king of Naples), 165, 170;
   De Evangelica Paupertate (written
   at his court), 170

Rome, 69, 70, 72; ancient, 4, 7, 13, 16, 25, 26, 32, 34–37, 38, 40, 45, 47–53, 56–61, 65, 72–73, 85–86, 88, 92, 97, 114, 140–44, 146, 165–66, 169, 194–95, 198–212, 233, 242, 254, 275, 283; and Bruni, 34–37, 44, 46, 50–53, 56–61; Capitol, 165, 169; Janiculum, 57; modern, 28, 35, 48, 49, 84, 92, 165, 169, 243, 246–47, 252

Romulus, 211, 212

Rossi, Pino de', 164n, 197n, 206, 207n, 208, 222n

Rubinstein, Nicolai, 11n

Rucellai, Giovanni, 280

Rupert (German king), 85

Rusellae (Etruscan city), 65

Salamis, 40

Salerno, 243

Sallust, 7n, 26, 27, 48, 72, 157, 165, 198, 202, 209, 212

Salutati, Coluccio, 18, 20, 21n, 70, 119, 121, 134–36, 147–48, 193, 210–14, 216, 224, 254, 287; and Cicero, 119–21; and Petrarch, 119, 135, 148; and Samminiato, 137
—works: *De Seculo et Religione*, 135, 210–13, 217, 225; *De Vita Associabili*, 135; *Epistolario*, 120n, 136n, 137n, 148n, 149n

Samminiato, Giovanni da, 137

Savonarola, 255, 284–85, 288

Scaevola, Mucius, 16, 40

Scarperia, Jacopa di Agnolo, da, 121n

Scipio Africanus Major and Minor, 16, 21, 26, 28, 35, 99, 100, 103–6, 110, 117, 125–28, 204, 207, 211, 254n

Scipio Nasica, 98

Seneca (Stoic philosopher), 19, 130, 148, 149, 162, 163, 165, 178, 181, 191, 192n, 196, 198, 200, 209, 216n, 236–37, 240, 249, 254, 263, 275–76

Servius (Virgil's commentator), 56

Sicanus, 55

Siena, 11, 65, 66, 74, 82, 86, 88, 89, 136, 152

Sixtus IV, Pope, 253n

Socrates, 106n, 166, 184n, 200, 277

Solomon, 169

Solon, 20, 120, 195

Sombart, Werner, 261

Son of Sirach, 111

Spain, 40, 204, 207

Sparta, 204, 205

Stefani, Marchionne de Coppi, 71n

Stevens, John N., 215n

Strozzi family: Filippo, 15, 59, 145; Palla, 15

Sulla, 40, 50–51, 58, 72, 212

Sylvester, Pope, 182

Tarquinia (Etruscan city), 65

Themistocles, 40, 249

Theodoric the Great (Ostrogoth), 104

Theophrastus, 99, 107, 118, 229n, 231

Thermopylae, 40

Thucydides, 32

Tiber, 54, 57

Tiresias, 54

Trattato del Governo della Famiglia (second half of Florentine Quattrocento), 279–80

Tuscany, 36, 53, 55, 59, 62–68, 74, 78, 81, 85–89, 114, 145, 163, 167, 192, 199, 200, 203, 209–10, 222, 247, 262, 285

Uzzano, Niccolò da, 5

Valerius Maximus, 165–66, 201, 206–9

Valerius Publicola, 242, 254n
Valla, Lorenzo, 49, 239
Varro, 19, 130
Vaucluse, 116, 117, 167–77, 180–81, 191, 247, 260
Veii (Etruscan city), 57
Vellutello, Alessandro, 23, 133
Venice, 6, 25, 86, 123–24, 177, 189, 195, 284n
Vergerio, Pier Paolo, 20, 29, 128, 196–97; and Cicero, 120–21, 127–28
Verona, 87, 88, 116
Vespasiano. See Bisticci
Villani family, 44, 77; Filippo, 44, 48, 55, 70, 72n; Giovanni, 44, 48, 49, 55, 69, 72, 77–79, 81, 84, 129; Matteo, 44, 77, 84
Vincent de Beauvais, 109–10, 111, 115
Virgil, 47, 54, 56, 60, 91, 179, 181, 198
Visconti family, 11–13, 82, 84, 86, 145, 173, 177, 241; Bernabò, 88;

Filippo Maria, 12n, 15; Giangaleazzo, 12n, 83–90; Giovanni, 84, 173
Volsci, 27
Volterra, 66, 74, 81

Widmer, Berthe, 123n
Wilkins, Ernest H., 180n
William of Malmesbury, 107n
Witt, Ronald, 10n, 135n

Xenocrates, 184
Xenophon, 91, 237, 261, 263, 267–68, 277

Zacchaeus, 219–20
Zama, 100
Zambeccari, Pellegrino, 136
Zanobi da Strada, 48
Zara (in Venetian Dalmatia), 124
Zeno (the Greek Stoic), 153
Zeno, Carlo (Venetian statesman), 124